BY AARON MAHNKE

Destiny: A Fairy Tale
Indian Summer
Consumed
Grave Suspicion

THE WORLD OF LORE
Monstrous Creatures
Wicked Mortals
Dreadful Places

THE WORLD OF
LORE

WICKED MORTALS

New York

AARON MAHNKE
WANTED
BODY SNATCHERS
MORPHINE
the world of
LORE
AND THIS IS...
REQUIESCAT IN PACE
NEW ORLEANS
WICKED MORTALS

2024 Del Rey Trade Paperback Edition

Copyright © 2018 by Aaron Mahnke

Published in the United States by Del Rey, an imprint of Random
House, a division of Penguin Random House LLC, New York.

DEL REY and the CIRCLE colophon are registered trademarks of
Penguin Random House LLC.

Most of the text in this work is based on the author's podcast, *Lore*.

Originally published in hardcover in the United States by Del Rey,
an imprint of Random House, a division of Penguin Random House
LLC, in 2018.

LIBRARY OF CONGRESS CATALOGING-IN-PUBLICATION DATA
Names: Mahnke, Aaron, author.
Title: The world of lore. Wicked mortals / Aaron Mahnke.
Other titles: Wicked mortals
Description: New York : Del Rey, 2018. | Series: The world of lore |
Includes bibliographical references and index.
Identifiers: LCCN 2018005235 (print) | LCCN 2018006700 (ebook) |
ISBN 9781524798000 (E-book) | ISBN 9781524798017 (paperback)
Subjects: LCSH: Murderers—Case studies. | Criminals—Case
studies. | Murder—Case studies. | Crime—Case studies.
Classification: LCC HV6515 (ebook) | LCC HV6515 .M24 2018 (print) |
DDC 364.3092/2—dc23
LC record available at https://lccn.loc.gov/2018005235

Printed in the United States of America on acid-free paper

Artwork designed by M. S. Corley

randomhousebooks.com

1st Printing

Book design by Simon M. Sullivan

For my girls.
You remind me every day that stories are like food:
we need it regularly, we each have our favorite
kinds, and making it can be a bit messy. I'm so
proud that both of you love stories so much, and I
look forward to the tales you will someday write for
me. I love you.

I believe there are monsters born in the world to human parents.

—John Steinbeck,
East of Eden

CONTENTS

HE WALKS IN SHADOWS

DEATH BECOMES HER

TOIL AND TROUBLE

A LITTLE PECULIAR

MAGIC TRICKS

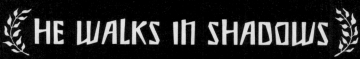
HE WALKS IN SHADOWS

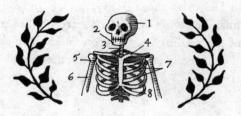

The Castle

ON JANUARY 17, 1894, a couple stood before a minister at the Vendome Hotel in Denver, Colorado. Henry Howard and Georgianna Yoke were about to be married. Standing near them was their witness, a woman named Minnie Williams.

The bride had come from Indiana to escape a scandalous reputation, and had found work in Chicago at a store owned by Henry. She was a tall, slender woman, about twenty-five years of age, with blue eyes and blond hair. And she was madly in love with Henry.

It sounds wonderful. It sounds perfect, actually. But there was trouble in paradise even before they met the minister there at the hotel.

You see, Henry was already married. He was, in fact, married to *two* other women. And Minnie, the woman standing as witness, was actually Henry's mistress of over a year. Even Henry's name was fake; his real name had been abandoned long before, and it would be months before Georgianna would discover who he really was.

Sometimes we think we know a person, only to discover that we were fooled. Community is built on trust, and that trust allows each of us to make connections, to let down our guard, and to feel safe. When that trust is broken, though, our minds quickly shift to disappointment and stress and outright fear.

Sure, it happens less often now in the age of Facebook and social media. But in the late 1800s, very little stood in the way of a person falsifying their identity, and Henry Howard—or whoever he was prior to that moment in Denver—had turned that skill into an art.

Few people knew this about Henry, though. In fact, few people could have imagined what deep, dark secrets boiled just beneath the surface of this smiling young groom. And when the world finally *did* find out exactly ten months later, they could barely contain their horror.

WARNING SIGNS

Henry Howard was born in New Hampshire in 1861 as Herman Mudgett. His parents were wealthy, well-respected people in their community, and their son was born into that privilege. But from an early age, Herman was a problem child, constantly getting into trouble.

According to Mudgett himself, as a child his classmates forced him to view and touch a human skeleton after learning that he was afraid of the town doctor. Their prank backfired, though, generating a deep fascination rather than frightening him off. And that obsession with death would only grow.

Soon the boy was expressing interest in medicine. One report claims that he would actually perform surgery on animals. Along with his excellent performance in school, he was able to pursue that interest and enter medical school, enrolling at the University of Michigan as H. H. Holmes in 1879. Far from home, and with access to resources that he previously lacked, college allowed Holmes to get creative.

He devised an easy way to make money—a drive that would fuel many of his future crimes. It involved stealing a cadaver from the medical lab. Holmes would disfigure the corpse and plant the body somewhere that gave it the appearance of being the victim of a tragic accident. Then, a few days later, he would approach a life insurance company with a policy for his "deceased relative" and collect the cash.

His final insurance swindle in Michigan netted him $12,500, but he knew his welcome was wearing thin. After collecting the money, he vanished, abandoning school and his new wife, Clara, and child, who never saw him again.

He moved around the country doing legitimate work, but also learning his way around the business world. He mastered the art of buying product on credit, avoiding the bills, selling the items, and then vanishing with the profit. Armed with that skill, he soon settled in Englewood, just south of Chicago.

It was 1885. Holmes was trying to avoid creditors from all around the country. But rather than vanish into obscurity, he chose to hide in plain sight. He married his second wife—bigamously, of course—and took a job at a local drugstore owned and run by Dr. Elizabeth Holden, whose husband was dying of cancer.

Holmes spent the next two years becoming more and more essential to Holden's business, paying her for ownership in the business and building relationships with the customers. When Mr. Holden finally did pass away, the payments from Holmes stopped, and Dr. Holden became upset, threatening to end their business partnership.

But nothing happened—because Dr. Holden mysteriously vanished. When asked about her disappearance, Holmes told the authorities that she had moved out west to live with family, right after she had signed over the business to him, of course. And the police bought the lie.

Holmes operated the drugstore as if nothing had happened, growing the business and continuing his chess game of evading creditors. But when the empty lot across the street became available, he couldn't resist the temptation. Holmes, you see, had bigger plans. The World's Columbian Exposition was scheduled to be hosted in Chicago in 1893, and he envisioned a hotel that could house the countless visitors who would travel to the area.

His project was lovingly called the Castle, which wasn't far from the truth. It was 50 feet wide and more than 160 feet long, taking up half of a city block. With three stories and a basement, it would eventually have over a hundred rooms within its walls.

And Holmes, ever the micromanager, took on the task of project architect, refusing to share the plans with anyone else.

Workers on the building asked questions, naturally, but when they did, Holmes would replace them. Most of the men working on the project never lasted for more than two weeks. All told, more than five hundred carpenters and craftsmen worked on the Castle.

True to form, Holmes managed to avoid paying most of them as well. He would accuse them of shoddy work and refuse to give them their wages. Some sued him, but he managed to put those cases off long enough that they eventually gave up.

Once the new building was completed, Holmes moved the drugstore to its ground floor and rented out space to other shops. His personal offices were located on the top floor, and the remaining space was rented out as temporary living quarters, marketed as a boardinghouse for young, single women.

The Castle was open for business. Unfortunately, not everyone who stayed there managed to survive the hospitality that Holmes offered them.

GONE GIRLS

When Mrs. Pansy Lee arrived from New Orleans, she rented a room at the Castle. She was a widow and had traveled all over the United States before arriving in Chicago to settle down. When Holmes learned that she had $4,000 in cash in the false bottom of her trunk, he kindly offered to keep it in his store vault for her. Mrs. Lee declined the offer, and vanished a short time later.

While some people came to the Castle for lodging, others were looking for work. One of the requirements that Holmes imposed was that all his employees were to have life insurance policies for the sum of $5,000. Holmes, remember, knew the life insurance business well.

When seventeen-year-old Jennie Thompson arrived from southern Illinois looking for work, Holmes saw an opportunity. She was young and pretty—the exact sort of blond-haired, blue-eyed beauty that he preferred—and he quickly gave her a job.

In casual conversation Jennie let it slip that her family didn't actually know where she was. She had told them she was traveling to New York, but the offer of a good job was enough to keep her right there in Chicago. She told Holmes that she couldn't wait to tell her parents about her good fortune. Before she did, though, he escorted her up to her room, and she was never seen again.

In 1890, Ned Connor arrived at the Castle looking for work. He traveled with his wife, Julia—unusually tall for a woman at nearly six feet—and their young daughter, Pearl. Ned was a watchmaker and jeweler, and Holmes hired him right away. But it was Ned's wife who captured his attention the most.

Holmes soon fired his bookkeeper and gave the job to Julia. Not long after, it began to be obvious that Holmes was more than a little friendly with Ned's wife. Ned, for his part, turned a blind eye. It seems he was glad to have a good job with steady pay and a roof over his head.

When Julia became pregnant, though, Ned took the hint. He packed up, filed for divorce, and left her and Pearl in the care of Holmes, who immediately took out insurance policies on both of them. But Holmes had a new problem: Julia knew the business *too* well, and she presented a threat to his illicit activities.

Holmes found a solution. He told Julia that he would marry her, but only if she would have an abortion. Julia resisted at first, but finally, on December 24, 1891, she gave in. She asked Holmes to put Pearl to bed, and then he led her to the basement, where he had a makeshift operating room.

Julia and Pearl were never seen again.

That same winter, Holmes summoned a man named Charles Chappell to his office. Chappell performed odd jobs around the Castle, but he had a particular skill that Holmes required. He was incredibly gifted in the craft of articulating skeletons.

Chappell arrived, and Holmes led him to a second-floor room, where the body of a woman lay on a table. According to Chappell's own testimony to the authorities, the body had been skinned like a jackrabbit. He assumed, since Holmes was a doctor, that he had simply been performing an autopsy on a patient, and pushed his doubts to the back of his mind.

Holmes paid Chappell $36 to strip the flesh off the body and prepare the bones for articulation. The finished skeleton was sold to Dr. Pauling of Hahnemann Medical College. Dr. Pauling would often look at the skeleton in his private office and marvel at how unusual it was to see a woman nearly six feet tall.

THE MURDER HOUSE

Eventually Holmes made a critical mistake. Ironically, it was his old love of insurance scams that caught up with him in the end. After he killed his right-hand man, Benjamin Pitezel, and attempted to pass the death off as an accident to the insurance company, the authorities caught wind of the crime and tracked him down.

He was finally arrested in Boston on November 17, 1894, ten months to the day from his wedding ceremony in a Denver hotel. Before his trial began, however, the Castle was mysteriously gutted by fire. Thankfully, the authorities had already been able to search the building, and after doing so they had given it a new name: the Murder House.

The authorities discovered that, like any boardinghouse of the time, the Castle had a reception room, a waiting room, and many rooms for residents to live in. But the building had more inside its walls than was expected. There were secret chambers, trapdoors, peepholes, and hidden laboratories.

Aside from the thirty-five guest rooms, the second floor was a labyrinth of passages. Some doors opened on brick walls, some could only be opened from one side, and others were hidden from sight completely. Trapdoors led to staircases that led to hidden chambers. There were even alarms in all of the rooms that would alert Holmes in his quarters if any of his prisoners tried to escape.

Some of the rooms were windowless and could be sealed off and made airtight if necessary. Some were equipped with gas jets that were fed by pipes from the basement. Others were lined with asbestos and had visible scorch marks on the floor.

Then there was the Vault.

It was a room that could fit a single person, and then only if they were standing. The walls inside the Vault were lined with iron plate, broken only by a handful of gas fixtures and a trapdoor that led to a chute. On the inside of the door was a single footprint, the size of a woman's boot. It was a homemade gas chamber that was designed to deliver corpses straight to the basement.

When the police descended to the lowest level of the building, they discovered that Holmes had expanded the basement beyond the foundation of the building and out beneath the sidewalk. He did this to make room for all of his equipment.

Here they found the dissection table, still splattered with blood. Jars of poison filled a shelf, and a large wooden box nearby contained multiple female skeletons. Built into one wall was a crematorium, which still contained ash and bone fragments. A search also found valuables that belonged to some of the victims: a watch that belonged to Minnie Williams, scraps of fabric, tintype photographs, and a ball of women's hair, carefully wrapped in cloth.

The bones of a child were found buried in a pit, and the remnants of a bloody dress were recovered from a wood-burning stove. When Ned Connor was asked to identify the fabric, he confirmed it belonged to his wife, Julia.

A rack designed to stretch bodies was also discovered. Beneath the dirt floor they found a vat of corrosive acid and two quicklime pits, used for quickly dissolving the flesh off corpses. There were human skulls, a shoulder blade, ribs, a hip socket, and countless other human remains.

Whatever the police had hoped to find that day, they were unprepared for the truth. In the end, they had discovered a medieval charnel house right beneath their feet.

MONSTERS IN MASKS

It's easy to feel safe in our own neighborhood, walking past the closed doors and manicured lawns. But what goes on behind those walls is never something that we can be sure of. Each and every person we meet wears a mask, and we're only allowed to peek behind it if they let us.

Society is built on the idea that we can trust the people around us. That we can take our neighbors, our family, even our coworkers at face value and enter into relationships with them. But with every relationship comes risk. We risk disappointment. We risk pain and betrayal. For some of us, we even risk our very safety.

European mapmakers of the fifteenth century would sometimes mark unexplored areas of their maps with a warning: "Here there be monsters." There's danger in the places we haven't explored. And while this was true then of undiscovered continents, it has always been true of humanity. Beneath the surface, behind the mask, hides the monster.

On May 7, 1896, after a final meal of boiled eggs, dry toast, and a cup of coffee, H. H. Holmes was led to the gallows at Moyamensing Prison. A black hood was placed over his head, and as the crowd outside the prison walls shouted their insults and jeers, he was positioned over the trapdoor.

When it opened, Holmes dropped and his head snapped to the side. But rather than killing him quickly, the rope had somehow broken his neck and left him alive. The crowd watched for over fifteen minutes as Holmes hung from the noose, fingers and feet twitching and dancing, before his heart finally stopped beating.

Holmes was buried in an unmarked grave in Holy Cross Cemetery, just south of Philadelphia. As per his request, there was no autopsy, and his body was buried in a coffin filled with cement. Holmes, you see, was afraid that someone would dig up his body and use his skeleton for science. He was probably right.

We don't know how many people he killed. Holmes confessed to a variety of numbers, even changing his story again on the hangman's platform. Some experts who have studied the missing-person reports of the World's Columbian Exhibition place the possible death toll as high as two hundred.

There's so much we don't know about Holmes, a man whose entire life seemed to be one elaborate lie built atop another, like some macabre house of cards. He will forever remain a mystery to us, a monster hidden behind a mask that was painted to look just like you or me. But one last insight into the man can be found in his written confession.

"I was born with the Devil in me," he wrote. "I could not help the fact that I was a murderer, no more than the poet can help the inspiration to sing. I was born with the 'Evil One' standing as my sponsor beside the bed where I was ushered into the world, and he has been with me since."

Black Stockings

MOST OF US have had the joy of being sick once or twice in our lives. It's part of the human experience, I suppose. We get sick, and then we get better. At least that's how it's supposed to work.

One thing I am constantly thankful for is the fact that we live in such a modern, enlightened age of medicine. We no longer use urine as an antiseptic, nor do we diagnose illness based on our astrological signs. But that wasn't always the case.

Gone are the days of bleeding ourselves with leeches, or trying to balance our humors to make sure our sanguine fluids aren't overpowering our melancholic fluids. And I'm probably not the only one who's happy that we no longer treat sick people with enemas of boar bile administered with metal syringes.

Yes, bile from a boar. I could not make this stuff up.

Our ancestors didn't know *why* certain things happened, but they sure did their best to explain them. Stories were created, myths were told, and superstitions took root. All of them were designed to explain why things happened, and these reasons, even if they *were* pure fabrications, somehow helped people deal with the realities of life.

Why was my child born deformed? Why did my husband's personality change overnight? Why did my entire family die from a plague last winter? These questions haunted people in ways we can't understand today, and they grasped for anything that would help them cope. They found answers in their common folklore.

Among the countless tales and stories told, there's one superstition from Ireland that saw more usage than most. You see, when something didn't seem right—when things went wrong and people suffered—in the minds of the Irish there was only one explanation that covered it all: changelings.

THE SUBSTITUTE

A changeling, according to the folklore of Europe, is a kind of fairy. Stories of them can be found in Germany, Ireland, England, Scandinavia, Spain, and many other European countries.

In all of those cultures, changelings have the same methodology: they are a substitute for a kidnapped human being. Either out of jealousy or great need, fairies were said to enter our world and make a trade without our knowledge. They would leave one of their own behind and return to the fairy realm, where the kidnapped human would live a happy, joyful life in paradise.

We have a great summary of changelings thanks to Irish poet William Butler Yeats. "They steal children," he wrote, "and leave a withered fairy—one thousand or maybe two thousand years old—instead. At times full grown men and women have been taken. Near the village of Coloney lives an old woman who was taken in her youth. When she came back at the end of seven years, she had no toes, for she had danced them off."

Changelings, according to the legends, can actually take one of three forms. The first is the kind Yeats wrote about, the senile and ancient fairy who is disguised as a child. Another type of changeling is an actual fairy child, and the third type is an inanimate object such as a block of wood or a carved log. This third type is sometimes known as a *stock*.

The logic, at least to someone in medieval Europe, was simple: if a child was born with birth defects, was sickly, or was ill-tempered, they were often thought to be the fairy substitute left behind when their real child was taken from their home.

If an adult went missing and was later found mysteriously dead, people would often assume that the body was really a bundle of sticks that have merely been enchanted to resemble their loved one.

Folklore blossomed on the subject. Old wives' tales and legend taught new generations how to spot a changeling, instantly providing both one more reason to fear every little change in a person's life and a clear sign of safety and hope they could cling to.

Even the overall well-being of a family could hinge on these creatures. Changelings, you see, were said to drain all luck away from a house, and by doing so, they would leave a family destined to struggle with poverty and misfortune, all while trying to care for a child they saw as a curse more and more every day.

When the stories focused on men and women who had been swapped out for a fairy, the symptoms were more psychological in nature. Signs of an adult changeling included mood swings, becoming argumentative, and losing interest in friends and family.

Changelings were said to have enormous appetites, eating everything they were given and then asking for more. It was said that if your infant preferred food from the larder rather than being nursed, there was a chance they weren't really your child at all.

While most changeling infants died in early childhood, those that survived were said to become dim-witted adults. Men and women who survived this long were sometimes called *ouphe,* which is where we get the word "oaf."

Thankfully, though, there were ways to test people to see if they were, in fact, a changeling. One method involved putting a shoe in a bowl of soup. If the baby saw this and laughed, it was seen as proof that the child was a changeling. Another method involved making a tiny loaf of bread inside half an eggshell, again meant to make the fairy laugh.

Once discovered, a fairy changeling could be driven from the house in a variety of ways, in which case the kidnapped human child or adult would be returned unharmed. One trick involved holding the suspected child over a fire, while another recommended forcing the suspect to drink tea brewed with foxglove, a poisonous flower. It was thought that as the person's body expelled the toxin through vomiting and diarrhea, the changeling would be forced to return to the fairy realm.

It sounds crazy to think that people would believe such stories, even centuries ago. Surely no one actually performed these tests or administered these treatments, especially to their own family, right?

Unfortunately, history teaches us that desperate people are capable of just about anything.

Drowned, Dipped, Burned, and Poisoned

In July 1826, a woman named Ann Roche from Tralee, County Kerry, in southwest Ireland, was caring for a four-year-old boy named Michael Leahy. According to her own testimony, the boy was unable to walk, stand, or speak. Convinced that he was, in fact, a fairy changeling, she bathed him in icy waters three times to force the fairy out. The boy drowned, she was tried by a court, and the court found her not guilty.

In 1845, a woman suspected of being a changeling was placed in a large basket filled with wood shavings and then hung over the kitchen fire until the contents of the basket ignited. In 1851, a man in Ireland literally roasted his child to death because he believed the boy to be a fairy. Three children were suspected of being fairies in 1857. They were bathed in a solution of foxglove and then forced to drink it.

Sometimes babies were left in or near bodies of water as a way of forcing the changelings to leave. In 1869, an exorcism was attempted by dipping a child three times in a lake in Ireland. Another woman actually left her infant on the shore of a lake and walked away, expecting the fairies to come and make the swap. Thankfully, she returned later to reclaim her child.

Sometimes neighbors stepped in when the parents of an obvious changeling did nothing. In 1884, while the mother of three-year-old Philip Dillon was out of the house, Ellen Cushion and Anastatia Rourke snuck inside. Philip, you see, could not use his arms and legs, and these neighbors saw that as proof enough of his condition.

One of the neighbors stripped the boy naked while the other stoked a fire. Then, when everything was ready, they placed him on a large shovel and held it over the flames. Little Philip survived, but he was severely burned by the incident.

We hate what we fear, you see. But rather than fade away as the nineteenth century moved on, the fears and superstition around changelings only seemed to grow in Ireland. And as hard as it might be to believe, things were about to get worse.

THE CLEARYS

In the late nineteenth century, each district in Ireland had a Board of Guardians. They were tasked with dispensing public aid, and one of the ways they did that was by building cottages to house rural agricultural workers. Many farmers had lost their land in the recent famine, and this was one way of helping alleviate some of the homelessness and poverty that had become so common in the country.

One cottage was constructed in Ballyvadlea, a small community of just nine homes and thirty-one people in County Tipperary. The family who was awarded the cottage moved in, but there was a problem. It seems that the house had been built on a rath, a low earthen ring. And while archaeologists know them to simply be remnants of an Iron Age fort, some of the Irish still thought of them as fairy rings, portals into another realm.

After the family moved in, odd things began to happen: cries in the night, noises that couldn't be identified, and a feeling of dread. It wasn't long before they picked up and left. In their stead, the cottage was given to an old retired laborer named Patrick Boland, who moved in with his adult daughter and her husband.

His daughter, Bridget Cleary, was unusual. In 1895, it was the men who controlled the family. Men were the breadwinners and the sole providers. But even though her husband, Michael, did well as a cooper—someone who makes and repairs barrels, a business that has always done well in Ireland—Bridget wasn't dependent on him. She had her own business, making dresses and keeping hens, and the income from those jobs was more than enough to meet her needs.

She was also said to be clever, flirtatious, and highly independent. So you can imagine how she must have annoyed her husband and caught the ire of the neighbors. And then there were the rumors of the affair she was having with another man. Bridget Cleary was a self-made, self-possessed woman, and everyone else was bothered by that.

I tell you all that because stories have layers. There's the meaning you glean from the initial telling, and then there's the rest of the story. The deeper you dive, the more things begin to make sense. And believe me when I tell you there's a lot about this story that fails to make sense.

On March 4, 1895, Bridget left home on an errand. She had eggs to deliver to the house of her father's cousin, Jack Dunne. It was a short enough distance that she decided to walk, but the weather turned sour while she was out. She spent the next day in bed complaining of raging pain in her head. She had chills and shivered constantly.

Dunne came by the little cottage to visit a few days later and found Bridget still in bed. He took one look at her and declared, "That's not Bridget." According to him, she was a changeling. Thankfully, no one believed him. Yet.

On March 9, five days after Bridget's trip in the cold, her father walked four miles to the nearest doctor and asked him to come help. Two days later, there was still no sign of the doctor, and so her husband, Michael, made the journey. After yet two more days of waiting, the doctor still had not come, and so Michael went again, this time making sure that he brought along a summons from the local health authority.

While her husband was out looking for the doctor, the doctor arrived unexpectedly. He did his typical house call checkup, prescribed some medicine, and then left. Still frustrated, the family called upon a priest to come by and give her last rites, just in case. Things weren't looking up for Bridget Cleary.

This was March 13, a full nine days since she'd taken ill, and so later that evening, neighbors and relatives gathered at the cottage to help administer fairy medicine in the form of herbs. Bridget refused the treatment, and they held a red-hot poker in her face until she complied.

Things got worse the following day. Cousin Jack Dunne had begun to spread word that Bridget had been taken by the fairies and replaced with a changeling. At his urging, a man named Denis Ganey was called to the house. He was known in the community as a "fairy doctor" and was well versed in treating cases such as these.

His treatments wouldn't necessarily fit into modern medical textbooks, mind you. They included the use of the hot poker, forcing the changeling to drink "first milk" from a cow that had just given birth, dousing the person in urine, and exposing them to flames. Bridget was slapped and held in front of the fireplace while her husband demanded that she state, before God and family, that she was indeed Bridget Cleary. Even though she answered yes, the gathered crowd didn't believe her.

Now, before I continue, there's something you need to understand about Michael Cleary's state of mind. While his mother had died when he was young, his father had passed away just hours before. He and Bridget were childless, and they lived with her father in a spare room in the nineteenth-century equivalent of public housing. His own wife was rumored to be cheating on him, and she didn't even need him to support her. Michael Cleary was adrift. He had come undone. Maybe that's what drove him to the edge of sanity.

The treatments continued late into the night. Friends and family began to ask to leave, but Michael was said to have yelled that no one was leaving until Bridget came home. He locked the door and placed the key in his pocket. If they could just get this right, he told them—if they could just drive the fairy out and be done with it—his Bridget would come home.

Again she was asked to declare her identity as a fairy, and Bridget refused. Historians don't know why. Maybe she was afraid. Perhaps her independent, stubborn nature prevented her.

Whatever the reason, her silence infuriated Michael. He stripped her to her undergarments and pushed her to the floor.

"Come home, Bridget, in the name of God," somebody was said to have cried as she lay near the fire.

"She's not my wife," Michael replied. "You'll soon see her go up the chimney."

With that, he doused her with lamp oil and grabbed a log from the burning fireplace, which he used to ignite the oil. Bridget Cleary burned to death on the hearth of her own kitchen fireplace in front of her husband and father, cousins, and friends. She was twenty-six years old.

Burning Questions

We haven't always known as much about the world as we do now. Compared to the centuries before our own, we live in a veritable golden age of knowledge and understanding. Science has eradicated much of the ignorance that once plagued us. And while I'm a fan of mystery and unanswered questions, that's not necessarily a bad thing.

Ignorance has been used as a justification for the barbaric, inhumane treatment of other people, to fuel our hatred of those who aren't like us. That kind of fear often becomes the agent of a dark transformation. Under the influence of fear, humans have a history of mutation, of changing into something grotesque and dangerous. We become monsters.

Fear drove Michael Cleary and the others to kill his wife. Fear of illness and disease, of mental and medical mysteries. Fear of the loss that seemed to be creeping ever closer to his household. Blinded by that fear, Michael Cleary lashed out with the only tool he had—superstition.

In many ways, it's beyond ironic that his fear turned him into someone else. In the end, perhaps he was the changeling.

After he forced one of Bridget's cousins at knifepoint to help wrap her body in a sheet, they carried her to a nearby field and buried her in a shallow grave. A short time later, some of the neighbors told the local priest that Bridget Cleary had gone missing. They said, in whispered tones, that it had been a fairy exorcism.

When the priest found Michael Cleary praying in the church the next day, he asked about Bridget.

"Is your wife all right?" the priest asked. "I heard she'd been sick."

"I had a very bad night, Father," Michael told him with a wild look in his eye. "When I woke up, my wife was gone. I think the fairies have taken her."

He was convinced she would return. He had plans to visit a nearby fairy ring and await her. She would arrive in a white gown on a pale horse, and he would cut her bindings with a blackened knife. His Bridget would come home.

The priest, to his credit, didn't believe a single word. He called the police, and a massive search was undertaken. On March 22, two constables found her body in the shallow grave her husband had dug just days before.

She had been badly burned, and lay in the fetal position, with her knees against her chest, arms wrapped tightly around them. Because her face had escaped the fire, a cloth sack had been placed over her head. All that remained of the little clothing she had been wearing was a pair of black stockings.

Bridget Cleary would never come home.

Covered Mirrors

I CAN STILL REMEMBER the first time I saw *Nightmare on Elm Street* as a child. Those tense moments in the dark. The thumping of my heart in my chest. The screams. But the decades have reduced much of those memories down to impressions and flashes of key images. The most important of those, of course, was the glove.

Freddy Krueger's glove was iconic. All leather and metal and fish knives. Just a glimpse of it was enough to send shivers down the spines of millions. It was one of a handful of weapons that became foundational to a new wave of horror movies that started more than thirty years ago.

There were others, of course. The chainsaw, with its screaming motor and biting teeth, filled many nightmares. The machete always takes me back to the hockey-mask-wearing Jason Voorhees from *Friday the 13th*.

There are many stories of a killer who uses a hook, from *I Know What You Did Last Summer* to an early episode of *Supernatural*. And who could forget the wooden stake that makes an appearance in almost every vampire movie?

But no tool of destruction has been more prolific—more *horrific*— than the ax. It's the stuff of nightmares, equal parts passion and skill. It's a near-mythic weapon that instantly inspires fear.

But a little over a century ago, those nightmares became reality.

Between January 1911 and April 1912, a killer traveled across western Louisiana and eastern Texas, and whoever they were, a trail of bodies was left on a scale beyond anything we can imagine today. They were crimes of intense passion and brutality. They were calculated and merciless. They were hate crimes to the core, focusing on victims of mixed race. And they were all committed with an ax.

The first murder took place in Rayne, Louisiana, in January 1911. While a young mother and her three small children were asleep in their beds, someone entered their home and brutally killed them all with an ax. Shortly after that, and just ten miles to the west in the small town of Crowley, the killer struck again. While Walter Byers, his wife, and their six-year-old son slept in their beds, their lives were ended.

There was a pattern forming—something beyond the victim profiles and the murder weapon—but it was still too early for the authorities to notice it. This was an age before the Internet, before twenty-four-hour news networks. Most information traveled along the railroad and took days or weeks to spread effectively. Which was unfortunate, because it allowed the killer to move on and continue his work.

Whoever he was, he didn't wait long before making his next appearance. On February 23, 1911, someone entered the home of the Cassaway family in San Antonio, Texas, and slaughtered everyone in their sleep, the husband and wife and their three children. There were never any signs of robbery. No vandalism or other evidence of a reason for the murders. Whoever the man was, he entered each home with one horrific purpose, and then moved on.

The killer took a long break after San Antonio, but when he reappeared he was back in Louisiana. On Sunday, November 26, 1911, in the city of Lafayette, all six members of the Randall family were butchered while they slept. The authorities said that each had been killed with a single blow to the back of the head, near the right ear. And the weapon, they claimed, was an ax.

The police arrested a woman named Clementine Bernabet, who claimed to have committed the crimes in Rayne, Crowley, and Lafayette. Her story was an odd mixture of voodoo superstition and cult mentality due to her involvement in something called the Sacred Church, but in the end the true killer proved her innocence by continuing with his spree while she remained behind bars.

In January 1912, Crowley experienced yet another tragedy at the hands of the Ax Man. Marie Warner and her three children were brutally killed in their beds, following the pattern of the previous murders. Two days later in the Louisiana town of Lake Charles, Felix Broussard, his wife, and their three children became the next victims. One blow to the head for each, just behind the right ear. But this was the moment the killer went off script.

He left a note. It wasn't incredibly helpful, but it did lend a small amount of humanity to the man behind the ax. The note read: "When He maketh the inquisition for blood, He forgetteth not the cry of the humble—human five."

No one knew what it meant. No one does to this day. But it helped the towns along the Southern Pacific Railroad line understand that it wasn't some mythical beast that was hunting them. No, the killer was a man. Still a monster, but of the human variety.

The death toll continued to climb. On February 19 it was Hattie Dove and her three children in Beaumont, Texas. On March 27 it was the Monroe family in the town of Gladden. On April 11 the killer returned to San Antonio to take the lives of William Burton and his family. Two nights later, in Hempstead, three more lives were taken.

The killer appeared one final time, in August 1912, in the home of James Dashiell of San Antonio. But something went wrong. Rather than never waking up again, Mrs. Dashiell opened her eyes as the killer missed his target. She screamed, and he ran, slipping away into the night.

And then, as if it had been nothing more than a hot wind blowing off the Gulf, everything just stopped. No more murders. No more blood. No more little coffins with no one left to weep over them. Just . . . gone.

But there's always another ax. There's always another family. And there's always another monster.

VILLISCA

Tucked in the southwestern corner of Iowa, between the middle and west branches of the Nodaway River, is the sleepy little town of Villisca. In 1912, this was the sort of town where everyone knew one another, if not by name then at least by face.

Local man Joe Moore had been the star salesman at a farm equipment business run by another Villisca native, Frank Jones, but had struck out on his own five years earlier, starting his own business. He and his wife, Sarah, had four children ranging from five to eleven years of age, and all of them were well loved in town.

On the night of June 10 their eldest daughter, Katherine, played host to a pair of local girls, Lena and Ina Stillinger, for a sleepover. With a full house, the family retired to bed, and soon all eight of them were fast asleep.

Just after midnight, however, a stranger lifted the latch on the Moore family's back door and stepped inside. Today, we don't think twice about locking all our doors and windows before going to bed, but in Villisca in 1912 that would have been overkill. Crime wasn't a problem, and everyone . . . well, we've already covered how friendly they all were.

Whoever it was that entered the Moore house that night closed the door behind him and then quietly picked up a nearby oil lamp. This was the type of lamp with a glass chimney on top, which protected the flame from gusts of wind. But the glass was also prone to toppling over if the lamp was tipped too far. Breaking glass makes noise, and that's probably why the intruder removed the lamp's chimney and set it aside.

He lit the lamp and turned the flame down as low as he could. Just enough light to see by, but not enough to wake anyone up. And then, moving as quietly as he could, he walked past the room where the two Stillinger girls slept, and slowly climbed the narrow stairs.

We know this because the town coroner did his best to later reconstruct the events of that night. We're told that the man first slipped into the room of Joe and Sarah Moore, who lay asleep in their bed. He set the lamp down. It would only get in the way when he started to use the other item he had brought with him: an ax.

When he raised the weapon over his head, it scuffed the ceiling of the room, but neither of the occupants of the bed noticed. He brought it down first on Joe and then on his wife. Two quick swings, two sickening thuds, and then it was over.

He next visited the Moore children, asleep in the second upstairs room. He quietly killed each of them with similar, quick blows to the head with the ax, before returning to the stairs. Back downstairs, he entered the room where the two guests slept, and completed his macabre mission.

No one awoke. No one screamed. No one was allowed a chance to warn the others until it was all over. But there are signs that one of the Stillinger girls woke up. According to the coroner, her body showed signs of movement prior to her death. Perhaps the noises upstairs woke her up. Maybe her sister screamed, or some other noise disturbed her sleep. But by the time she was awake, it was too late. She quickly joined the others in their horrible fate.

I wish I could say that the night's events were over, but the intruder—the killer, now—wasn't finished. After killing all eight of the people inside the house, he returned upstairs and systematically brutalized their remains with his ax. There are details I won't record—details that most of us can do without, no matter how strong some people's stomachs. But it is estimated that the killer struck Joe Moore's face at least thirty times before moving on to his wife.

When he was done with this, the man covered each of the faces of his victims. All eight victims, shrouded in clothing and bedsheets. Then he moved on to the mirrors in the house, draping each in turn with more cloth. Every reflective surface, every place where it might be possible to see eyes staring back at himself; he carefully and deliberately covered each of them.

They think the killer stayed in the house for a while after he was done. There were signs that he had taken a bowl and filled it with water, where he washed his blood-soaked hands. A little before 5:00 a.m., the man picked up the house keys, turned off the lamp, locked the doors, and then vanished into the red morning sky.

PATTERNS AND SUSPECTS

As it goes with so many small-town tragedies, the people of Villisca quickly went in search of someone to blame for the murders. One of the first suspects to be considered was Iowa senator Frank Jones. If you remember, Jones had been Joe Moore's boss at the farm equipment business just a few years before. When he left to strike out on his own, though, Moore had taken one of the most lucrative clients with him. There was no love between these two men. In fact, they used to cross over to the other side of the street to avoid passing each other.

There was also a rumor that Joe Moore had been having an affair with Frank's daughter. The theory—around town, at least—was that Frank hired a killer to get rid of Moore. He was never formally charged with the murders, but the news coverage ruined his political career.

Another suspect was local man Lyn George Kelly. Aside from being the town's Presbyterian minister, he was also a known sexual deviant with mental problems. This is a guy who had placed an ad in the local paper looking for a receptionist, and when women responded, he instructed them that they would be required to type in the nude. Super nice guy—if by "nice" you mean "crazy."

But crazy or not, he quickly admitted to the murders and to leaving town on a train the morning of their discovery. He was also left-handed, something the coroner had determined was characteristic of the killer. But there were problems, too. Kelly was five foot two and weighed a little over a hundred pounds. Not the "beast" people would have expected to find swinging an ax in the middle of the night. Unfortunately, Kelly later recanted his confession and complained about police brutality.

One final suspect was William Mansfield. It was believed by some that Frank Jones had hired Mansfield to do the killing, while others just believed the man worked alone. Mansfield had a criminal record, and at one point one of the detective agencies hired to investigate the murders claimed that he was even a cocaine addict. No one liked Mansfield.

And it seemed like he was really the guy. Mansfield had been suspected in two other murders prior to Villisca, which didn't help his case. One, in Paola, Kansas, had happened just four days before, and another had been committed in Aurora, Illinois. The locations of both of those murders were easily accessible by train, and both had been committed with an ax.

That's not all. Both of the previous murder scenes were eerily similar, too. In both homes, investigators found a lamp burning at the foot of the bed, glass chimney missing. Mirrors in both homes had been covered, and bowls of water used to wash bloody hands were found near the kitchen. No prints were found, though, suggesting a killer who was worried about being identified by prison records, something Mansfield would have understood.

In the end, however, Mansfield was able to provide an alibi. His name was apparently on the payroll records for a business several hundred miles away, making it difficult to believe he could have traveled to Villisca to swing the ax.

Someone did, though. Which means the killer got away. He caught a train, skipped town, and landed somewhere else. Who knows where the train might have taken him.

A CONVENIENT CHOICE

The ax is about as iconic as it gets. Some of the oldest man-made tools that scientists have discovered are hand axes, suggesting that their form and function is somehow part of our subconscious. They fit our needs, and perhaps they fit our nature as well.

In Villisca, like countless communities around the world at the turn of the last century, the ax was about as commonplace as the hand-pumped well or the wooden outhouse. Everyone had one, and everyone took them for granted. It was incredibly common to see them lying on a person's porch or protruding from a large piece of firewood in the yard.

Which means that there would have been no need for the Villisca ax murderer to carry his weapon with him. It was a weapon of convenience. It was the easy and logical choice. The perfect tool for the perfect crime.

As a result, our scary stories are full of those brutally sharp iconic weapons. Their vicious arc is the stuff of nightmares. And for the Moore family, those nightmares became real.

We encounter William Mansfield one more time in the historical records. Shortly after his trial and release, a man named R. H. Thorpe from nearby Shenandoah came forward with a story. According to him, he saw a man fitting Mansfield's description board a train the morning of the murders within walking distance of town.

Maybe it was someone else. Maybe it was Mansfield himself, caught in his own lie. There's no record that the authorities followed up on that lead, but other things followed him in the years to come.

In June 1914, a full two years after the events in Villisca, Mansfield was arrested once more, this time in Kansas City. The reason: his former wife, along with her parents and her infant child, had been found dead in their home in Blue Island, Illinois. According to the authorities, they had been brutally murdered in their sleep during the night.

The killer had used an ax.

On the Farm

IN 1943, ABRAHAM Maslow gifted the world with his list of five core essentials that every human being has in common. Today we call the chart Maslow's Hierarchy of Needs, and it's still a framework for how we understand and study much of human behavior today.

The list includes a few obvious entries, such as our physiological needs and our desire for love and affection. There are deeper concepts, too, like self-actualization and esteem. They're just as important, but a bit harder for many people to understand at first glance.

But it's the last item on the list that I want to focus on. It seems almost too obvious to be there, but at the same time, it has a bit of everything. It's basic, yet complex. It straddles the line, and maybe that's why it's so important to all of us.

What is it? Safety. Humans like to feel safe. Our pursuit of safety is core to who we are as people. It's not unique to humans, for sure—animals are very good at finding and building homes wherever they can—but it's undeniable that safety drives a lot of our decisions.

And rightly so. We deserve to feel safe. One could argue that it's a subset of freedom: when we are fully in control of our own lives, a portion of that control will always be diverted toward safety.

We find safety in many different places, though. We find it in a group of friends, because, as every horror movie has taught us, there's safety in numbers, right? We find it in places, like work, our schools, and religious buildings—although those are admittedly much less safe today than they were a generation ago.

It's in our own homes, though, that we find the most safety. We nest there, in a sense. We build a cocoon around ourselves that protects us from the weather, from outsiders, and from harm.

Tragically, though, sometimes that's not enough.

WELCOME TO THE NEIGHBORHOOD

No one liked Andreas Gruber. They thought the old farmer was greedy, and the public perception of the man was that he was rude and cranky. He was an old, crusty farmer, and no one around him appreciated that very much.

Gruber was sixty-three, and his wife, Cäzilia, was seventy-two. They lived on their farm about forty miles north of Munich, between the small German towns of Ingolstadt and Schrobenhausen. It wasn't their farm, though. No, it belonged to their daughter, thirty-five-year-old Viktoria, who lived there on the farm with them along with her two young children. Her daughter, Cäzilia, was seven, and Joseph was two.

And it was Joseph's birth that really got the neighbors talking. Viktoria's husband, Karl, had left to serve in World War I in 1914 while she was pregnant with their daughter. According to all reports, he never returned and died there in the trenches. So who fathered Joseph?

Local gossip, fueled by a dislike of Andreas Gruber, claimed the boy was a product of incest between Viktoria and her father. The birth certificate, though, simply listed the initials L.S., leaving the boy's paternity a mystery to wonder and whisper over.

The farm provided ample privacy from the gossip, though. It sat in a large clearing in the thick German forest, close enough to nearby Kaifeck to be part of the village, yet far enough away to be outside the normal flow of life there. *Hinter*, as the Germans would say. The farm was *hinter,* or behind, the village of Kaifeck, so most called it Hinterkaifeck.

They still interacted with the village, though. Young Cäzilia attended school six days a week there, the postman delivered mail to the farm regularly, and a local woman even lived with the Grubers as their maid. From everything I've read about the family, they seemed to be nothing more than ordinary. Sure, they were broken in certain ways—Viktoria's lost husband and Andreas's reputation as a greedy crank were hard to miss—but overall they were just one more German farm family doing their best to get by.

In the autumn of 1921 the Grubers' maid quit her job there on the farm. She claimed, of all things, that the farm was haunted. She'd heard noises when no one else should have been around. She'd noticed items that had been moved, items that no else would admit to shifting. She never felt alone.

It took a while to find a replacement, and in the meantime, winter arrived. Life on the farm became more insular. There were no crops to tend to, so the Grubers cared for their animals and stayed warm. But little things were beginning to happen that caught their attention. Things that shouldn't be happening, and it made them wonder if maybe, just maybe, their old maid had been right.

They began to hear those same noises in the attic. Andreas even found a newspaper in the house that he had no memory of buying. When he asked his wife and daughter, they were just as baffled. And then one of the house keys went missing. It was unsettling, to say the least.

In late March 1922, though, Andreas noticed the most unusual thing. He'd been outside the house, perhaps to fetch something or to check on the exterior of the house. The night before had given them another fresh layer of snow on the ground, so perhaps he needed to inspect the roof. We don't really know.

As he walked from the house to the barn, Andreas claimed he saw footprints in the snow. They started at the edge of the forest and covered the distance between the trees and the house, ending there. Perhaps a traveler had passed through in the night. Maybe a local had been walking through the snow and gotten lost. It happened from time to time. But what was odd about the tracks to Andreas was that they didn't go back. They just ended there.

We know all of this because Gruber himself told some of the locals while he was in town the next day. He was clearly disturbed by the things he had seen, but none of his neighbors had experienced anything similar.

That was the last time anyone saw the old farmer alive.

THE SCENE

The first clue that anything odd was going on, at least to the people of Kaifeck, was when little Cäzilia failed to show up for school on Saturday, April 1. The next day, the entire family was absent from church, where they attended—pardon the pun—religiously. Cäzilia missed school on Monday as well.

Finally, when the postman arrived on Tuesday, he found Monday's mail still on the porch where he had left it. This drew his suspicion, and he mentioned it back in the village. The people there put the pieces together and decided something had to be amiss. So later that day, a group of neighbors gathered together, and they quickly set off to visit the farm.

You know how muffled and quiet it can get outside when there's a lot of snow? As if the sounds of the world around you have been muted and hushed? I imagine that those men were keenly aware of that unnatural silence, standing there outside the Gruber farmhouse that day.

One of the men shouted out for Andreas or anyone else in the house to come out and speak with them. They just wanted to make sure everyone was safe and well. But no one answered. Just more of that muted, snow-covered silence.

Not giving up, one of the neighbors—a local man named Lorenz Schlittenbauer—led the group to the barn. It was daylight, so perhaps Andreas could be found working in there with the animals. But when they opened the door, they were greeted by a grisly sight.

There, on the straw-covered floor, lay the bloody bodies of Andreas, his wife and daughter, and young Cäzilia. It was clear that something horrible had happened to the family, and Schlittenbauer quickly walked from the barn to the house, which were connected by a door. Inside, he found more bloodshed.

Maria Baumgarten, the new maid who had started work on the farm the previous day, lay dead in her own bedroom. Little Joseph, last to be found, had met the same fate. It was a scene of devastation and gore, and it left the men stunned.

Within a matter of hours, investigators from Munich arrived to go over the scene and gather evidence. They wanted to piece together what had happened, to discover the story, and to find clues that might point to the person or people responsible. What they did uncover, though, was far more disturbing than answers.

It appeared that each of the adults in the barn had been led there one at a time. Whoever the killer had been, they had appeared to call each person into the barn alone, where they executed them with a farm tool known as a mattock, a sort of pickax used for cutting. Each blow to the head was powerful and deadly, and each victim most likely died instantly.

The bodies inside the house had the same type of wounds. Maria and Joseph were found in pools of their own blood, their skulls crushed by their attacker. As far as the police were concerned, whoever wielded the weapon knew how to use it, and did so without hesitation. This was cold-blooded murder, without a doubt. The trouble was, the weapon seemed to be missing. It was just . . . gone.

Other aspects of the crime didn't seem to line up with logic. For one, there seemed to be no motive behind the actions of the killer. It was known to a few in the village that just weeks before, Viktoria had withdrawn all of her savings, borrowed more from her dead husband's sister, and brought the cash home. She told people that she planned to invest in the farm. She even made a large 700 mark donation to the village church.

All of the remaining money was still there, in the house. The killer hadn't taken it. Nor had they taken any of the other valuables that filled the farmhouse. Nothing was stolen. Whoever had called the Grubers into the barn—whoever had swung the pickax and ended all of their lives—hadn't been interested in money.

Another detail that seemed odd was the condition of the house and farm. In most instances, a killer will flee the scene after the crime has been committed. But here, there were signs to the contrary. The animals in the barn appeared to have been fed and watered throughout the weekend. And not by an amateur, either; whoever had tended them knew his way around a farm.

But most disturbing of all were the reports from neighbors that smoke had been seen rising from the chimney of the farmhouse all throughout the weekend. Food had been eaten, and one of the beds had been slept in.

It was hard to believe, but the facts didn't lie: the Gruber family's killer hadn't run. Instead, he had stayed in the house long after their bodies turned cold, as if nothing had happened at all.

THEORIES

The question, of course, was a simple one: who could do such a thing? But this was 1922. CSI wasn't a thing that existed yet. There was no DNA analysis available to the investigators. Even fingerprint identification was too young to have reached the farmlands of German Bavaria. But even if there had been better tools, there were other obstacles to uncovering the truth.

The local men who initially stumbled upon the bodies, led by Lorenz Schlittenbauer, had disturbed much of the crime scene. While the maid and young Joseph had each been covered with cloth by the killer, the bodies in the barn had been stacked like lumber. On top of this macabre pile, the killer had placed an old door, and then hay had been scattered all over it in an attempt to hide it.

So when Schlittenbauer entered the barn with the others, he actually lifted the door and began to move the bodies, making a full and accurate investigation impossible. According to those who watched him, Schlittenbauer lifted and moved the corpses with no emotion or hesitation, as if the sight of it all didn't bother him. Or wasn't new to him. And it was that, along with some other subtle clues, that quickly moved him to the top of the list of suspects.

Why would he do this? Well, he told one of the men that he moved the bodies because he was looking for his son. Think back for a moment. Remember the questionable parentage of young Joseph, whose birth certificate simply listed one L.S. as the father? Numerous neighbor testimonies made it clear that Lorenz Schlittenbauer was that man.

And that went a long way toward explaining why he'd led the searchers from the barn into the house: he'd been looking for his son, Joseph. But according to some of the men with him that day, the door between the barn and the kitchen had been locked. They knew that because Schlittenbauer pulled a key from his pocket and unlocked the door. Which was more than a little curious, seeing as how Gruber had mentioned in town that one of his house keys had gone missing.

One final bit: the family dog was seen by the postman on the day before, where it had been tied to a corner of the barn. When the men arrived on Tuesday, though, they found it in the barn, wounded but alive. When it saw Schlittenbauer, the animal barked uncontrollably.

All of the clues seem odd and out of place. They make your mind perk up and feel like something deeper was going on, but at face value they prove nothing, and that's the frustrating part. The dog might have just been barking because of the bodies. Schlittenbauer might have had a key simply because he was the Grubers' closest neighbor. Like I said, these clues were subtle. And that's why he was never formally charged with a crime.

As for motive, some people believe that Viktoria had sued Lorenz for support, and the man had refused. Clearly, Viktoria needed money shortly before the murders, as her bank withdrawal suggested. But historians are doubtful. The most likely reality, they believe, is that Joseph's father was none other than his grandfather, Andreas, and the arrangement with Lorenz was simply an effort to save face in the village.

Alternative theories have also been suggested. There are some who believe that Viktoria's husband, Karl, did not, in fact, die during World War I. No body was ever recovered or sent home, and a friend of Karl's even testified later to seeing him alive in the mid-1920s. Some people wonder: could Karl have had a hand in the murders, perhaps out of anger toward Viktoria's relationship with Schlittenbauer while he was away at war?

I've even read another theory that claims Andreas had been waiting for an important letter of some kind. I can't find more than a mention of it, but what if the killer and the letter were connected? That might explain why he stayed in the house for days after the murders. He'd been waiting to intercept whatever the letter contained.

One last thought: by all accounts, the killer had been in or around the Gruber home many times before the events of March 31. The Grubers' former maid had quit her job because she said she felt the place was haunted. There had been the unrecognized newspaper. The odd noises. The missing key. Weeks and weeks of unusual activity that eventually led up to the day of the murders.

The day, mind you, that the new maid started working there. Maria Baumgarten had been killed just hours after arriving for her first day on the job. It makes you wonder: did her arrival upset the plans of whoever it was that seemed to be stalking the Gruber family?

Did she see him, and pay with her life?

A SAFE PLACE

Hinterkaifeck has the feel of a cabin in the woods, the centerpiece of many a horror film and novel. A place of retreat, far from the demands and prying eyes of the outside world, where we could go to get away. A place where we can find safety in the middle of an unsafe wilderness. A home away from home.

We want to feel safe, and thankfully most of us do. But there's just enough risk on the tails of the bell curve that we're always left wondering, "What if . . . ?" And that's how fear works. It sits in the dark corner at the edge of our minds and watches. We know it's not going to step out into the light, but we can feel it glaring at us from the dark.

I can't help but wonder if the Grubers ever had that sensation during those last few months. If maybe there had been times when Andreas just couldn't shake the feeling that someone was watching him. Did Viktoria have moments when she felt like she wasn't alone? We'll never know the answers to those questions, unfortunately.

One more tiny mystery: the physician who performed the autopsies on all six victims had their heads removed and sent to Munich for further study. Some reports claim that a clairvoyant was part of that research, but I can't find proof of that.

Their bodies were buried nearby, in what is now modern-day Waidhofen, but their skulls remained in Munich, and were eventually lost in the chaos of World War II.

Today, the farm in the woods is little more than a memory. All that is left today is a small memorial. But over the year that followed the tragedy there, it stood empty, like a crypt in the middle of that clearing in the forest, a constant reminder to the neighbors who passed by of the people they lost, and of the violence that had visited their small village.

That might be why they finally tore it down in 1923. Maybe they couldn't stand to look at it again. Maybe it needed upkeep that required going inside, and no one was willing to do that. Maybe they just wanted to move on and forget.

Whatever the true reason was, it was only after the farm was torn down that the murder weapon was finally discovered. One of the men found it among the debris at the top of the pile, mixed in with items that had been in storage.

It had been hidden inside the house all along, in the last place anyone would look: the attic.

Supply and Demand

BURIAL, LIKE DEATH, is supposed to be permanent. The tradition has a weight, a finality. The very act of placing our dead in a hole in the ground, and then covering them with pound after pound of heavy, damp soil . . . well, it's one of the most powerful metaphors of everyday life.

When we bury our dead, we bury the past. We dig deep and place something precious—some*one* precious—out of reach from society. And the vast majority of the time we do all of this in graveyards, places that are themselves viewed as sacred and set apart. Burial, for a huge portion of the world, is the end.

Graves, as eternal as they seem, are sometimes disturbed. Most of the time, the buried are unburied by accident. We assume this when we talk about the uncovering of ancient burial sites in places like Rome or London, often as a result of modern construction projects and development of long-abandoned property.

For example, the London skyscraper known colloquially as the Gherkin stands on the site of the 1,600-year-old grave of a girl from the Roman era of the city. The remains of King Richard III were found in 2012 beneath a parking lot in the city of Leicester. And just last year, a very old burial site was discovered beneath a portion of New York University. Sometimes the dead are disturbed.

Sometimes, though, it's on purpose. In ancient times the goal was often grave robbing. Nearly all of the tombs in the Valley of the Kings in Egypt were robbed of their treasures long before Egyptologists began to study them. When there are valuables on the line, humans have a way of moving past the sacredness of the grave and digging in—literally.

While most graves have been opened either purely by accident or intentionally by curious scholars, some have been dug up for darker reasons. In the eighteenth and nineteenth centuries, that reason had a noble veneer that concealed a more sinister activity. They called it body snatching.

In Demand

Something was happening in Edinburgh in the late 1700s. The Scottish Enlightenment had been transforming the culture and attitude of the city, and things were beginning to shift.

Edinburgh, you see, was becoming a major center for learning. And along with growth in the fields of literature, philosophy, mathematics, and economics, one of the pillars of that growth was medical science. If you wanted to become a physician in the late eighteenth century, chances are you were planning to move to Edinburgh.

One of the old medical terms that I think gets glossed over these days is the idea of the operating theater. Today that's the room in a hospital where surgeons perform sterile medical procedures. But two centuries ago, it looked a lot more like a real theater, which is where the name came from.

Educators would stand in front of a tall table, and the students would sit in tiered rows so that they could all have a good view. And what they'd be watching, in most cases, was human dissection. It wasn't sanitary, but nearly all of the subjects were already dead, so sterilization was a lot less important. The key for all of these medical students was to see the inner workings of the human body up close and personal.

Remember, these were the days before MRIs and radiography. If you wanted to know how a part of the human body worked, you needed to look inside, and that required cutting. Believe it or not, there was some debate among medical professionals as to whether this was actually a moral thing to do. But in the end, the need to learn far outweighed all other reasons.

The result was a huge demand for corpses. If you were going to teach a class that involved dissection, you needed a fresh body. The trouble was that the laws of the land vastly restricted where teachers could get bodies from. Thanks to an act of Parliament in 1752, the only bodies that could legally be used for dissection were those of executed murderers. By the early 1800s, though, fewer and fewer executions were happening.

At the same time, demand for corpses was a bit ... um ... *bloated.* Just London itself had over seven hundred medical students, and each of them was required to dissect at least three human bodies. You can see the problem, right? To help, a new criminal was born out of this turmoil: the resurrectionists.

These were the people who were willing to dig up freshly buried corpses and sell them to the colleges and universities who needed them. They were a creative bunch, truth be told. Sure, some of them would do the deed the typical way, digging straight down to the coffin, but that quickly became impossible. You see, people didn't like it when their loved ones were dug up and dragged away.

To combat the grave robbing, some unique preventative measures were implemented. Oftentimes family would organize a team of adults to literally sit beside the grave 24/7 for the first two weeks. Their goal was to guard the grave while the body beneath had time to decay enough to become undesirable to the resurrectionists. In other cemeteries, stone watchtowers were built, and guards were hired in place of family, working the *literal* graveyard shift.

Some buried their dead in metal coffins, locking them against thieves and animals alike. Others were interred in standard graves but were then covered with stone slabs or metal mortsafes, a sort of iron cage that protected the grave from being disturbed. In fact, if you stroll through Greyfriars Kirkyard in Edinburgh today, you'll see a number of them still protecting their occupants. Some

Internet posts will tell you that those were installed to keep zombies in their graves. Those Internet posts are dumb.

The resurrectionists were able to work around a lot of those techniques, though. Often times they'd start digging from a good twenty or thirty feet away and approach the grave through a tunnel from the side. After removing the headboard of the coffin, they would loop a rope around the head of the occupant and pull them out. And this would all happen right under the nose of a hired guard or a grieving family member.

Once they had the body, the clothing and personal belongings were stripped off and returned to the grave to avoid felony charges, and then these body snatchers would make their way to their favorite medical educator and make the sale. It was wrong on many levels, but it was common. And in Edinburgh, where more physicians trained than in most other cities, it was nearly an epidemic.

Despite that, though, it was still really difficult to get a corpse when you needed one. The resurrectionists worked hard and managed to supply hundreds of fresh bodies each year, but the educational need was nearly insatiable. And like any moment in human history when the market has demand that outpaces supply, people went looking for a creative solution.

And boy, did they find one.

A Dead Giveaway

The two Williams met in a boardinghouse in 1826 and quickly realized how similar their pasts were. If you stepped back and thought about it, it's as if they were destined to meet and work together.

The younger William, William Hare, was born in 1807 in northern Ireland. He grew up in close proximity to the Newry Canal, which cut through the countryside from Carlingford to Loch Neagh, where the coalfields were. He worked for a time at the local canal in Poyntzpass driving a team of horses along the route, but that job came to an end when he killed one of his employer's horses in a fit of rage. As a result, Hare packed up and left Ireland, taking his skills—and temper—with him to Scotland.

He'd been working on the Union Canal when he met a local man named Logue Laird who ran a boardinghouse for the destitute and the homeless. He was new to Edinburgh and this seemed like the best chance to get his feet on the ground, so he moved in. And that's how he met Logue's wife, Margaret. When Logue died in 1826, William married Margaret and the couple stayed in the boardinghouse.

At the same time, another William was working his way toward the boardinghouse. William Burke was also from Ulster in northern Ireland. He'd managed to move through a series of odd jobs, and had married and started a family. In 1817, though, he left them behind and emigrated to Scotland, where he began working on the Union Canal.

During his time in Edinburgh, Burke met a woman named Helen, and the pair made plans to move west and start a new life together. Instead, chance intervened and they were invited by Margaret Laird to stay at the boardinghouse, in one of the spare rooms. And that's when the two Williams met.

We know very little about their friendship. They both worked on the canal, so I can imagine them as the stereotypical factory buddies, walking home from work together, stopping at the local pub for a drink on their way. At the very least, sharing the same home and job brought them together at a level that was beyond casual.

On November 29, 1827, Margaret Laird stepped into the room where her husband sat. She had an expression on her face that was a knot of frustration and horror. One of their lodgers, an elderly man, had passed away during the night. Margaret had found him dead in his cot, a horrifying experience for most people. This tenant had no family that they were aware of, and no valuables worth selling, which was disappointing because the man also owed her for the past few months' worth of rent.

That's when Hare had an idea. He approached Burke and told him what had happened, and then presented an idea that required the man's help. What if they sold the body to a medical teacher? There were rumors on the streets that physicians were paying good money for fresh bodies, and it was hard to get fresher than this, no doubt. They'd be rid of the body, and might recoup the lost rent in the process. It was a morbid win-win scenario, but these were morbid men.

Law required the body to be buried, so they filled the coffin with firewood, buried that, and snuck the corpse away to Edinburgh University. There they were directed to a doctor named Robert Knox. Knox had been an army physician at Waterloo and had been teaching independently at the university for a little over a year with hopes of obtaining a full-time professorship there.

Knox taught a lot of anatomy classes, all of which required fresh cadavers. As a result, Knox had a large network of providers, teams of body-snatchers all across the city who were robbing graves and bringing him every cadaver they could get their hands on. Still, the demand from the growing class sizes was outpacing the supply, which left Dr. Knox with a problem.

When Burke and Hare approached him that night in November 1827, Knox took full advantage of the opportunity. He asked no questions, and the men were polite, but you have to imagine that Knox suspected something unusual. After all, the body was still clothed. And yet . . . he had needs, didn't he?

The two men went home that night with £7 in their collective pockets—in modern American money, that's close to $1,200. The rental debt was covered, and there was profit left to go around. But that much money, earned with such relative *ease* . . . well, it was hard to not think about the possibilities.

And that gave the men a killer idea.

MAKING A KILLING

It wasn't an original idea. There'd been rumors for years of disappearances, horrifying tales that were used to warn children to beware of strangers. The youth of Edinburgh were disappearing, they said, and you could be next if you weren't careful, so watch out.

Others whispered of abduction by Gypsies, or children spirited away by illegal slavers, but all of it was just gossip, xenophobic rumor masked as fantasy. At the core of it, though, was a grain of truth, which is why some members of the medical community—as well as politicians in London—were already discussing the warning signs. Soaring prices for dead bodies meant *someone* was bound to cross the line eventually.

I'm telling you all of this to help you understand something important: Burke and Hare didn't invent what they were about to do. They weren't the first, although they were arguably the best at it—which is why, years later, their names would be synonymous with the act. But they weren't pioneers by any means. They were just early adopters of that famous Wayne Gretzky lesson to skate to where the puck is going, not to where it's at right now. Except here the puck was a cadaver. I know, I'm stretching the analogy a bit. Work with me here.

A month after selling their first cadaver to Dr. Knox, Margaret told the two men of another tenant in the house, a man known as Joseph the miller, who was sick in his room. Burke and Hare paid him a visit, and after getting him drunk on whisky, they smothered him with a pillow. That body earned them a full £10 from Dr. Knox and zero suspicion. So they kept going.

With no more sick or dying tenants under their roof, Burke and Hare started to frequent the local taverns looking for poor, lonely travelers or members of the invisible layer of Edinburgh society. In February 1828 they met an elderly woman named Abigail Simpson and offered her a room at the boardinghouse for the night. Once behind closed doors, the whisky and pillow were used again, with the same results.

Even Margaret got in on the action, apparently by helping to bring victims home to the two men. They aimed for travelers who appeared poor, alone, and in search of assistance, and then played to those needs. Each visitor to the house was treated the same: whisky and suffocation.

Sometimes Burke and Hare worked together as a team, as they had with the first victim, and other times they split up and worked alone. They were in a line of work that required Goldilocks conditions, after all: the right person, in the right place, with the right needs, at the right time. It wasn't necessarily chance, but it wasn't all skill, either. Still, they were getting good at it, and they'd turned it into an art.

The men were dressing well now, and many of the locals near the boardinghouse had noticed this. Each new cadaver came with a bigger payday, and both men were living large as a result. But it wasn't always easy money. Long stretches of time would go by between victims, and sometimes it was easy to doubt whether their lucky streak would continue.

It was after one of those dry spells that Burke and Hare happened to bump into an old friend named Mary Haldane. Mary was an older woman who had once lived in the boardinghouse with them but had since moved out to find a better life. But she was also a drunk, and the men knew an opportunity when they saw one. Here was a victim who would have no problem with glass after glass of whisky.

After waiting for her to pass out that night, they smothered her to death, and then took her body to Dr. Knox the following morning. A few days later, Mary's daughter Peggy came searching for her missing mother. A local grocer had told her that he'd seen Mary in the company of Hare, so she knocked on their door.

Margaret answered the door and recognized Peggy immediately. Together with Burke's wife, Helen, the two women did their best to proclaim complete ignorance of Mary's whereabouts, but when the men heard them, they panicked. If they sent her away, she'd only go to the police. No, they needed to offer her some form of hope, some solution to her desperation.

Hare stepped into the hall and interrupted the conversation. He could help, he said. In fact, he knew where Peggy might look to find her mother. Peggy's eyes opened wide with hope, and then Hare stepped aside with a sweeping arm.

Would she care to come in and talk about it over a drink?

Burke and Hare continued on this way for months, and as they did, the death toll climbed steadily higher. And then, on October 31, 1828, Burke was in the local grocery store when an elderly woman named Mary Docherty stepped in. She was newly arrived from Ireland and had come to Edinburgh looking for her son. Burke heard her accent and saw how frail she was, and knew he had found his next victim.

He struck up a conversation with her, and after discovering where she had been born and what her last name was, he pretended to be distantly related through his mother's side. Mary fell for it. She was far from home, after all, and very alone. She had no travel companions, no money, and no place to stay, and so Burke kindly offered to lead her to the boardinghouse, where she was welcome to stay the night.

There was a problem, though. The inn was full, so to speak. They'd given their last room to a small family earlier in the week. James Grey was a former soldier, and he'd brought his wife and small child with him. Burke offered to find them temporary lodgings elsewhere for the night so that Mary, his newly discovered relative, could stay.

The Greys agreed and moved out for the night. After they'd gone, the drinking started. It was an evening full of dancing, shouting, laughter, and many, many songs sung at the top of their voices. Mary kept up nicely despite her old age, and each of them got as drunk as possible, which led to a fistfight between Burke and Hare.

There's some debate about whether the fight was real or planned, but the outcome worked in their favor nonetheless. In an effort to stop the fight, Mary stepped between the men and was knocked to the floor. Too drunk to get back up, she simply passed out where she lay, and that was the opportunity the men had been waiting for. They strangled her and then hid her body in her room between the bed and the wall, where a small pile of straw had been placed.

In the morning the Greys returned to eat breakfast at the boardinghouse, and they asked about the old woman. Gone, Burke told them. He claimed she'd gotten a bit too rude thanks to the alcohol, and they had been forced to turn her away in the night. Ann Grey thought it a shame, but shrugged and then stepped into her room to retrieve the stockings she'd left on the bed the afternoon before. And that brought her within sight of the pile of straw.

Burke panicked and demanded she leave it alone. She had been smoking a pipe at the time, and he shouted something about the straw and fire, and Mrs. Grey didn't like his tone. Something about it all seemed odd, and the seed of suspicion took root at that moment.

Later, through a series of mistakes, misunderstandings, and errors in judgment by Burke and Hare, the Greys found themselves in the big house all alone and very, very curious. So Mrs. Grey started to search the room again. Beneath the pile of straw, beside the bed she planned to sleep in that night, she was shocked to find the cold, dead body of the missing old woman.

The police were called to the house. The men managed to get the body out before their arrival, but it was too late. The Greys later identified Docherty's corpse in the possession of Dr. Knox, sealing the case. Burke and Hare were arrested, and their eleven-month killing spree—a run of murder that claimed seventeen victims in total—was finally brought to an end.

Hare proved to be more open with the police than Burke, and he managed to strike a deal with them. He turned king's evidence, agreeing to testify against his partner and tell the police everything that had happened, all in exchange for immunity from prosecution. So when the trial began on Christmas Eve in 1828, it was Burke alone who received the death sentence.

He was hanged a month later. It was a cold winter day, and torrential rain pounded the cobblestones outside the courthouse. But no one cared about the rain. A crowd of nearly twenty-five thousand gathered to watch the killer drop, and cheered at his death.

The following day, Burke's body was dissected at Old College in front of a sellout crowd. For over two hours, Dr. Alexander

Monro led his anatomy lecture using the former body-snatcher's corpse as a teaching tool, while groups of students were led through in waves to give everyone a chance to see the infamous killer.

During the dissection, Monro stopped for a moment and retrieved a piece of parchment and a quill. The students watched him in total silence as he dipped the quill and began to scratch out a note: "This is written with the blood of William Burke who was hanged at Edinburgh on 28th January, 1829 for the murder of Mary Docherty. This blood was taken from his head."

BURYING THE PAST

Some people have referred to Burke and Hare as the most famous grave robbers in history, but the truth is that they never once opened a grave. They never even stole a body, in the true body-snatcher sense. Faced with a supply and demand problem, Burke and Hare created their own inventory. Enterprising, yes, but not grave robbing in the traditional sense. As a result, seventeen people lost their lives, and all but one of them—Mary Docherty—ended up on the table in a medical theater.

There was a silver lining as a result of their deeds, though. Just three years after Burke's execution, Parliament passed the Anatomy Act of 1832, which opened the door for medical doctors and anatomy teachers to find enough cadavers for their work. Bodies could now be donated, and unclaimed corpses from prisons and workhouses could also be used.

We know about the last days of Burke and Hare, but what I'm more curious about are the ten months before their arrest—how two poor men living in Edinburgh's Old Town managed to lie to themselves all that time, to justify their actions and then strut around town in expensive clothing. I'm interested in the psychology of it all, how they slept at night. Because it couldn't have been easy.

These men were engaged in something that came with layer upon layer of moral debt. They were luring in needy people with the promise of help, which was bad enough on its own. Then they were ending their lives. Finally, they denied them the burial they deserved. How does a person process those deeds and live with themselves after the fact? William Hare was never tried and convicted for his crimes, so one can assume he lived for decades with all of this weighing on his conscience.

Maybe, though, just maybe, he did try to make things right. You see, something odd was found in 1836, just seven years after Hare's release. Outside Edinburgh is a rocky hill known locally as Arthur's Seat, and in June of that year, some boys were on the northeast side hunting for rabbits.

In a moment of distraction, one of them began to scale part of the rocky face of the hill, when he lost his footing and slipped. He instinctively reached for a handhold and caught the edge of a slab of stone that had been wedged in a crevice. When the stone fell away, it revealed a large, man-made hole in the hill.

The boy leaned in, trying to make sense of what he could see inside. There were shadows and moisture and odd shapes. And if he wasn't mistaken . . . wood. He reached in, brushed away the cobwebs, and pulled one of the objects out.

It was a coffin. A tiny wooden coffin, decorated with tin and carved from a single block of wood. Inside was a wooden doll about four inches long, dressed in a tiny shirt and trousers, with a face carved on the round head. The boy put the coffin back, and then counted. There were a lot of them. All coffins, all occupied by a tiny figure, all buried with care.

The final total was a curious number, to say the least. There were *seventeen* of them.

That Axman Jazz

ETWEEN MAY 1918 and October 1919, there was a jazz fan on the loose in New Orleans.

Wait; that's not right. Let me try that again.

Between May 1918 and October 1919, there was a *killer* on the loose in New Orleans.

On May 22, 1918, while Joseph Maggio and his wife, Catherine, were asleep in bed, someone broke into their home and killed them. They lived above their retail space, where they sold groceries and ran a bar, but the killer didn't seem to be interested in the valuable food and alcohol in the shop below. He came, it seems, for them.

He cut their throats with a razor blade, most likely because it was quiet. But after he was done, the killer took his ax and proceeded to bash the heads of both victims to an indefinable mess. Maybe it was to hide the killing wound. Maybe it was to let out some sort of personal rage he felt toward them. No one knows. History just remembers the crime scene.

Catherine died instantly, but Joseph actually managed to survive through the night until his brothers Jake and Andrew discovered him. But he only held on for a while, dying just moments after they arrived. And so the police were brought in.

The authorities found the razor and traced it back to Joseph's brother Andrew, who was quickly arrested. But the facts didn't line up. There were, however, multiple reports of an unknown man lurking near the Maggio home prior to the murders. And so the police released Andrew and went looking for the real killer.

Unfortunately, the killer was already on the move.

DAS AXMAN

One month later, on June 27, Louis Besumer and Harriet Lowe were asleep in the apartment behind Besumer's grocery store when a man quietly walked into the room. The stranger then struck both of the sleeping victims in the head with an ax he had found elsewhere in the apartment. Both suffered fractured skulls and were taken to the hospital.

Besumer survived, but Harriet Lowe died a little over a month later, on August 5. That same day, one Mrs. Schneider—twenty-eight years old and eight months pregnant—was taking a late afternoon nap. She awoke to find a dark figure of a man standing over her. The man proceeded to beat her head and face. She too survived, and weeks later she gave birth to a healthy baby girl.

On August 10, Joseph Romano, an elderly man who lived with his two nieces, was attacked by a man with an ax. The two women saw the attacker and described him as dark-skinned and heavyset. But that didn't explain how he entered the house, as the only point of entry was a single missing panel that had been chiseled out of the home's door.

Charles Cortimiglia, his wife, Rosie, and their infant daughter, Mary, were all attacked on March 10, 1919, while they slept. A bloody ax was found on the back porch, near the door—the door, mind you, that had a missing panel.

Three days later, on March 13, the New Orleans *Times-Picayune* received a letter from someone claiming to be the killer. Here's a sample of what it said:

> *They have never caught me and they never will. . . . Now, to*
> *be exact, at 12:15 next Tuesday night, I am going to pass over*

New Orleans. In my infinite mercy, I am going to make a little proposition to you people.

Here it is: I am very fond of jazz music, and I swear by all the devils in the nether regions that every person shall be spared in whose home a jazz band is in full swing at the time I have just mentioned. If everyone has a jazz band going, well, then, so much the better for you people. One thing is certain, and that is that some of your people who do not jazz it on Tuesday night will get the axe.

The city complied, and jazz was played across town that night in homes and social clubs. True to his word, the killer spared the people of New Orleans. But just for the night.

More attacks followed. Steve Boca—another grocer, oddly enough—was attacked on August 10. Sarah Laumann was the next victim, on September 3. But it was the final attack, on October 27, that left the darkest stain on the city's memory.

That night, Mike Pepitone's wife was pulled from sleep to the sound of her husband screaming. She ran to his bedroom and found him covered in blood that flowed from a massive head wound. But she also saw the killer.

And then it was over. The killer disappeared. No one went to trial. No one was held accountable for the murders that plagued the city for nearly two years. It all just came to an end, like the silence after the final notes of a jazz tune.

And that was the end . . . or maybe not. You see, on December 2, 1920, a man was walking through the dark streets of Los Angeles—two thousand miles from New Orleans—when a figure stepped out of the shadows. The figure held no ax, though. This time it was a gun, and a moment later, Joseph Mumfre lay dead on the street.

Mumfre, you see, was originally from New Orleans. He was an ex-con who had been released from prison just before the ax murders had begun in 1918, and he had moved to LA just a week after the murder of Mike Pepitone.

The killer stood over Mumfre's body, gun in hand, while sirens drew closer and closer. There was no panic or flight from the scene of the crime. So when the LA police arrived minutes later, it was a simple matter to take the killer into custody.

Her name was Esther Albano, but we would know her by another name: Mrs. Mike Pepitone.

The Altercation

HENRY LYONS WAS in a difficult situation. It all began with a disagreement his friend Giles Cleft had with Cleft's ex-wife. They had never really gotten along, and Lyons had at first assumed that this was merely one more fight in a long string of moments of domestic unrest.

The couple had been married for just four years, although some records say twelve. They even had a child together. But by 1867, the couple had legally separated, and Cleft's ex-wife had moved out with their three-year-old daughter and into the home of one Thomas Farrant.

This didn't make Giles Cleft happy for a number of reasons. First, Giles was fifty-three, but his former spouse was a mere twenty-eight, and Farrant—the man she now lived with—was in the prime of his life at a youthful twenty-five. Farrant was mildly successful, selling fruit there in Bristol, while Giles lived in a less desirable lodging house. And Giles believed that when she moved out, his ex-wife had run off with some of his own personal belongings.

Oh, and Farrant was Giles's great-nephew. Needless to say, he was feeling slighted, and he was angry about that. So the day after Christmas in 1867, Giles made his way over to Farrant's home, and he brought Henry Lyons along with him. I'm not sure why. Bodyguard? Witness? Wingman? It's hard to say for sure.

Lyons, though, waited downstairs, while Giles headed up to ask for the stolen belongings. I would imagine it was quiet at first. Then there was a bit of shouting. And then more yells, along with crashing and shrieks from the younger woman. At some point in the fight, Lyons decided he should check in on the disgruntled couple, and so he headed up to join them.

He walked in on a scene ripped straight from the pages of a Victorian murder mystery. Giles had broken one of the legs off the bed and was beating his former wife with it. The child wailed in the corner, obviously frightened. And despite the cold December air, the small window was wide open.

Lyons moved instinctively. He stepped between the two and managed to allow the woman a chance to escape out the door to safety. She came back a couple of minutes later for the child, and then vanished again. And it was somewhere in between those brief moments when people outside began to scream.

Eyewitnesses reported that a man had fallen out the window of the upper story of the building. The man toppled nearly thirty feet to the pavement below, landing headfirst on the stone lip of a cellar window before crumpling into a lifeless pile on the pavement. Within moments the man was dead.

The man, it turns out, was Thomas Farrant, Giles's nephew and the object of much of his anger. It goes without saying that Farrant died as a result of the fall, and so, as one might expect, an investigation began into his death. How, everyone wanted to know, did Farrant end up falling out of the window?

One theory is that Farrant climbed out the window to escape Giles when he heard the older man screaming through the door. But there are issues with that idea. Farrant was young and strong, and it was his own home. Why flee? Also, the window was very small, less than two feet square, so crawling through it would have been extremely difficult if his goal was to stand up on the other side.

The alternative theory, though, was that someone had thrown him out the window. Lyons claimed that when he arrived on the scene, the room was empty except for Mr. and Mrs. Cleft. Giles himself told the police that he didn't hear a sound from anyone other than his ex-wife. As far as he could tell, Farrant had never been there.

The witnesses on the street below were clear, though: Farrant fell only after Mrs. Cleft had exited the building. So Farrant had been pushed out his own window. But who did the pushing?

All signs pointed to Giles Cleft, the disgruntled ex-husband. Upset over his wife's theft. Angered over her choice of roommate. Outraged at his lot in life. Whatever the reason, it would seem that Mr. Cleft had a motive, single-handedly grappled with Thomas Farrant, and shoved him out the window. Except there was one little detail that made that hard to believe.

Giles Cleft was blind.

Drained

B ELA KISS, WHO was born in 1877, moved to the Hungarian town of Czinkota in 1900. This was long before the town was absorbed into Budapest. He worked as a tinsmith, although we don't know much else about him beyond that. He rented a home in a cozy neighborhood and lived alone.

He was alone because his wife, Maria—a woman fifteen years younger than he—had reputedly found herself a lover and the pair had run off together in 1912, leaving Kiss to carry on by himself.

As a result, Kiss hired an elderly housekeeper named Mrs. Jakubec to come take care of the cleaning and chores while he worked. He gave her a tour of the house, pointed out all of the important features, and walked her through her responsibilities. His private office, though, was off-limits.

That was where he sat and corresponded with his lady friends. His housekeeper had seen some of the sealed envelopes on their way to the post office but never had the opportunity to read them. And Kiss occasionally brought home a young woman, but no woman ever came back for a repeat visit. Maybe he had a commitment problem, or maybe they didn't care for him in person. It was hard to say for sure.

Mr. Kiss thought that political change was coming, though, and he told others that he wanted to be prepared. He'd gone as far as to collect metal drums, and he said he was filling the large barrels with gasoline, "just in case." And by 1914, he was proven right. World War I broke out, and he was required to enlist and serve in the military. He handed his house keys to the housekeeper and told her to take care of the place.

And then two years went by.

Eventually the landlord decided he was probably never going to see Bela Kiss again, and began the process of making the home available for rent to a new tenant. He traveled to the home in July 1916 and immediately found the barrels of gasoline. After two years of war, it didn't take a genius to recognize a valuable commodity, so he called the local police department to make the fuel available to the government.

Maybe he asked for payment, or maybe he donated it in an effort to earn some goodwill. We don't know the motivation, but we *do* know the outcome. Soldiers arrived at the house to take possession of the fuel drums but wanted to inspect them before hauling them off. So one of the soldiers poked a hole in the lid of one drum. And then backed away.

The odor that escaped was powerful, and full of the scent of decay and rot. It wasn't gasoline, that much was immediately clear, and so they opened the drum and drained it. Inside, they found the body of a woman. They drained another drum and found another body. Over and over, body after body, more and more women were discovered, each the victim of strangulation.

In all, the bodies of twenty-four women were found on the property. The housekeeper was called in for questioning, and although she didn't know any more than the police did, she did point them to his private office door, the door she had never been allowed to unlock. So the police got inside.

On the surface, it was very office-like. Bookshelves lined the walls, and a desk sat in the middle of the room. But in the desk the police found a journal of his correspondence with over seventy-four women, along with a photo album and some letters that were never mailed. Some used false names, and some went as far back as 1903. Kiss, it seems, had been living a secret life. He'd been writing to women who posted in the marriage columns of local newspapers, luring them to his home, and then killing them. And no one had ever suspected a thing.

Of course, calls to the military were made, looking for the man, but there was no immediate information. And then, in October of that year, the military sent word that Kiss was recuperating in a Serbian hospital. Officers were sent to capture him, but by the time they got there, Kiss had somehow placed another man's corpse in his own bed and slipped out of the building.

He was never seen again.

Or maybe not. Four years later, a French soldier encountered a man who used one of Kiss's false names. A man who bragged that he was pretty good at strangling people. A man who looked a lot like the description of Bela Kiss. Police were alerted, but the man managed to disappear before they arrived.

In 1932, a man who fit his description was seen stepping out of the subway station in Times Square in New York City. A police detective with a photographic memory claimed he recognized the man from old photos but couldn't get close because of the crowd.

Four years later, someone reported that a man who looked just like Kiss was working as a janitor in an apartment building on Sixth Avenue. Police were sent to look into it, but when they arrived, the janitor was gone. After that, his trail goes cold.

One last thought: there was something odd about each of the victims found in those fuel barrels that day in 1916. Yes, they'd been strangled to death, but they all shared another wound.

Right where you might expect, each victim had twin puncture marks on the side of their necks. When the bodies were further examined, one last clue was discovered.

Each woman had been completely drained of blood.

A Miner Thing

JAMES GRAHAM WAS a miller in Durham County, far to the north in England. It was a hard and grueling occupation, one that involved long days in the mill, operating the basic machinery involved in grinding grain down to flour. Sometimes the mill was powered by wind, sometimes by the waters of a stream or river. No matter how it all worked, though, it was, for all intents and purposes, the earliest form of a factory job.

One night in the winter of 1631 he experienced something unusual. He had just put one final load of corn into the mill and had come downstairs to leave for the night when he stopped in his tracks. There, standing on the floor of his mill, was a woman. The doors had been locked, so he wasn't sure how she'd gained access, but it seemed as if she might need his help.

This woman, according to Graham's description, was hideous. This was a result of the wounds—five, in fact—on her head. Blood covered her pale face. Most frightening of all, though, was what she said to him.

She told him her name was Anne Walker. No, she didn't need help, despite her injuries. She was already dead, you see. She'd been murdered, and she knew who had committed the crime.

Graham didn't press Anne for information; she gave all of that up very freely. It was almost as if she was trying to report the crime in an official capacity. As if she were seeking help in putting the matter to rest. After capturing Graham's attention and telling him what had happened, she named names.

She had worked as a house cleaner for her cousin, John Walker. He owned a nearby estate, and Graham recognized him by name and reputation. But Anne had become pregnant by him, and as a result, he had promised to have her removed to a private place where she could finish her pregnancy and give birth away from the prying eyes of the community.

One night John Walker sent one of his men, Mark Sharp, to take her to that special place. Sharp had worked as a coal miner, so at first she didn't think it unusual when he led her to a nearby coal pit.

Once there, though, he took up one of the pickaxes and struck her down. Five blows to the head, over and over again, until she was dead. Then he buried her body in the pit, hid the weapon, and disposed of his now-bloody leggings and shoes.

Graham was the only person she'd been able to find and tell about her plight, and that made her a bit more desperate than most ghostly visions. So desperate, in fact, that she threatened him. Unless Graham went to the local magistrate and reported what she'd told him, she promised to haunt him.

Graham might have been frightened, but he was also a tired, busy man. So rather than do anything about it that night, he went home. But not wanting to be haunted by her, he made it a point for the next few days to not stay in his mill alone past sunset. Which he managed to do for some time.

Finally, though, on the night of December 20, Graham made the mistake of overstaying in the mill. As promised, Anne Walker returned and repeated her demands. Which turned out to be enough for Graham. The very next morning he visited Sergeant Hutton, the local magistrate, and told him of the crime.

I can imagine Hutton was skeptical, but he also knew of the disappearance of young Anne Walker. Many of the locals had whispered that prior to her disappearance she'd appeared pregnant. So he entertained these details and went looking for the body. If it was where the miller claimed it was, there might be something to his story.

Later that morning, he arrived with some helpers to search the old coal pit and dig through the soil. After a while, they made a grisly discovery: Anne Walker's pregnant, decomposing body, with a face covered in blood from multiple wounds to the head. They also found the pickax, and the leggings and shoes belonging to Sharp.

Immediately he and a team of strong men located Sharp and Walker and took them both into custody. They were put on trial, and Judge Davenport found them guilty based on the physical evidence. Afterward, they were sentenced to be hanged.

As you might expect, James Graham was relieved to have helped. He brought two criminals to justice, after all. As a result, Anne Walker—perhaps appeased by the actions of the miller and the trial that followed—went silent.

She was never seen again.

Homecoming

THEY CALLED HIM the Handsome Bandit, and he *was*. Good-looking, well groomed, and—according to the stories—quite the charmer. Don't judge a book by its cover, though; smooth, yes, but this man was a smooth *criminal*. Born in 1845, he was wanted for murder and robbery in two states before the age of sixteen. And it only got worse from there.

But that life of crime came with a string of prison terms. The first was a seven-year stay in state prison in Missouri, ending with his release in 1890. He was back in 1893 for fourteen more years. And then, as if he hadn't learned his lesson yet, he was arrested and convicted for burglary in 1908, spending one more year behind bars.

After that, he told them he was done. He was ready to behave. But crime was like a well-worn path in his life, and it was far too easy to slip back into the rut. So on New Year's Eve in 1910 he put on his best suit, freshly polished shoes, and the bowler hat he always wore, and headed out into the cold Chicago air.

When he entered the packed saloon on West Sixteenth Street, he pulled a gun and shouted for everyone to fill his sack with their cash and jewelry. And he almost got away with it. At the last moment, though, a police officer walked in and caught him in the act. Shots were fired. Bullets tore through the clothing of both men.

But only the Handsome Bandit toppled over. He died a few minutes later.

Some people see more than a shoot-out, though. Some believe there were *other* forces at work. It was a curse, they say, for betraying one of America's most notorious serial killers. And even though that killer had died fourteen years earlier, it was more than logical that the Handsome Bandit, Marion Hedgepeth, was his newest victim—from beyond the grave.

Who was he? Well, Hedgepeth knew him as Henry Howard, but that, of course, was just an alias. To you and me, he'll always be known as . . . H. H. Holmes.

ABANDONED

The man that history has come to know as H. H. Holmes certainly built a legacy for himself. Except his legacy was filled with secret chambers, trapdoors, gas valves, and a list of victims that some historians think exceeds two hundred innocent lives. And we've heard his story here before.

Well, part of it.

You see, the lion's share of historical attention always falls on the Castle, the apartment complex built by Holmes that functioned more like a dungeon than home sweet home. We're filled with a morbid fascination regarding his methods, his madness, and his mastery of the art of murder. But in an effort to uncover what went on behind the walls of the Castle, we miss an entire chapter in his story.

But first, a reminder: it was the 1893 Chicago World's Fair that brought his victims into his web. Some came for work, some for pleasure, and some for a chance to start a new life. Most of them were young women, and upon arriving they needed a place to stay. Holmes gladly accommodated as many of them as he could. And thanks to his methods, his tenant turnover rate was . . . well . . . *brisk.*

When the World's Fair ended on October 30, 1893, it was like the fire hose had been turned off. Rental income, along with that steady flow of new victims, dried up almost overnight. What *didn't* stop, though, was the knocking on the door by his creditors, who were starting to circle closer and closer, like vultures around a dying animal.

So Holmes did something unthinkable: he abandoned ship. Think about it. He'd spent years building the Castle, planning his crimes, and then slaughtering dozens—perhaps *hundreds*—of people there. But it was either face the creditors and give them access to the building or make a run for it while he still had a chance.

And he didn't run alone. Holmes had a helper named Benjamin Pitezel, who served as his right-hand man, and there was no one Holmes trusted more. Life hadn't been kind to Pitezel, though. Jobs had been hard to come by, and the work he performed for Holmes wasn't really the sort that left him feeling good about himself. Add in the pressures of supporting a wife and five young, hungry children, and it's no wonder he had a reputation for being an alcoholic.

So in early 1894 the two men made a run for it, hoping to find work on the road. And their first stop was Fort Worth, Texas. You see, one of the women Holmes had killed months earlier, Minnie Williams, had conveniently signed over her inheritance to him. It was a sizable sum, and he planned to collect it. But he and Pitezel quickly discovered that the authorities in Fort Worth were a bit too nosy for their taste, and they gave up.

Before leaving Texas, Holmes managed to use forged documents and counterfeit money to purchase several train cars full of horses, and then he traveled north with them. Once in St. Louis, he sold them, but the authorities there caught wind of it and tracked him down. By July 1894 he'd been arrested and sentenced to prison under the false name of Henry Howard.

It was during his time in prison that he got to know Marion Hedgepeth, the Handsome Bandit. Hedgepeth seemed like a smart man. He was experienced and well connected, so Holmes began to tease more and more information out of him. Specifically, he was looking for a crooked lawyer who could help him get away with future insurance fraud, and offered $500 for a solid tip. Hedgepeth claimed he knew just the man for the job.

After Holmes's third wife, Georgianna, bailed him out, he quickly moved on and forgot the deal. He reconnected with Pitezel, who'd recently brought his wife and children to St. Louis to resettle, and reached out to the attorney Hedgepeth had told him about. The man, Jeptha Howe, agreed to meet, and soon the three men began planning.

Howe would later declare Holmes to be "one of the smoothest and slickest men that he had ever heard tell of." He was impressed with the killer's intellect and his ability to think around challenges. And they were going to need that for their next scheme.

Holmes, you see, wanted to die. Well, not really, but he wanted it to appear that he had. And for a number of really good reasons. There was all that evidence hidden away in the Castle, his ever-growing criminal record, even the curious relatives of his victims. All of it threatened to catch up with him. It would be better if he just died, if only on paper.

Then there was the financial payoff. Because, of course, he had a life insurance policy. So Holmes and Pitezel traveled to Rhode Island, where they watched the local morgues for a body that looked enough like Holmes to fool the authorities. When they found one, the corpse was taken to the beach near one of the many luxury resorts and burned.

Holmes somehow managed to get the corpse identified as himself, and soon after, his crooked lawyer filed the claim with the life insurance company. But after everything they'd gone through to get to that point, the plan began to fall apart. The insurance company didn't have a good feeling about the identity of the victim and refused to pay on the policy.

Now, Holmes couldn't very well fight for the claim himself. There was no way to prove the body really was his own other than the physical similarities. But the insurance company wanted irrefutable proof, and neither Howe nor Holmes could give them that.

So instead he and Pitezel dropped it and moved on to Philadelphia. Holmes had a new idea, but it was going to take a lot of work to set up. And to do it, he would lean heavily on Pitezel for help.

But as everyone knows, if you lean too hard, you're liable to fall over. And that's exactly what began to happen.

But Holmes wouldn't go down alone.

A BODY DOUBLE

This time it was Benjamin Pitezel's turn to die. It would be another insurance scam, involving yet another body double. But this time they needed to do it right, and Holmes had finally figured it out.

You see, the insurance company would want solid proof. And a fake Pitezel wouldn't be enough, because just pointing at a body and claiming it was a specific person no longer worked. Instead, Holmes believed that the body needed to be found in a place only Pitezel should be. The proof, Holmes believed, would be in the *location* of the body, not the appearance.

But all of this required a long game. Pitezel used a false identity to rent a storefront at 1316 Callowhill Street. The business would be a patent office and inventor's lab, perfect for a growing city at the height of the second Industrial Revolution. Then Pitezel sent for his wife and children, who soon arrived to complete the picture of normal domestic life.

At some point in late August, Pitezel bumped into a man named Eugene Smith, who was a carpenter looking for work. Pitezel told him about his inventor's laboratory, and invited him to come by the following week to discuss employment. And on the afternoon of September 3, 1894, that's just what Smith did.

When he knocked on the shop window, no one answered, but the door was unlocked and so he let himself in. He probably shouted hello into the empty room, a bit of confusion in his voice. He probably walked a few steps in, to see if the man he'd come to meet had somehow not heard him. And that's when the smell reached his nose.

It was the scent of a charnel house, the acrid, bitter smell of burned flesh. Which would probably have sent most of us running in the other direction. But Smith needed a job, and it was an inventor's workshop, so he probably just told himself it was part of some experiment, and forced his feet to take him deeper in.

He pushed a curtain aside, stepped into the back room, and then stopped. There was a body on the floor, surrounded by a pool of crimson. The clothing looked familiar, but the head was horribly burned, almost beyond recognition. Almost. If he squinted, he was pretty sure, sort of, that it might be the man who asked him to come by that day.

So he called the authorities, gave his statement, and then left them to their job. And the Philadelphia police fell for it. They connected the dots between Smith's story and the name on the shop lease papers, and stamped their seal of approval on the corpse's identity. Which was what Holmes and the others had been waiting for.

Howe filed the paperwork with Fidelity Mutual Life Association, and soon the men were looking at a check for $10,000. Their hard work had paid off. Holmes gave Howe a quarter of the money, and another $500 to Pitezel's wife. Her husband had gone into hiding, which was pretty obvious given the circumstances.

Except it was all a lie. After all, Holmes was very good at lying. Benjamin Pitezel wasn't in hiding, and he would never return to claim his share of the money. Because he was dead.

You see, while Pitezel was carrying out his part of the plan, Holmes had begun a second scheme behind the man's back. It began with forged letters to Pitezel from his wife, Carrie. Holmes knew Pitezel was an alcoholic, and he knew that stress at home would set the man off. So he sent fake letters to him at the shop, hoping they would cause Pitezel to get drunk. And it worked.

Early on the afternoon of September 5, just a few hours before Eugene Smith showed up for his job interview, Holmes entered the shop and found Pitezel in a drunken stupor. Think about that for a second. I know it's easy to hear all of the commentary on how skilled Holmes was and brush it off as hyperbole. But this was a man who would make Dexter jealous.

So with a bit of smug satisfaction, he took a length of rope from the closet and tied Pitezel's hands and feet. Then he retrieved a bottle of benzene, a clear liquid used as an industrial solvent that also happened to be incredibly flammable. And then . . . well, why don't we let Holmes himself describe what happened next.

"I proceeded to burn him alive," Holmes later wrote. "So horrible was this torture that in writing of it I have been tempted to attribute his death to some humane means—not with a wish to spare myself, but because I fear that it will not be believed that one could be so heartless and depraved."

But that was Holmes in a nutshell, after all. Heartless and depraved. Anything and everything was nothing more than the means to an end. And that end was almost always money.

So when he handed Carrie Pitezel the $500 and lied to her about her husband, he did so with joy. He later told the police that he'd wanted to kill Pitezel since the moment he'd met the man. Morbid or not, Holmes was feeling pretty good about his long-term goals.

But he wasn't done yet. First, he took the money back from Carrie Pitezel, telling her that he wanted to invest it for her. She handed it over without an ounce of worry. Then Holmes gathered everyone in his little community—his third wife, Georgianna; Carrie Pitezel; and the five Pitezel children—and ushered them onto a train out of town.

Wait, I'm sorry. I just called them his "community." In reality, they were all potential witnesses. Eyes and ears that might notice something inconvenient to his plans. And as stereotypical as it might sound to our Hollywood-influenced minds, Holmes didn't want any loose ends.

The witnesses, you see, would have to disappear.

A HOUSE DIVIDED

It wasn't as easy as pushing everyone onto a train and leaving town. If only it were. No, Holmes had a problem: there were enough adults in the group that, if they got to talking, they might start putting the pieces together, which would be a very bad thing for him.

So Holmes flexed his manipulative muscles and managed to split them into three separate groups. He booked his wife, Georgianna, in one train car, Carrie Pitezel in another with her oldest and youngest children, and then the three middle children—Alice, Nellie, and Howard—in a third.

Over the next few weeks, the group traveled in the most bizarre fashion, all painstakingly managed by Holmes. And the entire time, Carrie Pitezel and Georgianna were unaware of each other's presence. When they stopped in various cities, Holmes would rent houses or rooms for them all that were just close enough but never together, often keeping Carrie separated from her children.

They seemed to travel everywhere. Indianapolis. Detroit. Cincinnati. New York. Holmes led them all across the eastern half of the United States. He even slipped up into Canada for a short time, spending a few days in Toronto, where he rented a house at 16 St. Vincent Lane.

Not long after, at one of their many stops, Carrie Pitezel asked Holmes if she could see her children, but he told her no. He'd left them with an old widow back in Indianapolis, but promised they'd be reunited soon enough. Which was another lie. One that Carrie fell for.

The last big move happened in early November 1894. He sent Georgianna to stay with her parents back in Indiana, and then took Carrie Pitezel to Vermont. He rented her a house in Burlington before heading east to New Hampshire to visit his own elderly parents. Rumor says he also paid a visit to his first wife, Clara, and even bought their son a suit.

But this deeply tangled web of lies that Holmes was stringing together was about to come unraveled. Weeks before, you see, Fidelity Mutual had become suspicious about the insurance claim that Holmes had collected on. It's not that they doubted the identity of the body. No, it was the manner of death. They didn't believe it was an accident.

So they hired an investigator named Frank Geyer to help. Geyer was a member of the Pinkerton Detective Agency, sort of a private security and investigation company founded by Allan Pinkerton back in 1850. And when Geyer was handed the job, he dug in deep, quickly discovering that Henry Howard, the false name used by Holmes, had a record.

That name took him to Missouri, where he interviewed Holmes's old cellmate, Marion Hedgepeth, the Handsome Bandit. The man, you'll recall, that Holmes had promised to pay $500 before changing his mind. Feeling cheated, Hedgepeth was more than eager to return the favor, so he confessed everything he knew about Howard to Geyer.

After that, it was a matter of following the clues, of which there were few. Holmes was good at being invisible, after all. But Geyer was good at his job. Maybe it was the paper trail left by Georgianna when she bailed Holmes out of prison, or their marriage certificate. Whatever it was, Geyer found it, and was soon headed to Indiana to find her parents.

Imagine his surprise when he found Georgianna herself. And she led Geyer to Carrie Pitezel in Burlington, who in turn told him that Holmes had recently headed to Boston. Geyer moved quickly; on November 17, 1894, he and his associates finally caught up with Holmes, and took him into custody.

It was only after Holmes had been locked up in a Philadelphia jail cell on charges of insurance fraud that two significant things happened. First, the janitor for the building that Holmes had abandoned in Chicago decided to go to the police and tell them about the parts of the building that were off-limits. Which, of course, evolved into the investigation that's taught us everything we know about the Castle.

But the second was Carrie Pitezel's request for Geyer to find her three missing children—Alice, Nellie, and Howard. His first stop was Detroit, but he found no sign of them there. He did, however, find evidence that some of the floorboards had been pulled up, where a shallow hole had been dug in the dirt.

It wasn't until Geyer arrived in Toronto that his investigation began to gain traction. Interviews led him to the cottage at 16 St. Vincent Lane, where a neighbor recalled seeing a man with two little girls. A man, he said, who had borrowed a shovel to dig a potato patch. When the true meaning sank in, Geyer must have felt sick.

The bodies of Nellie and Alice Pitezel were found beneath several feet of loose dirt. They'd been murdered, that much was clear, but how it had been done was a mystery. It was only after Geyer and the others discovered the large trunk in one of the upstairs bedrooms, and the rubber tubing that ran between it and a gas pipe, that the story came into focus: miles from his precious Castle, H. H. Holmes had crafted a temporary gas chamber to murder the Pitezel girls.

But eight-year-old Howard Pitezel was still missing, so Geyer pressed on with urgency. Desperate, he traveled back to Indiana, where he interviewed hundreds of people with the hope of finding the house that Holmes had rented there near Indianapolis. Some estimates claim Geyer followed up on over nine hundred leads, and that persistence eventually paid off.

With a better understanding of how Holmes operated, Geyer had the house and property searched with incredible diligence. When they identified a bone fragment in the fireplace as human, the entire chimney was dismantled, which slowly exposed what little remained of young Howard. Later, under oath, Holmes described how he had drugged the boy, killed him, and then burned his body piece by piece to destroy the evidence.

Howard Pitezel was the last innocent life to be taken away by the hands of H. H. Holmes.

HOMECOMING

Herman Mudgett spent his life building a tower of lies: his business ventures, his love affairs, his insurance scams, and his trail of bodies across so much of North America. Maybe that's why his Chicago murder castle is such a powerful image in our minds—that warren of body chutes, gas chambers, and torture rooms was a physical reminder of that world of lies.

So it's no surprise that at the end of it all, he headed back toward the only real life he had ever had. The only place where there were no lies: home. Maybe, just maybe, there was a small part of him that wished he could start over and do things differently. Then again, maybe not.

After his execution on May 7, 1896—an execution that didn't go according to plan, mind you, with his body writhing at the end of the noose for over fifteen minutes—Mudgett was finally buried in Philadelphia's Holy Cross Cemetery. At his request, his body was placed in a simple pine coffin, which was then filled with cement. After it was placed in the grave, more cement was poured on top.

There are rumors, of course, that Mudgett faked his death. That he somehow escaped to live on in Europe. Even as I write this, three of his great-grandchildren have announced plans to exhume his remains and test them, just to be sure.

But whether or not the body in the grave truly belongs to the man we call H. H. Holmes, there are those who believe that his evil was so deep, so horrific and powerful, that it managed to live on. That the noose and cement weren't enough to stop him from killing again.

The first was a physician who testified during the trial, Dr. William Matten. He died of blood poisoning shortly after Holmes was buried. The trial judge died next, followed by another of the medical witnesses.

One of the priests who visited with Holmes in his final hours died mysteriously near his own church, and a member of the jury was killed in an unusual electrical accident. Even Frank Geyer, the man who brought Holmes to justice, became seriously ill after the trial, although he somehow managed to survive.

There were others, too. The father of one of the victims who passed away suddenly. The Fidelity Mutual Insurance office that burned to the ground. The prison superintendent who committed suicide. And of course, the death of Marion Hedgepeth in December 1910.

They call it the Holmes Curse, and it's built on a premise that's difficult to push aside completely, no matter how rational we might be: some people, it's said, are just too evil to die. For those who believe it, it paints a horrifying picture.

H. H. Holmes, the heartless and depraved architect of the Chicago murder castle, might not be done after all.

 DEATH BECOMES HER

All the Lovely Ladies

OR THE PAST few decades, a vast global audience has been rediscovering ancient fairy tales through the lens of the animated films pioneered by Disney. They've simplified and popularized some of the bigger stories, such as *Cinderella* and *Aladdin*—and brought needed attention to lesser-known tales like *The Little Mermaid* and "The Snow Queen," which Disney titled *Frozen*.

But when I was growing up and watching the classics, what struck me the most wasn't the animation or the music but the common appearance of that one key figure in so many tales: the evil woman of power. We can see versions of her in *Sleeping Beauty* and *Snow White,* and she's fresh and modern as the wealthy socialite Cruella De Vil in *101 Dalmatians*.

It's a common thread in folklore, in some form or another. Sometimes she's a cruel stepmother, while other times she's the witch in the faraway castle. Everywhere we look, the image of the woman who rules through violence and fear is right there, waiting for us.

There are a few reasons why women, not men, have been featured as the most frightening fairly tale villains throughout the ages. Some experts say that it's because mothers have tended to be the most powerful authority figure in the lives of children throughout history. Making their fictional counterparts evil was an easy way to make the danger seem the most understandable to young minds.

Others point to a patriarchal system built to teach everyone that power should only belong to men, which might just be the biggest fairy tale of them all. Throughout history, when women have taken on positions of power, they've shown themselves to be just as wise and benevolent as men. Sometimes more so.

But that hasn't caused the archetype to vanish from folklore. In many ways, folklore as we know it wouldn't even exist without these powerful women, good or bad.

It's in the edge cases, though, where life too closely imitates art, that things get complicated. Because tucked into the dark corners of history there are stories of real women, with real power, who have caused real, heart-pounding terror.

Sometimes the evil queen is real.

Torturous Beginnings

Standing on any of the streets in the small Slovakian village of Cachtice might make you long for an idyllic European life. Tall hedges front each of the homes, and you can catch a glimpse of satellite dishes on most of the houses. Expensive cars sit in the driveways, and there's an overwhelming feeling of culture and class, a sense of an older time. It's hard not to love the lush greenery, the ancient stones, and the centuries-old buildings.

It sounds perfect to me. And maybe it is, if that's your thing. But just a mile and a half away, inside a dark forest and set up on a rocky hill, sits something that pushes Cachtice into the realm of fantasy: a ruined castle.

The relationship between the castle and the village is fairly symbiotic today. Prior to restorations about a decade ago, tourists were known to actually camp inside the crumbling walls, and locals have even held cookouts there. But four hundred years ago, things were different. And it all started with a little girl.

When Elizabeth married a young count from a noble family in 1575, the count's family gifted the young couple with an estate of their own. Not that Elizabeth needed charity. Far from it. She was born into an influential family of her own, who ruled over a part of Hungary called Transylvania, now part of modern-day Romania. Her family had produced knights, judges, and a cardinal in the Catholic Church. Her uncle was even the king of Poland. It was safe to say that Elizabeth had powerful connections.

When she and Count Ferenc married in 1575, she was just fourteen and he was twenty. By his own mother's admission, Ferenc wasn't the sharpest tool in the shed, but he sure was athletic, and in the years to come he would develop a reputation as a hero of war.

Because her lineage outranked his own, though, she kept her surname rather than taking on that of her husband. As a result, history would forever remember her as Elizabeth Bathory.

Just a note: if you've ever read about Elizabeth, you might have assumed her surname is pronounced BATH-OH-REE, but you'd be wrong. It's BOW-ter-REE. Trust me. I did my homework on this. But it's not because of her name that she's still whispered about. It's because of the things she did.

Prior to Elizabeth's wedding, in the time between her engagement and marriage to Ferenc, it was rumored that she had become pregnant as a result of an affair with someone of a much lower social station. Her future husband took care of the situation in true sixteenth-century fashion, though. She was moved to a secluded manor house to give birth to the baby—a daughter, it is said—while Ferenc located the father and punished him.

The punishment, it seems, was to have him castrated, and then a pack of dogs was set loose on him, tearing him to pieces. It was very possibly a culturally appropriate thing to do, according to the time and place of the events, but I can't help but imagine that even if it was, it was probably just as barbaric and horrifying to the people who heard about it then as it is to us today.

Unexpectedly, though, this small bit of torture seemed to intrigue young Elizabeth more than it should have. Some historians think that it was this spark that set something ablaze inside of her: a hunger to punish others and, some say, a thirst for blood.

Just four years after their wedding, Count Ferenc was named

the chief commander of all Hungarian troops, and led them into battle frequently during the course of the thirteen-year war with the Ottoman Empire, called—get this—the Long War. And it was while he was gone that Elizabeth took over running the castle and the lands around it.

But it was also around that time that rumors began to spread through the village near the castle. Today they sound to us like the setup to a horror film or maybe the basis of some dark fantasy novel, but in the late 1500s this was reality, not fiction.

The village would receive frequent visits from staff from the castle on the hill. And these representatives of the count and countess would recruit a small number of young women—girls by today's standards, really—and take them off to serve in one of many roles in the royal household.

These were coveted jobs, don't get me wrong. That wasn't the problem. Any young woman in any Hungarian village would dream of being asked to serve in the castle of the nobility. Outside was a life of poverty, hunger, disease, and filth. Inside those stone walls, though, there was hope. Hope of safety. Hope of a daily meal, and of living conditions that were better than those of the livestock outside.

That wasn't the problem. No, the problem, as far as the people of the village were concerned, was that their daughters never came home.

NOBLE BLOOD

The truth of their disappearance was more horrible than anyone in the village might have imagined. And according to some reports, it all began not long after the count and countess were wed in 1575. It was shortly after that, when Ferenc was frequently away at war and Elizabeth was in need of help, that she brought on a small team of personal servants and helpers.

It was reported that they both loved to treat their servants horribly. Maybe it was the couple's aristocratic upbringing, or their privilege left unchecked. What we do know is that it was when

Elizabeth hired an older woman named Anna Darvulia that things began to get darker. Anna, according to reputation and testimony in Hungarian court documents, was said to be a witch, but at the very least was known for her violent, almost sadistic nature. And as the months and years went on, Anna became the prime facilitator of Elizabeth's love of torture.

One document describes how Elizabeth and Anna would take servant girls outside in the middle of winter and force them to lie naked in the snow. Then they would pour cold water over their bodies and wait for it to freeze on their skin. When they were satisfied that the girls' bodies had become cold enough, they would leave them there to die.

In the spring, it was more of the same. Instead of the cold fields, though, girls were brought out in the heat of the day, stripped naked against their will, and then covered in honey. Then Elizabeth would watch as insects, drawn by the sweet nectar, would crawl over and bite the young women.

Later, a large room was set up in the lower level of the castle so the torture could be practiced year-round, and it was there that witnesses claim the countess would have watched the mouths of servants sewn shut, or sharp instruments forced under their fingernails. And she did it all, it seems, for the pure enjoyment of the experience.

In 1604, after a long struggle with an unknown illness, Count Ferenc passed away. Before doing so, he made legal arrangements that the care of his wife and children should fall to Elizabeth's cousin György Thurzó, the count palatine of Hungary. He was one of the most powerful men in the kingdom, and to Ferenc it seemed like a wise decision.

Elizabeth was also apparently a very lonely person. Years without her husband by her side, of running the castle and surrounding villages on her own, of being the prime figure of authority in a world where few women enjoyed such power—all of it was incredibly isolating to her. Which made Ferenc's death that much more difficult to deal with.

After nearly twenty-nine years of marriage, she was well and truly alone. The loss reportedly left the countess deeply depressed and antisocial, and her response was to retreat to her quarters, where she stayed in bed for long periods of time. That didn't mean the torture had to stop, though. In fact, her loss and loneliness only seemed to escalate it.

Elizabeth had begun to believe that human blood could help her remain young and healthy. Maybe it was the recent loss of her husband that forced her to face her own mortality. Perhaps it was a bit of forgotten local folklore. Some have even suggested that she discovered the idea by accident after a particularly bloody torture session. Whatever the reason, she became obsessed with blood.

Rather than go out, she had Anna bring servant girls to her room. There she would cut them, have portions of their flesh burned with hot metal, and even bite them on their bodies, sometimes even their faces. But her hunger for violence came with a price, and as a result, these poor young women from the village became scarce.

Like an addict, she adapted, and started to bring in more and more women of noble birth. She started with daughters of the lowest order of noble families—those with the least amount of wealth and power—but slowly worked her way up the aristocratic chain. And that, more than anything else, was what became her undoing.

After hearing some of the rumors from a member of his royal court, the king of Hungary assigned a trusted advisor to investigate the matter. And his choice was, whether by chance or intention, Count György Thurzó, Elizabeth's cousin and legal caretaker. So in the autumn of 1610 he made the journey to Cachtice.

His arrival was a surprise to Elizabeth and her team of attendants. That might be one of the reasons his investigation was so successful at uncovering the truth. But the countess might also have just become careless; she *had* been carrying on her violent, torturous habit for three decades, after all. It's easy for *anyone* to convince themselves they'll never get caught after that long.

Whatever the reason, when Thurzó arrived, it was immediately clear that something dark had been taking place. Before long, he knew why. What he unearthed, though, was almost beyond belief.

DAMNED AND TRIED

Upon his arrival, Thurzó assigned his two notaries to begin gathering evidence to support the claims that the king had heard rumors of for years. But rather than being difficult to find, the witness testimony began to flood in. Maybe the people sensed an end to the countess's evil reign. Maybe they finally found hope. As a result, over three hundred people stepped forward to offer testimony against her and her team of helpers.

And it wasn't just the village commoners who spoke up, either. Witnesses included priests and nobles, as well as staff from a number of the countess's estates. Some spoke of the rumors they heard whispered within the walls of the castle, while others came forward to say that they had witnessed some of Elizabeth's torture sessions firsthand. They described the exposure outdoors, the sharp tools and hot metal, even the biting.

Other servants had only seen the bodies, but they all admitted that the cause of death was always clearly obvious: death by torture. And those bodies began to turn up, too. Some were found in local graveyards, while others were located in various rooms in the castle, where they'd been hidden. Charred human bones were found in a number of fireplaces, and other remains were unearthed on the castle grounds.

While the physical evidence was literally being uncovered, so too was the elaborate network that the countess used to gather her victims. Most of the testimony pointed to her team of servants, including the alleged witch Anna Darvulia, but there were others. Elizabeth had contacts in the surrounding villages that were responsible for finding new women for her to torture. Sometimes the women were hired away as servants under the promise of good wages and fair treatment. Other times, they were simply abducted outright.

Finally, Count Thurzó had all the evidence he needed to begin a trial, but there were problems from the beginning of that process. For one, Anna apparently died before the trial could start. Rumors swirled around her role in the string of crimes, ranging from chief executioner to witch and even to Elizabeth's secret lover. She was someone Thurzó wanted to arrest more than all the others, but her death made that impossible.

So he turned to the remaining team of servants. Along with the countess herself, this entire group of accomplices was arrested on December 30, 1609, and then held for trial. In January 1610 the evidence was presented, testimonies were heard, and cases were made.

In the end, the group was charged with the death—the murder by torture, mind you—of roughly eighty servants. Servants who once had traveled to the castle with hopes of a better life. Servants who, through no fault of their own, had become the object of the Countess's desire. But that's the irony of it all: Elizabeth Bathory, you see, never went to trial.

No, because of her high rank and political power, the countess never stood trial. She was the reason for it all, and yet as each one of her personal attendants were tried and convicted, she remained untouched. Like so many of her other abuses of power over the years, she was immune to the full force of the consequences.

Yes, she would be punished, but not to the degree that her helpers were. Each and every one of them was convicted, and in each case, they were sentenced to be executed. All except for the countess.

But not before many of them had a chance to speak for themselves. During the trial that built the argument and laid out the crimes, one servant claimed that she had special access to Elizabeth's quarters. And during one recent visit, while her mistress was away, she had discovered a journal that the countess kept. A private journal, hidden from sight and because of that excluded from the evidence presented in the trial.

In this journal, the servant girl claimed, was a list. The names, as best as Elizabeth could remember, of each and every victim of her love for torture. It didn't come as a surprise to most of the court that the countess would do something like that, though.

This was a woman who killed for pleasure, who reveled in the bloodshed. Some even claimed she literally bathed in that blood.

No, what was shocking about the journal was the number of entries. While the court was presented with evidence for eighty or so murders, this servant claimed that the secret journal, which she had seen with her own eyes, exposed the true extent of Elizabeth's evil.

According to her, the list had over 650 entries.

Evil Alone

Evil has a way of coming in all shapes and sizes, it seems. No matter where we look, there are those who have served to build the legends that we all have come to fear over the centuries.

Thankfully, the evil queens of Disney have seemed to live lives a lot less bloody than Elizabeth Bathory's, although that's probably not the best place to start. The folktales that inspired many of those movies are almost just as bloody at the countess herself. In that, she's not alone.

There are skeptics, though. Some think that the accusations brought against her were fabricated by powerful relatives in an effort to take her land and wealth. It is established fact that the king of Hungary himself owed the countess a large sum of money, and many of the key testimonies during the trial came from people with much to gain from her arrest and imprisonment. Even her own cousin, Count Thurzó, benefited from her public downfall.

Even though she escaped being put on trial and avoided the executioner's ax that awaited her faithful helpers, Elizabeth Bathory didn't go unpunished. She lived on. So did her personal quarters, which can still be toured today thanks to some recent restoration work that the castle has undergone.

Two of the four towers have crumbled to the ground, and there's no longer a roof protecting the interior from the elements, but you can still walk through the lower-level chamber where all of the torture was said to have taken place, as well as the wing of the fortress where the countess lived.

In the end, whatever the truth might have been—no victims, eighty, or over six hundred—Elizabeth Bathory has gone down in history as the "Bloody Countess." But her life didn't end with honor and accolades. There was no one to see if her beauty treatments had worked. No one to keep her company or to endure her torture. No one to talk to at all.

Because after the trial, she was placed in her personal quarters, and every single window and door of that room was bricked up, locking her permanently inside. With nothing more than a slot in the door for food, the Bloody Countess lived out the last four years of her life in what must have been nothing short of a nightmare to her.

Complete and utter isolation.

Lost and Found

TEENAGERS HAVE A tendency to get up to mischief when they're bored. It's as true today as it ever has been. So when four teenage boys found themselves with a spring afternoon on their hands, they did what any English lad might have done in 1943: they went poaching.

They were only hunting for birds' nests, really. It was April, and spring meant nests full of eggs. So they went exploring in their area of Stourbridge, there in the Midlands of England. Over the course of that afternoon, their search brought them to a private park known as Hagley Woods. And that's where they saw the tree.

It was a massive elm, with an overgrown trunk that looked more like a hedgehog than a plant and thin, wispy branches that stuck out toward the sky. Some called it a wych elm. It was strong, it was climbable, and—most important—it was perfect for nesting. So one of the boys scaled the side of it.

When he reached the top and began to look for nests, he found something entirely different: a skull was staring up at him from the hollow center of the tree. The boy assumed it was from an animal and plucked it free from the branches. That's when he noticed how large it was, and the patches of hair that were still attached to it. Human hair.

This grisly discovery kicked off one of the biggest unsolved mysteries in modern England. Beneath the skull, lodged in the hollow center of the tree, was a complete skeleton. It belonged to a young woman of unknown origin and unknown identity. No one stepped forward to claim the body. No killer was ever found. But the public fell in love and named her, and to this day, people still wonder, "Who put Bella in the Wych Tree?"

Humans, you see, are fascinated by dead bodies. They're the centerpiece of countless mystery stories, and a vivid reminder of our own mortality. We can see that fascination in both the innocent wonder of films like *Stand by Me* and the gruesome realism of *CSI*.

Real life, though, is more complex. It's darker than we'd care to admit. And while the odds are good that most people won't ever stumble upon a dead body, it's a lot more common than you'd expect.

Corpses should be hard to come by, but unfortunately, that couldn't be further from the truth.

UNLIKELY PLACES

In February 2013, a number of guests at the Cecil Hotel in Los Angeles called down to the front desk to complain about the water in their rooms. Some described how the shower would run black before clearing up. Others companied of the odd taste and odor. And that age-old complaint that we all know and love—poor water pressure—popped up time and time again.

So the maintenance crew was sent up to the roof, where the hotel kept water tanks used to supply the rooms. And it was in one of the tanks that they discovered a body. A human body, no less, which had been there for weeks.

It turned out to be a missing woman named Elisa Lam. Her parents had reported her missing in early February, but she had last been seen there in the hotel on the thirty-first of January. And it was her decomposing body that had been altering the hotel's water supply.

Finding bodies in unusual places isn't a new thing, though.

And it's not uncommon, either. In January 1984 three students from Columbia University were walking home to their dorm when they passed an old carpet, rolled up and discarded on the side of the street. Now, like a lot of you, I've been to college, so I think we can all agree that curbside discoveries are frequently wonderful: a random desk, or an ugly couch that's way too comfortable to be ignored. So it's hard to blame these three students for bringing the rug home.

When they unrolled it, though, they found a body inside. The man, roughly twenty years old, had been shot to death, as was evident from the bullet holes in his forehead. Needless to say, they didn't keep the rug, and the police were brought in to do a full investigation.

In December 1982, staff were called to a room in a motel in North Bergen, New Jersey. The occupants complained of a powerful odor in the room, and they weren't the first. For a number of days leading up to the call, each guest had complained of the same thing. And it seemed to be getting worse.

The motel staff finally discovered why. It was the body of Gary Smith, who had been killed by his auto-theft partners and stuffed inside the bed in the room. They had poisoned his hamburger, and then strangled him when he failed to die fast enough for their liking. Afterward, they hid the evidence beneath the mattress.

In 2011, Abbeville National Bank in Louisiana began renovations to their second floor, an area they had used for storage for decades. Running between the storage area and the active bank facilities was a chimney, and it was just inside the first-floor fireplace that workers discovered a few small bones.

Climbing inside the fireplace and looking up, they found the source. A body, now little more than a skeleton, had been lodged in the flue. Dental records connected the skeleton to a man reported missing twenty-seven years earlier, in 1984. The man had a criminal record, and had been in trouble with the law shortly before his disappearance. Police can't prove why he was in the chimney, but given the proximity to the bank, they feel it's safe to guess that he had been trying to rob it, Santa Claus style.

In November 2011, Russian police raided the home of a historian named Anatoly Moskvin. Inside, they found twenty-nine life-sized dolls, all women, all dressed in fancy clothing. But they weren't dolls at all. Moskvin, it turns out, was a grave robber with a fetish.

For years, the historian had been visiting cemeteries all over western Russia—as many as 750 by some counts—and occasionally brought home corpses that interested him. All were females between the ages of fifteen and thirty, and all had been dead for a very long time.

It seems, if we're to believe the newspapers and media outlets, that stumbling upon a corpse isn't as rare of a thing as we might expect. Maybe it's a product of the times. With more and more people on the planet, I suppose the odds keep going up that we'll eventually open a wall or dig a garden bed and find a body.

But some bodies are intentionally harder to find. Some killers go to great lengths to hide the evidence of their dirty deeds. And that's really the core of these stories, isn't it? Because hiding a body is about more than just making an object disappear; it's about concealing a crime and escaping the consequences.

The trouble is, when those hidden bodies *are* found, their stories often reveal the greatest horrors of all.

BORN A THIEF

She wasn't always known as Kate Webster. Sure, when she gave birth to her son in 1874, that was the surname she passed on to him. She claimed to have married a sailor named Webster, but he had died. A decade earlier, though, she had been someone else entirely.

Kate Webster was born Katherine Lawler to a poor family in a small Irish village in 1849. While most children might have helped out at home, or perhaps played with toys, Katherine grew up fast. She spent her childhood learning to pickpocket. And judging by how the rest of her life played out, it was a skill she'd been born with.

At the age of fifteen she was caught and imprisoned for a short time, but by seventeen she managed to steal enough money to secure herself passage on a boat to England. But she didn't use the journey as a chance to make a fresh start. No, Katherine Lawler just kept upping her game.

Within a year of arriving in Liverpool, she was caught stealing and sentenced to four years in prison. Once released, she found work cleaning houses in London, as well as working as a prostitute. And then she became pregnant.

The father, according to Kate, was a man she called Mr. Strong. He'd been her friend, her lover, and her partner in crime for many months, but when he learned of the pregnancy, he abandoned her. Her son, John Webster, was born in April 1874, and those who knew her couldn't help but wonder: would this help Kate change her ways?

The answer, it turns out, was a clear and obvious no. Rather than seek reform, Kate simply evolved. She would rent a room in a boardinghouse, and once there, she would begin to sell off the furnishings in her room. When everything was gone, she'd move on and repeat the crime elsewhere.

Another thing she repeated, sadly, was prison time. In 1875, while her son John was only a year old, Kate began serving an eighteen-month term in Wandsworth Prison there in London. It was one of many stints in police custody, even though she moved around a lot and used various aliases to disguise herself. And all the while, her friend Sarah Crease helped by watching and caring for young John.

Some think Sarah was an enabler. That she gave Kate the freedom to live her life of crime without the burden of parenthood. But others view Sarah as a hopeful friend. She saw a young boy who needed looking after, and she did her best to help out. She also tried to get Kate a real, honest job, something that had the potential to turn the woman's life around.

In 1879, Sarah's employer asked if there was someone who could do some house cleaning for a friend of hers, a woman named Julia Martha Thomas. Mrs. Thomas lived in the Richmond area of London. She was a widow in her mid-fifties and had a reputation for being a little strict and prone to anger. But it was a job, and Sarah immediately suggested Kate Webster.

The relationship between Webster and Mrs. Thomas began cordially enough but quickly devolved into daily arguments. Webster claimed that Thomas would follow her around and criticize her work, while Mrs. Thomas claimed Webster came to work drunk most of the time. Needless to say, it wasn't a match made in heaven, but the two women tried hard to make it work.

After a little over a month, Julia Thomas decided it was time to cut Webster loose. Kate, to her credit, tried to change. She begged for just a few more days of employment, and for some unknown reason, Thomas agreed to the terms. But the relationship was eating at her like an ulcer and she couldn't stop thinking about it. She thought that Kate was stealing from her, but she didn't have proof yet. And she feared for her life.

On March 2, 1879, Thomas showed up at church clearly upset. She'd just had another argument with Webster, and it had shaken her deeply. Her friends there claimed that Thomas seemed distracted and agitated, and she left early to go attend to matters at home.

But Kate was waiting there for her, and this time, they would trade more than angry words.

Mischief Managed

Julia Thomas thought the house was empty, but she went searching for Kate Webster anyway. They had unfinished business, and it was time Kate found someplace else to work. It was settled, at least as far as she was concerned.

While Thomas was upstairs in the hallway, Webster stepped out of a dark room and attacked her employer. The two women struggled for a moment, and then Kate gave the older woman a shove. Thomas tumbled down the staircase, where she slammed into the floor below. With her skull now fractured and bloody, she began to scream where she lay.

Kate was immediately concerned that the neighbors might hear. There was a busy pub next door, and if someone happened to hear the shouting, Kate was sure to be discovered and arrested. Launching herself down the stairs, she sat on the injured woman's chest and began to squeeze her throat with both hands. She wanted the screaming to stop. She *needed* it to stop. And after a few tense moments, it did.

Julia Thomas lay dead on the floor of her own home, and Kate Webster had graduated from theft to murder in the course of just a few heartbeats. But Kate was stronger than her fears, and she knew she had to act fast.

She grabbed a razor, a meat saw, and a carving knife, and set about cutting Thomas's body into pieces. Later Webster would admit that while she believed she had always had a strong stomach, this work in particular tested her limits. There had just been so much blood, she later told the police.

Webster put the pieces into a large copper laundry kettle and boiled them in an attempt to reduce them to a more manageable state. It was essentially rendering, the process where meat is cooked until the fat and protein separate. Witnesses would later come forward and talk of the stench coming from the home, but no one complained at the time. This was London in the late nineteenth century; perhaps people were just a little more forgiving of odd odors back then.

When the boiling was complete, Webster fished each part out from the remaining lard and placed them all into a box she found in the home. Most of them, that is. She couldn't seem to fit the head and one of the feet, so she had to get creative. She tossed the foot into a local trash heap, but the head was more problematic. In the end, she found a Gladstone bag—something like an old physician's handbag—and stashed it inside there.

And then she cleaned the house, removing as much of the evidence as she could that something horrible had taken place there. It took her two full days to do it, but when she was finished, she put on a dress from her former employer's wardrobe and went to the pub next door to meet a friend for drinks.

This friend, a Mrs. Porter, later told police that Webster arrived at the pub carrying a large black bag. She kept it with her almost the entire evening, as if it contained something very valuable to her. Oddly, though, Webster excused herself from the table at one point, and when she returned a short while later, the bag was gone.

Webster's next order of business was to get rid of the box that contained what remained of Mrs. Thomas, so she enlisted the help of Mrs. Porter's son to carry it out of the house and to nearby Barnes Bridge. He carried the heavy box all the way to the bridge, and then she sent him home, claiming that a friend was on the way to meet her there.

This boy would later tell police that, as he was walking away, he heard a large splash. It was as if something heavy had been tossed into the river. Webster had disposed of the body, and I can't help but wonder if she perhaps sighed with relief when the box finally dipped beneath the surface of the Thames and vanished from sight.

The following day, though, things got more complicated. Unaware that the box containing Mrs. Thomas had floated to the surface and drifted to shore overnight, Kate Webster dug in deeper. She took on the identity of her former employer while beginning to sell off all of the items in the house. Old habits die hard, apparently.

And it was about this time, according to a later witness, that Webster stepped outside and spoke to a pair of neighborhood boys. She had two bowls in her hand, and they were steaming hot. She told them it was lard—from a pig, she added—and they were welcome to have it for free if they wanted it.

The boys ate two bowls each.

Kate, Meet Justice

While the police were investigating the discovery of the box full of body parts, they had no clues that might point them to the killer responsible. It even took them a bit of time to figure out that the parts were actually human, rather than butcher cast-offs. But even then, all they could be sure of was that the victim had been a middle-aged woman.

Kate Webster, meanwhile, was making money hand over fist. She sold off the smaller items first—the jewelry, the knickknacks, even her victim's gold teeth—and then began to spread word that the furniture was for sale as well. And that led to an agreement with a local man, who arrived on March 9 with a small group of men to help him carry the items out of the house.

A neighbor woman saw the activity and approached one of the men. "Who ordered the removal of these items?" she asked him. The man simply turned and pointed to Kate Webster, who stood on the front steps of the house. "She did," he replied. "Mrs. Thomas."

When the police finally arrived, they entered the house and immediately found signs of something tragic. A charred finger bone in the fireplace. Bloodstains on the floor. Splatters of grease or lard around the copper kettle. But the one thing they wanted to find—the killer—was nowhere to be seen. Kate Webster had skipped town.

In the end, the authorities tracked her down in Ireland. She'd taken her son and made her way back to her hometown as fast as she could. When she arrived, she was still wearing clothing and jewelry taken from Mrs. Thomas. But her stay there was short-lived. The local chief of police—the man who fifteen years earlier had put her in jail for the first time—recognized her in the bulletin from Scotland Yard, and took her into custody.

Everything after that moved quickly. Webster was transported back to England, and at every train stop between Liverpool and London, crowds gathered to jeer and shout at her. By March 30, she had been formally charged with murder.

Of course, she tried to lie her way out of it. This was the woman who had changed her name dozens of times to outsmart the police. Who had moved into room after room and sold off the possessions inside. She was a thief and a liar, so it was only natural for her to try talking her way out of this, too.

First she blamed the murder on Henry Porter, the husband of her friend from the pub. When his alibi held up, she shifted the blame to the man who had come to buy the furniture from the Thomas house, but he too was easily dismissed. When it appeared that she wouldn't be able to squirm out from under the charge of murder, she took credit for the crime, but claimed that she had done it only because others told her to.

In the end, none of it worked. The formal trial began on July 2, 1879, and six days later, the jury declared her guilty. The judge, a man named Justice Denman, sentenced her to be executed.

When asked if there was any reason why she should not be executed, Webster told the judge yes, insisting that she was, in fact, pregnant. A new jury of women was gathered together along with a physician, and after examining Webster, they declared that the pregnancy, like everything else the woman had said, was also a lie.

She returned to Wandsworth Prison, where she had served time before working for Mrs. Thomas, and it was there that she wrote her formal confession. She described all of the details of the murder, right down to how she burned the internal organs to get rid of them, how she chose her tools, and even how she removed the head.

On July 29, Kate Webster stepped onto the platform inside the prison's execution chamber, a building ironically nicknamed the "Cold Meat Shed." The governor announced the time, a priest administered late rites, and then she was guided onto the trapdoor with a sack over her head. Afterward, she was buried in an unmarked grave there at the prison.

The records of Wandsworth Prison contain the names of 134 people who were executed over a span of 110 years. Kate Webster was the only woman on that list.

What Once Was Lost

It's hard to nail down the real reason behind our fascination with death, but it's safe to at least make a guess. Death puts our mortality on display. No matter how hard we try to avoid it as a topic, to ignore its slow, steady approach from the distance, we can't seem to get away from it. Whether we want it or not, death will come for us all one day.

And the dead body stands as that singular, visceral reminder of that death. In the horror movies, it's the clue that's dropped in our laps early on in the film. It highlights the danger our heroes find themselves in. It represents what's at stake, what could happen if they fail, and the true power of the killer.

When the London police pulled the box containing the remains of a woman from the cold waters of the Thames, they didn't know a lot. But they did know one thing: there was a killer in London, and whoever it was needed to be stopped. Thankfully, they managed to do just that.

But in a wild twist of irony, the body of Julia Thomas has been lost. It might have been a result of the way evidence was handled in the late nineteenth century, or the state of decay when the remains were found. Whatever the reason, there's no grave for Julia Thomas. No tombstone with her name etched into the surface. Her body was lost, then found, and then finally lost again.

Well, most of it. As luck would have it, the neighborhood where her house once stood has gone through some renovation. In October 2010, a wealthy London homeowner was having an addition built in his backyard when the work crew unearthed something small and white.

It was a skull. The teeth were missing, but there was a fracture to the back of the head. And after doing a bit more research, investigators determined that the structure that once stood in the homeowner's backyard was a stable. A stable behind the pub that stood next door to the home of Julia Thomas.

Her body might be lost forever in the pages of history, but the head that Kate Webster had tried so hard to get rid of has finally been recovered.

Oh, and the wealthy homeowner who stumbled upon the skull? None other than English naturalist Sir David Attenborough.

Negative Consequences

THE CON ARTIST. The master thief. When they're good, we tend to use words usually reserved for creative geniuses. They are people who have taken their skills and elevated them to a form of art, however criminal those skills might be.

And Hollywood *knows* we love them, too. After all, these flawed and complicated characters make for great movies. Blockbusters, even. *The Italian Job. The Usual Suspects. Ocean's Eleven.* There's something oddly attractive about criminals, isn't there?

Take Sophie Levy. She was born in 1848 and managed to steal her first purse by the age of six. By twelve, she'd been arrested for shoplifting. By twenty, she'd been locked up in New York's Sing Sing Prison three separate times. Soon after, she married an internationally renowned safecracker, and together they pulled off jobs, spent time in prison, and somehow also managed to raise a family.

For the next thirty years, Sophie perfected her craft. She made shoes with hollow heels so she could smuggle diamonds between Amsterdam and New York. She sold fake gold bricks. She even learned to speak French and then traveled to Europe, where she picked jewels right off the wealthy elite, bringing in close to $4 million in modern American dollars after just one year of work.

When she wasn't picking pockets, though, Sophie was luring

married men into her web. Once she blackmailed a man for the equivalent of what would today be half a million dollars. Another time she walked into a fancy building, approached the first CEO she could find, and threatened to reveal their torrid affair. The man paid her off immediately.

Sure, Sophie took money from the men she tricked, but that was about it. Yes, they lost some dignity. And yes, they probably had a lot of explaining to do back home. But their lives were never at risk. Sophie's victims, for all intents and purposes, made it out alive.

Some, though, haven't been so lucky.

THE OUTSIDER

Right about the time that Sophie Levy was arrested for the first time in 1859, a woman named Brynhild Størset was born in Selbu, Norway. We don't know a lot about her childhood, but there are a few important details that survive to this day.

Secondhand reports from the area tell us that Brynhild was an angry child. We can speculate why, but speculation won't give us more details. She was angry, and spent her childhood living as an outsider without friends. But she was smart. Everyone remembers that. Brynhild, they always said, was a clever girl.

In 1877, at the age of eighteen, she went to a local dance to confront a young man who had gotten her pregnant. But rather than agree to help her, he attacked her. During the altercation, he knocked her down and kicked her. As a result of the injuries, she miscarried the child, but despite this, the young man never faced criminal charges.

Those who knew her said that her personality changed after that. She grew darker, more brooding. Angrier, if that was possible. And more determined. Interestingly, shortly after the attack, the man who had kicked her became sick and died. Stomach cancer, they said. But maybe also his just reward.

In 1881, Brynhild made the shift that so many of her fellow Norwegians had made: she moved to America. Her sister had moved there a few years earlier, so Brynhild traveled to Chicago and reconnected with her. And she also changed her name to Belle. Once settled, Belle found work, and she also found a husband. Mads Sørenson was a fellow Norwegian immigrant, and together as husband and wife, they worked toward a better future.

Within two years of their marriage, the couple had opened a candy store and had five children living with them, including a foster child named Jennie Olsen. It's not clear if Belle was the mother of any of the others or if Mads brought them all into the marriage, but it certainly made life interesting.

But business was challenging, and the couple struggled to make ends meet. Then, two years later, the shop unexpectedly burned to the ground, and the resulting insurance money helped support them. For a while, at least.

We need to step aside for a moment, though. Set Belle on the back burner; we'll come back to her, I promise. But first I want to talk to you about insurance. For you and me in a relatively modern world, insurance is a common idea. Insurance on property. Insurance on lives. All of these types of policies, at the basic level, are designed to pay money upon tragedy. But it hasn't always been commonly accepted.

In the early 1800s, life insurance was mostly seen as *taboo*. Exchanging money for human life just didn't sit well with most people. So for decades, it was a major struggle to sell life insurance policies. And then, after a massive 1840s advertising campaign in major cities across in the country, something clicked and the industry took off. By the late 1800s, life insurance had moved from taboo to common sense.

Interestingly, there was someone else living in Chicago at the same time as Belle: a serial killer known as H. H. Holmes. And while his story is told in this book, there's one aspect of his crime spree that's relevant to this story. Holmes, you see, loved to scam insurance companies. As a medical doctor, he found that faking the death of policyholders with real, stolen corpses was a relatively easy crime. And he made a killing at it, no pun intended.

But by 1896, Holmes had been caught, tried, convicted, and executed. Which meant his story was all over the newspapers in town. And maybe, just maybe, that news coverage gave Belle some inspiration. Because in 1900, a lot of tragedy struck her family, and all of it netted her insurance money.

First, part of their home burned down early in the year. Tragic, yes, but Belle collected on the home's insurance policy. Then, in June, two of the couple's five children died. The cause of death was listed as "acute colitis," which basically manifested as nausea, diarrhea, and intense pains in the lower abdomen. The couple buried their children, and Belle collected their life insurance policies.

And finally, a little over a month after the children passed away, Belle's husband died unexpectedly. *His* death drew more suspicion, though. There were two reasons for that.

First, one physician diagnosed the man while he was still alive as suffering from some form of poisoning. The symptoms will sound familiar to you, too: nausea, diarrhea, and abdominal pain. Another doctor, though—one who was a personal friend of Belle's, incidentally—blamed it on an enlarged heart. And that's the cause of death that was officially recorded.

The second oddity was the insurance paperwork. It seems that July 30, 1900—the day her husband actually died—was the only day that his two separate life insurance policies overlapped each other. Meaning, they were both valid and binding, but only within a small, twenty-four-hour window.

Together, they netted Belle a sum that would be equivalent to a quarter of a million dollars today.

FARM LIFE

With life now a bit more complicated, and with a lot more eyes on her as a result of the mysterious deaths in her family, Belle decided to pack up the remaining three children and move away. Of course, she also had a small fortune to fund that move now.

She didn't go far, though. In 1901, she purchased a forty-acre farm in La Porte, Indiana, about seventy miles to the east of Chicago. And it's during the process of buying the home and moving to Indiana that Belle met a man named Peter Gunness. Like her, he was a Norwegian immigrant. He worked as a butcher. And he was a widower with two young children.

Their relationship blossomed after the move. By April 1902, Peter and Belle were married, and set about converting her property into a pig farm. Just a week after the wedding, though, there was an accident. While Peter was outside working, his youngest daughter suddenly died. No one could determine a cause of death, but it should be noted that Belle was the only other person in the house with the child at the time.

If Peter suspected anything, he didn't act like it. The couple carried on with the pig farm and raised Peter's remaining daughter alongside Belle's other three children. They cured bacon and made sausage right there in the farmhouse, selling it all locally. And then, in December, Peter had an accident.

Belle told two versions of what happened. At first, she claimed Peter had bent over near the stove to pick up his slippers and was injured by a pot of brine. Then she changed the details. A meat grinder had fallen off a shelf and hit him on the head. And her wavering, her indecision . . . well, it drew suspicion.

Belle was immediately arrested and put on trial for murder. After failing to prove anything with concrete evidence, though, she was set free. Which didn't sit well with the neighbors. They knew Peter. He'd been a competent man and a skilled butcher. He wasn't prone to accidents as preventable as a meat grinder to the skull. Peter's brother agreed as well, and had Peter's only surviving daughter sent away to live with family in Wisconsin.

Still, Belle kept on with the farm, despite all the hostility. She hired a farm hand named Ray Lamphere to take over Peter's job. And she collected on Peter's life insurance policy, a payday that would be worth over $80,000 today. Then life on the Gunness farm got quiet . . . but only for a while.

Sometime in late 1906, neighbors noticed that it'd been a while since they'd seen Belle's adopted daughter, Jennie Olson. Belle told them Jennie had gone off to school in California. About that same time, Belle placed an ad in a widely distributed Scandinavian American newspaper. Here's what she posted:

> Comely widow who owns a large farm in one of the finest districts in La Porte County, Indiana, desires to make the acquaintance of a gentleman equally well provided, with view of joining fortunes. No replies by letter considered unless sender is willing to follow answer with personal visit. Triflers need not apply.

In other words, Belle wanted men who were rich, single, and willing to travel right to her front door to prove it. Which doesn't sound suspicious at all, does it? Right. And you thought Craigslist was sketchy.

The first man to answer the ad was George Anderson, from Missouri. He arrived at the farm, and the two had dinner together. Of course, she asked him how much money he had, and he confessed that he wasn't actually rich at all. Later that night, he awoke to find Belle standing over his bed, a crazed look in her eyes. He jumped out of bed, quickly dressed, and bolted out of the house. He never looked back.

The personal ad proved to be incredibly successful. Over the course of most of 1907 and through early 1908, a number of men responded to Belle's request. John Moe traveled all the way from Minnesota, carrying more than a thousand dollars with him to help pay off her mortgage. About a week after he arrived, John Moe went missing.

Frank Riedinger journeyed from Wisconsin and promptly disappeared. Ole Budsberg, also from Wisconsin, was seen just once—at the La Porte bank, of all places—and then he, too, vanished from the public eye. Belle and Andrew Helgelien exchanged letters for months before he finally traveled to see her. He disappeared shortly after, and Belle made more large deposits at the local bank.

And through it all, there were odd stories being whispered around town. Once a delivery man named Clyde Sturgis reported that he'd delivered a number of oversized trunks to Belle's farm throughout the year. He was amazed at how strong she was, tossing the trunks onto her shoulder and walking into the house with them.

Others reported that the farmhouse's shutters were always closed. And on more than one occasion, locals passing the farm in the middle of the night said they saw Belle working outside.

According to each report, she'd been digging holes. In the hog pen.

WHERE THERE'S SMOKE

Toward the end of these disappearances, in early February 1908, Belle fired her farmhand Ray and replaced him. According to her, Ray was madly in love with her, and jealous of the men who visited. Ray had trouble letting go, though, and about a week later Belle appeared at the courthouse to request that Ray be declared insane.

It didn't work, though. Ray was cleared and set free. Then he continued to stalk Belle at the farm. He was arrested for trespassing at least once, and Belle continued to express fear. He was threatening her, she said. She was afraid for her life and the lives of her two children.

Then in late April the new Gunness farmhand, Joe Maxson, awoke to the smell of smoke. He stepped out of his room to find the entire house filled with flames. The man managed to escape out his bedroom window, but by the time help arrived, the farmhouse was a smoldering pile of burned timber. And no one but Joe, it seems, had made it out alive.

The wreckage of the house was searched for survivors, and what they found was gruesome. The two Gunness children were found dead in their beds. Another body, that of an adult woman, was also found. But there was a problem: the body didn't have a head. And that made it difficult to identify as Belle Gunness. So they tried other methods.

First they allowed neighbors to view the corpse. All of them, without fail, said that the shape of the body didn't seem like it could have been Belle. Then her clothing measurements from the local department store were compared to the body, and those, too, came up incorrect. As far as the police were concerned, the body's identity was a mystery.

They did have one piece of evidence, though, that helped them get a better picture of what happened that night. A local boy came forward and claimed to have seen Ray Lamphere running away from the farm just before the fire. That was enough for the police. Even though he adamantly denied it, Ray was arrested and charged with murder.

That said, they still weren't sure whom he'd murdered, apart from Belle's children, of course. But before they could get answers, they encountered more questions. After searching the wreckage, the police found a set of fake teeth belonging to Belle. Maybe she hadn't survived after all.

Soon after, the new farmhand pointed out some of the work Belle had ordered him to do recently in the hog pen. There were a number of low spots that she'd claimed were old refuse pits, and she'd she told him to bring in soil from another area of the farm and fill them in. After the fire, though, he was a bit more suspicious.

So the police brought in a team of men to dig it all back up. When they did, they found something horrific: corpses. Lots and lots of corpses. They identified the bodies of Jennie Olson and Andrew Helgelien easily enough. A head was uncovered that belonged to Ole Budsberg.

They found John Moe's body, too. Body after body began to appear in the dark soil, confounding everyone present. But a lot of what they found was too badly decayed to allow for identification. Partly, they say, because most of it had been fed to the hogs first.

Hogs, mind you, that became sausage . . . which became someone's meal.

The counts vary depending on which historian you read, but between the physical evidence uncovered in the hog pen and the reports of missing men from the previous two years, most think that Belle Gunness was responsible for the murder of over forty people. Most had shown up as a result of her personal ad, and most showed signs of strychnine poisoning. Then they were butchered and buried in the yard, sometimes with quicklime, sometimes without.

And this revelation put a lot of her personal tragedy into question. Had her first husband really died of an enlarged heart, or had he been poisoned? And what about her children, or her second husband? It seems that Belle had been active—and *deadly*—for over twenty years, and no one had any idea.

Well, almost no one. Ray Lamphere clearly knew something. That's probably why Belle tried to get him committed and locked away. Lucky for him, it hadn't worked. But he *had* been guilty of setting the farmhouse on fire. So in November 1908, seven months after his arrest, he was sentenced to twenty years in prison. He died a year later from tuberculosis.

Thanks to the false teeth found in the remains of the house, the court decided that the headless body belonged to Belle Gunness. Those remains were prepared for burial, and then transported back to Chicago a short while later.

She was buried beside her first husband, Mads.

THE GAME

It would be nice to believe that the consequences of a life of crime always catch up with the criminal, but that's not always the case. It's poetic, sure, but unrealistic.

Yes, we have examples like Sophie Lyons. She did hard time for her crimes, serving at least fifty short prison sentences before the age of fifty. What's fascinating about Sophie, though, is that after that last stint in prison, she went clean. So clean, that she wrote a book about her life as a warning to other criminals. Crime, according to Sophie Lyons, doesn't pay.

For the rest of her life, she used her fame and sizable fortune to help prisoners seek reform. She offered rent-free housing for former inmates who wanted to change their lives. She went from being the infamous "Queen of the Underworld" to serving as Santa Claus to the inmates of Sing Sing every Christmas, delivering gifts that she bought with her own money. According to her, "any crook who wants to go straight can do it."

But some crooks don't want out of the game. They just want a fresh start somewhere else, where they can pick up where they left off. Belle Gunness was clearly one of those criminals. Looking back, we can see a woman who most likely poisoned the man who kicked her at the dance in Norway when she was eighteen. In Chicago, she killed her husband, and two of his children. And then in Indiana . . . well, you get the idea.

As I said already, Ray Lamphere died in prison a year after he was sent there. But before he did, he made a deathbed confession to Reverend E. A. Schell. And just a few months later, Schell revealed what Ray had told him. It's enlightening, to say the least.

According to Ray, he did indeed burn the house down. That much was true. But he did it because Belle told him to. In fact, she helped him, and the headless body was part of that plan. Belle, he said, had lured a woman to the farm with the promise of a job as a housekeeper, and she'd poisoned her before cutting off her head.

Even the children were a lie. They hadn't died in the fire, as everyone suspected. No, Belle had smothered her two remaining children prior to the fire because, according to Ray, they had started to ask too many questions. Questions about all the men who had visited the farm. Questions about their disappearances. And questions about all the money.

Belle, you see, had amassed a fortune. Between all the men she'd lured to her farm and each of her past insurance frauds, it's estimated that she raked in a massive total worth over $6 million today. And right before the fire, she went to the bank in town and withdrew it all.

If Ray was telling the truth, Belle Gunness didn't actually die in the fire. Her body wasn't the headless corpse pulled from the wreckage. She wasn't the one buried beside her first husband in a Chicago graveyard. She vanished. But Belle Gunness wasn't the type to quit the game and go straight like Sophie Lyons. If she moved, she took her wicked web with her.

In 1931, an elderly Los Angeles woman named Esther Carlson was arrested and brought to trial for murder. She was a Norwegian immigrant. Her victim was a Scandinavian man. And the crime involved poisoning the man for his money. If all of that sounds familiar to you, then you've been paying attention. And so were the police in Los Angeles, so they sent a photo of Carlson to the authorities in La Porte, Indiana.

Now, it had been decades—thirty years, in fact—so the memory of anyone who might have known Belle was a bit fuzzy. An old neighbor of hers took a glance at the photo and said, yep, the woman sure did look similar. Same build. Same face. Same weight. But he couldn't be sure. And the Belle that he knew had a wart on her face. This new woman, Esther Carlson, did not.

The police refused to give up. They reached out to the photographer and asked for the original negative to the picture. Even back then, in 1931, it was common to retouch a photo. The Photoshop software, after all, is modeled after photo manipulation techniques that did just that sort of work, dating back over a century.

When they received the negative and opened the envelope, they were amazed at what they saw. There, right on Esther Carlson's face, was the wart. Belle's old neighbor had been right, after all.

Sadly, Belle Gunness—if it was, indeed, her—managed to slip away one last time, although this would be her final escape. You see, shortly after the photo was identified, Esther Carlson became sick with tuberculosis.

She died before her trial could begin.

The Sweet Embrace

IN 1841, AT the age of seventeen, Lydia married an older man named Edward, and they went on to have seven children. Two decades later, though, her youngest child died of an intestinal illness. A year later, her husband died of consumption. Less than two months after that, three more of her children passed away. Fever and respiratory illness were blamed for those.

Over the next two years, her last three remaining children would also die of horrible illnesses. And every time it happened, Lydia would be there, taking care of them and making them comfortable. A cup of hot chocolate. A glass of cold water. Medicine for the pain.

She married again, but two years later, that new husband also passed away. The attending physician said it was most likely cholera that did it. But Lydia found a way to move on, marrying again in 1870, to a man with three children. She had a family once more.

Months later, their youngest died. Then the next oldest. A year after that, the last child passed away. All under the care of poor Lydia. So when her husband died next, one doctor decided to look a bit deeper. Past the sympathy and bedside manner of the three-time widow. Past the tragedy of so much illness and death. And what he found was horrifying.

For eight years, Lydia Sherman had been slowly killing everyone around her with poison. In fact, her last husband had enough arsenic in his system to kill three men. It wasn't accidental or a product of carelessness. Lydia Sherman, the "Derby Poisoner," did this for fun.

Some historians think the driving force behind all of it was a deep desire to care for people. To be their anchor through horrible illness. In some twisted way, she wanted to help. In the end, though, she gave new meaning to the phrase "killing them with kindness."

It's a vulnerable place to be, on the edge of death. When illness or suffering have worn you down to a thread and you need to be cared for by someone else, you're at their mercy. In some instances, your life is *literally* in their hands. Without a doubt, that's a lot of power.

Power that some people have taken way too far.

Door to Door

When Peter showed up on the doorstep of the Boston Female Asylum in February 1863, he was a complete and utter wreck. He was a tailor with a fondness for the bottle, but that was a relationship he had a difficult time controlling. It's hard to fault the guy, though; life had certainly thrown a lot of speed bumps his way.

Sometime after their third child was born, Peter's wife, Bridgette, died from tuberculosis, leaving him as the sole provider for three daughters. His oldest, Nellie, would eventually be committed to a state mental institution, where she would spend the rest of her life.

Rumors about Peter Kelley swirled around the bustling city of Lowell, causing him all sorts of troubles. He was usually described as angry, alcoholic, and more than a little insane, earning him the nickname "Kelley the Crack." But he hadn't arrived at the Boston Female Asylum to get help. No, he'd come to abandon his daughters.

And they took them. This place was essentially a hybrid between a prep school and an orphanage. Girls would arrive young, be taught basic skills and manners, and then be placed out into local homes as indentured servants who had to work off long contracts. It was a hard life, there's no doubt about it.

The oldest Kelley girl, Delia, took four years to be placed, but we don't know why. Maybe she was rebellious. Perhaps she protested against the slavery-like conditions that awaited her. All we know is that she went on to become a prostitute and eventually died after a life of too much drinking.

The youngest, Nora, was placed much faster. In November 1865, less than two years after arriving, she found herself moving into a new home. In fact, it was a return to her hometown, Lowell, which must have offered at least a small bit of comfort in the middle of all that chaos.

The family took her in and gave her a new name, although there's no record that she was officially adopted by them. Still, from that point forward, she would be Jane. And Jane had a tough climb ahead of her.

The family had their own daughter, Elizabeth, but from everything I can find, the girls did not get along. Jane was an orphan with no social status. Elizabeth, though, was well-off, secure in her place in life, and set to inherit everything. Imagine the sibling dynamics between Cinderella and her stepsisters and I think you'll get pretty close.

The next twenty years were hard for Jane. She grew up. She learned about running a household. Her foster mother, Ann, passed away, but rather than Jane finding herself free to go and build her own life, Ann's daughter Elizabeth took over the household—and Jane's contract. She was stuck.

She also watched the country recover from the Civil War and move on into what historians call the Gilded Age. It's a fancy term for an explosion of wealth in America beginning in the 1870s, but it also hides a dark underbelly. Yes, the rich became mega-rich, building massive estates in places like Newport, Rhode Island, but the poor only spiraled further downward.

So when her contract was completed in 1885, Jane moved out and decided to follow her dreams. What she wanted—what she *needed*—was a chance at a better life. A way to elevate herself above the poverty she seemed destined for. And she found her answer at Cambridge Hospital, where she went to attend nursing school.

But that's where things got complicated. Because Jane had a darker side, and her training only seemed to draw it out. Perhaps we can blame that on her rough childhood, or her deep desire to prove the elites around her wrong. Maybe she just wanted to be in control. Whatever the reason might have been, Jane became a problem very quickly.

At first it was just the lying. She claimed that her father lived in a far-off land, and that royalty had asked to hire her after school. She told lies about her classmates and managed to get others into trouble for things she herself did. Some of them were even expelled as a result.

But the patients loved her. Some say it was her smile, how she would take care of their needs so cheerfully. They felt cared for and attended to, and that was an important skill for any nurse. And Jane excelled at it.

The truth, though, was a lot less pleasant. Once, during her training in Cambridge, she was heard to say, "There's no use in keeping old people alive." Which might explain how fast and loose she was with the drugs she administered to them.

Today we live in a world very good at controlling dangerous medication. Pharmacists keep narcotic painkillers under lock and key. There are strict rules built around our complete understanding of how these drugs work. But remember, this was the 1880s. Jane and her fellow students didn't have the benefit of all that expanded knowledge.

In fact, some drugs were completely misunderstood. Morphine, for example, wasn't seen so much as a painkiller back then as a sleep aid . . . albeit one that was highly addictive. So much so that a former Confederate colonel named John Pemberton created a coca wine—a sort of tonic made of wine and cocaine—as a medicinal cure. When the city of Atlanta passed prohibition laws in 1886, Pemberton swapped out the wine for carbonated water, but the cocaine stayed in the beverage for almost two more decades. Today Pemberton's drink is still sold as Coca-Cola, but the medicinal roots are long gone.

Jane, though, wasn't looking for a solution. In fact, she saw great potential in the veritable treasure trove of drugs at her disposal. Morphine, yes, but also strychnine, mercury, arsenic, and atropine. All of which were widely available, liberally used, and highly poisonous.

And it was right there—at the intersection of Jane's training, her access, and her twisted ideals—that something horrifying was about to be born.

The Freelancer

Morphine was Jane's gateway drug. It was the tool that led to darker things. As a nursing student, Jane would often administer the sedative to elderly patients and watch them slip into a coma. And then she would stand over them or sit beside them and wait for their last breath. It was her favorite part.

As nursing school equipped her with more knowledge, Jane added tools to her kit. The stimulant atropine was the perfect pairing to morphine because it seemed to counteract the visible signs of poisoning. The patients who died under her care were more often than not completely overlooked, tragic victims of heart failure or complications from diabetes.

Jane was getting away with murder—and making it look easy, too. But at the same time, she was failing miserably at hiding her other, less horrifying crimes. She continued to tell lies about her coworkers, to steal from patients, even to steal drugs from the hospital. And it eventually caught up with her. In the summer of 1890, Jane was kicked out of Cambridge Hospital before she could complete her degree.

Oddly, she stayed in town and set up shop as a private nurse. Which led to glowing recommendations from the physicians she interacted with. Which, led to—I kid you not—a *job offer* from Cambridge Hospital. Yeah, the school that kicked her out ended up hiring her back.

It didn't last as long as she wanted, though. Within months, one of the doctors on staff took notice of the disproportionate number of deaths that happened on Jane's watch. He assumed she was incompetent and fired her.

Today that would be the end of it. The future would be a lot less bright, and it certainly wouldn't involve caring for others as a professional nurse. But this was a different time, in the darkness before the age of the Internet and social media. Paper trails were a lot harder to follow, and all you really had to do was to move on and start over.

That was the spring of 1891. Jane was thirty-two and still had a lot of faith in her ability to sell her services as a private nurse. For the next four years, that's exactly what she did. She lived in a spare room at the home of an elderly couple in Cambridge, although when necessary, she would move into the homes of her patients until they no longer needed her.

Business, it turns out, was good. Due to her round figure, cheerful mood, and ever-present smile, people began to call her "Jolly Jane." Her patients loved her, and their families felt as if she really, truly cared for their loved ones. And maybe she did. Jane was twisted and broken, after all, and so to her, what she did *was* care. She was a matchmaker, in a sense, guiding them into the sweet embrace of death.

Her favorite remedy was a glass of European mineral water that she imported from Budapest. She would mix in a combination of morphine and atropine and then let the drugs do their work. Not just for patients, though; no, she also used this trick on her own landlords, the Dunhams, first poisoning the husband and then two years later doing the same to his widow.

Jane, it seems, was the sort of person who brought her work home with her.

Every summer, though, she got away from it all. She packed up from her room in Cambridge, Massachusetts, and traveled south to the Cape Cod area, where she rented a cottage from an older couple, Alden and Mattie Davis. It was a way to get away from city life and enjoy the fresh air and ocean waves.

But it wasn't all pleasure-seeking. Jane did her fair share of work there on the Cape, helping out when locals needed medical advice or a quick remedy. And they loved her for it. She would stay on for a few months, help the community in her spare time, and then move home to Cambridge at the beginning of winter.

At the end of the summer of 1899 Jane received a letter from her original foster sister, Elizabeth, and invited the older woman to come visit her there on the Cape. By then, Elizabeth was married to a man named Oramel Brigham and enjoyed all the benefits of wealth and privilege that Jane had dreamed of.

On August 26, the two women spent the afternoon at the beach, soaking in the sunshine and salty air, and then returned home for their evening meal. Jane, always the thoughtful hostess, produced a cold glass of European mineral water and handed it to Elizabeth. The older woman, thirsty from the warm day, downed it quickly.

When Elizabeth fainted a half hour later, Jane helped her to bed and quickly became the professional, experienced nurse that everyone believed her to be—except for the poisoning part, I suppose. She was attentive, and did her best to make the older woman comfortable.

As Elizabeth became worse and worse, though—as that cocktail of toxic medication sent her body into fits of seizures and pushed her in and out of sleep—Jane actually moved closer to the bed. She wanted to watch. She wanted to see it all happen, to see her foster sister suffer. And she did it all with a smile on her face.

Then, when the end seemed near, Jane took her obsession one step further. She climbed in bed with Elizabeth and laid herself down right beside her. Later, she would describe those final moments with a cold, clinical frankness that betrayed the sheer horror of it all.

"I held her in my arms," she said, "and watched with delight as she gasped her life out."

A FAMILY IN NEED

Jane left the Cape that autumn and returned to normal life in Cambridge. But it was more than that. She also left the emotional high of murdering her foster sister Elizabeth, only to slip back into her less eventful life as a private nurse. Which might explain why she went looking for a change.

In January 1900, only a few months after returning home, Jane caught word that an old friend of hers, Myra Connors, had become ill. She rushed to the woman's apartment to help her, but not out of some altruistic design to care for a friend. No, Myra had something that Jane wanted, and this was her chance to take it.

Myra worked in town as a dining hall matron at St. John's Theological School. It was a job that came with a lot of perks, such as an apartment on campus and even a housekeeper. It wasn't much, but it represented the "high life" that Jane had always wanted for herself. After all, if resentment of that sort of life fueled her murder of Elizabeth, perhaps murder could also be her way of achieving it.

Jane arrived at Myra's apartment at the end of January. By February 11, her old friend was dead, and thanks to a bit of sweet-talking and straight-up lying, Jane managed to take her friend's job and home. But it didn't last long. Just a year later, she was fired for the most ironic reason of all time: poor workplace ethics.

So, back to nursing she went. She rented a room from Mr. and Mrs. Beedle, an elderly couple in Cambridge, and settled into her old routine. And by routine I mean killing patients by day and slowly poisoning her landlords at night. This went on for months without a hint of trouble until the summer of 1901, when Jane heard a knock at her door.

When she opened it, it was Mattie Davis. If you remember, Mattie and her husband, Alden, were the older couple who rented a cottage to Jane during her summers on the Cape. Mattie, it turns out, had traveled up to Cambridge to see her daughter and thought she would stop by Jane's to settle some business from the previous year.

Jane, you see, hadn't been paying the full rent for years, claiming she would make up the difference later. But that deficit had begun to add up, and by the time Mattie Davis knocked on Jane's door, her tab was roughly $500. Throw in economic differences and inflation, and that's roughly $15,000 in modern money.

Jane smiled that warm, jolly smile of hers and welcomed Mattie inside. It was unusually hot outside, and with the sun blazing bright in the sky, it was better to have the conversation in the cool shade of her sitting room. Then Jane slipped away for a moment and returned with a tall, refreshing glass of mineral water for Mattie.

A short while after the older woman had finished her drink, Jane offered to walk to the bank with her and withdraw the funds to pay her debt. Mattie smiled and stood up—and then sat back down as waves of dizziness washed over her. She didn't feel well, she told Jane. She didn't feel well at *all*.

Jane kindly sent for Mattie's daughter and helped the older woman to a bed. When a physician arrived, she worked alongside him to find the cause of the illness and restore Mattie's health. But it was a frustrating experience; one minute she would be in a deep sleep, and then next she would be awake and having seizures. No one could make rhyme or reason of it all. No one, that is, except Jane.

When no one was looking, she was dosing the woman with her usual cocktail of medication, reveling in the chaos and suffering it was creating. And she did this for an entire week, at the end of which she gave Mattie one massive dose of morphine and then let the drug do its job. Mattie Davis died a short while later.

What happened next was a whirlwind of damage control and covering her tracks. First Mattie's two daughters—Genevieve and Minnie—converged on Jane's house and asked for her help. Their father, Alden, now widowed and heartbroken, needed someone to look after him. They loved and trusted Jane, and wanted her to travel to Cape Cod and take care of him.

I think it serves as a powerful testimony to just how confident Jane was in her ability to fool the people around her. She had just killed their mother, and yet here they were, practically begging her to go help their father. She must have felt like a kid in a candy store, thinking of all the fun she would have. So she agreed and traveled south.

Jane wasn't done, though. In fact, as far as the Davis family was concerned, she was only just getting started. When she arrived at Alden's home on Cape Cod, everyone in the family was glad to see that Jane, their favorite nurse, had come to help. She was a ray of hope in the midst of their darkness.

But Jane would quickly prove to be something else entirely: an angel of death.

FALL LIKE DOMINOS

Jane's arrival at the Davis home was met with a sigh of relief. She was very good at her job, after all, but Alden Davis and his two adult daughters were still completely unaware of just how much Jane was very good at. So they opened their home and welcomed her in.

For what she had planned, Jane needed to build a case. She needed the answers to be obvious when people started asking questions. And they were certainly going to be asking a lot of questions. People around her always did. So she set about planting evidence that could help her later on, convenient reasons why people might be dying.

She started by setting random fires throughout the house. And I'll be honest with you, I'm not really sure what her plan was with those. Maybe it was an attempt to just get it all over with and kill everyone at once. But that wasn't Jane's style. I think she just wanted the family members to suspect each other of being a bit unstable.

She told Minnie, the older of the two sisters, that she'd seen Genevieve in the garden shed, just sort of standing there, eyes focused on a box of rat poison. She told Minnie that she was worried about how her sister was handling the loss of their mother, and suggested that they all keep an eye on her.

Less than a week later, on July 26, Genevieve was dead. When the family went looking for answers, Jane brought up the rat poison again. She even told someone else that she'd seen a syringe on the young woman's bedside table. Perhaps, she suggested, it was simply a tragic suicide. And having planted those stories days before, everyone seemed to accept it.

Not that it was easy. This would be the second family funeral within a month, and that was a lot of emotional weight to carry around. Obviously, Alden Davis and his last remaining daughter, Minnie, were devastated, as well as being more than a little numb throughout the funeral. Jane, though, was doing much better. In fact, she later told people, "I went to the funeral and felt as jolly as could be. And nobody suspected me in the least."

Two weeks later, another Davis was gone. This time it was the father, Alden, and the stories that were whispered painted an innocent, if tragic, picture. He'd already been old and unhealthy. Add in the loss of his wife and one of his children, and, well, it was just a bit too much for him to handle.

After that, there were three people left in the Davis household: good old Jolly Jane herself, Minnie Davis Gibbs, and Minnie's ten-year-old son, Jesse. It was a precarious place to be, with all of the tragedy that had occurred and the town filling up with questions and theories. But Jane held on and stayed the course. Her work—however horrible it was—wasn't finished just yet.

When she found the right moment, Jane asked Minnie about the debt she had owed her parents, wondering if perhaps, in light of their recent deaths, that debt might be forgiven. Minnie was appalled and refused to even consider it, and that, I think, left Jane with only one option to pursue.

Just four days after the death of her father, Minnie went to bed sick on the afternoon of August 12. It seemed to be digestive, but all she'd had before feeling ill was one of those early Coca-Cola-type drinks known as coca wine. She was emotionally drained and overstressed, and had certainly needed something to settle her nerves. But as I'm sure you've already guessed, that beverage had been prepared by Jane.

The nurse did her best to help by heavily medicating Minnie. By that evening, she was in a deep sleep, completely unresponsive and unaware of her surroundings. Then, right before her usual bedtime, Jane did something entirely unexpected. Rather than toying with her victim a bit more, she prepared a syringe with a massive dose of her morphine cocktail, and then injected it into Minnie.

Then she walked upstairs and gathered Minnie's sleeping son,

Jesse, in her arms and carried him back down. I'm sure she woke him up, either on purpose or just through the sheer act of lifting him. And then she sat down beside Minnie's bed, Jesse on her lap, and watched as the woman's body spasmed and violently convulsed.

Poor Jesse could do nothing but watch as his mother died, right before his eyes.

Later, the family doctor would scratch his head and chalk Minnie's death up to severe exhaustion. The town was stunned. An entire family—two generations of the Davis clan—gone in just six weeks. The local newspaper ran the headline "Entire Family Wiped Out." And yet Jane had already left town.

Later, when her past had caught up with her and she had nothing to lose, Jane was a bit more honest about her true feelings on the events that summer in Cape Cod. After being asked how she felt about killing so many people so quickly, her answer was delivered with that trademark smile and a twinkle in her eye.

"I made it lively," she said, "for the undertakers and gravediggers."

ALL CAUGHT UP

It takes a lot of trust to place ourselves into the hands of a caretaker when we're sick. Illness has a way of taking away our power. We are at our weakest and most vulnerable. So it's understandable to want that caretaker to be someone we know and trust. On so many levels, the Davis family did absolutely nothing you or I wouldn't have done in their shoes.

Then again, trust is a funny thing, isn't it? We assume the people around us are who they claim to be. That they have our best interests at heart. That they care. But all too often, the faces we see are nothing more than a mask that hides a darker purpose. A mask very much like Jolly Jane's cheerful smile.

I wish Jane's story ended in the Davis home. I really do. This is where we all want it to end, I think. She'd already done so much—taken so many lives and caused so much pain and suffering—and now an entire family was gone. For most stories, this would be more than enough.

She kept trying, but her luck seemed to have run out. While still near the Davis family, she asked Minnie's widower if she could be his housekeeper, but he declined. Next she headed north to Lowell to try to seduce the husband of her late foster sister, Elizabeth, but that plan also fell apart. Perhaps as a cry for attention, she took a dose of her own morphine, but she was discovered and taken to a hospital.

But she wasn't the only newcomer there with a secret. One of the patients in a nearby room was not who he claimed to be. The man, who had entered the hospital pretending to be ill, was actually a detective hired by Captain Paul Gibbs, the father-in-law of Minnie Davis. The detective was there to watch Jane, because Captain Gibbs had some suspicions about the nurse's true nature.

Back on Cape Cod, the old captain was putting those suspicions into action by having the body of Minnie Davis exhumed. He was looking for evidence of foul play, and it wasn't long before they found it. Jane, who had since left the hospital to stay with friends, was arrested on charges of murder and brought in for questioning. It was finally over.

The trial, though, exposed just how horrible her spree of healthcare killings had been. According to Jane herself, she had murdered at least thirty-one people that she could name, but there were dozens more whose names she could not recall or had never known. Some estimates put the total somewhere close to a hundred.

Jane was declared morally insane by the court, and on June 23, 1902, she was transferred to the Taunton Insane Hospital in Massachusetts. It's said that she entered the facility fully confident she would recover and be set free, but time proved her wrong. Her smile slowly slipped from her face, and was replaced by outbursts of yelling and complaints about everything around her. She even suspected the hospital staff of poisoning her food, and in the end, refused to eat. She passed away on August 17, 1938, at the age of eighty.

There's irony in her final years, of course. This woman—

a nurse who claimed to care for so many while actually delivering death to them in a glass of water—found herself in the care of other nurses. It's no wonder she suspected the staff of sinister plots; she had authored nearly a hundred deaths with that same pen of trust and power.

They say old habits die hard, and that's very often the case. Sure, Jane had been removed from society, but it was a lot more difficult to remove the thing that made her Jolly Jane. One last tale provides us with chilling proof of that.

Years after Jane died, one of the nurses who had cared for her there in Taunton told a story about one experience she'd had. Sometimes, she said, Jane would wave her over to her chair with a twinkle in her eye. And then she would point toward the door.

"Get the morphine, dearie, and we'll go out into the ward."

And then, with a wide grin, she would add, "You and I will have a lot of fun seeing them die."

TOIL AND TROUBLE

Half-Hanged

SIMEON SMITH WAS one of the early settlers of New Hampshire in 1772. He built a farm there on the border between Wentworth and Warren, and held a local office. By trade, he was a tailor, but like a lot of men of that decade, he fought with the Continental Army.

It's easy to look back at Simeon Smith as a typical pioneer from the late 1700s. He was patriotic and a stereotypical New Englander, for sure. But few people in town liked him. Why, you might ask? Because Simeon Smith, according to the local stories, was a sorcerer.

It was said that Simeon would saddle and bridle a random neighbor, and then ride them all over the countryside. Just to spite them. When women were having trouble churning butter and it simply wouldn't work, it was because Simeon Smith was in the churn, they said.

If children in town behaved badly, it was because he had bewitched them. He could become as small as a gnat and move through the keyholes of your locked doors. He could become larger than a giant, and would stalk through the forest at night. Or so they said.

Stories like these were common in early America. They are a weird mixture of fact and fiction, of historical truths and hysterical superstition. In an effort to explain the unexplainable, sometimes neighbors and prominent figures were thrown under the proverbial bus.

The era between the mid-fifteenth and late sixteenth centuries was precarious for many people. This wasn't the age of Harry Potter; witchcraft wasn't something that was spoken of lightly, or with a sense of wonder and excitement. It caused fear. It ruined lives. It made good people do bad things.

All in the name of superstition.

BLAME THY NEIGHBOR

Superstition was common in the late 1600s. If something odd or unexplainable happened, the automatic response from most people was to blame the supernatural. But most scholars agree that these beliefs were merely excuses to help people deal with neighbors and family members they didn't care for. If you didn't like somebody, it was common to accuse them of witchcraft.

In the most famous historical example of this, the witch trials of Salem, Massachusetts, we can see a clear pattern in the events. Many of those accused of being witches were wealthy and held religious beliefs that were different from their accusers. Once a suspect was convicted, their estate would be confiscated by the court. And in a community that was known for property disputes, grazing rights, and religious arguments, that became a recipe for disaster.

What happened in Salem happened elsewhere around New England, just on a smaller scale. Neighbors accused neighbors constantly. Stories were told. Lives were ruined. It was the way of things, I suppose. Not ideal, but not uncommon, either.

In one story, from Exeter, Rhode Island, a farmer was said to have been carting his lumber to market when a cat ran across the road. For some unknown reason, this farmer immediately jumped to the conclusion that the cat was actually a neighbor of his, a woman who he insisted was a witch. She had transformed herself into a cat in order to meddle in his business.

This farmer was fast on his feet. Not only did he see the cat running and then make the connection to his witchy neighbor, but he managed to pull out his gun. He was said to have fired a silver bullet at the cat—something well known at the time to be effective against witches—and struck his target. At that very moment, according to the story, the suspected witch fell in her own home, breaking her hip.

In the town of Salem, New Hampshire, a man decided that his cow looked strangely different from how he remembered, and he made the most logical conclusion he was capable of: his neighbor was a sorcerer, and the man had bewitched his cow.

Folklore dictated the solution: he cut off the cow's ears and tail and then burned them. Soon after, the farmer's neighbor was found dead, victim of a house fire.

In West Newbury, Vermont, a farmer had settled in for the evening beside his fireplace. Perhaps he was enjoying something alcoholic and refreshing, or maybe he was trying to read a book. While he was there, he witnessed what he called "spectral shapes" that danced and moved in the flames.

This farmer immediately thought of one particular woman in town, a woman known to be a witch, and he took some tallow and beeswax and sculpted a careful likeness of her. Then, taking a branch from a thorn bush, he pierced this little figurine before tossing it into the fire. At the same time, across town, the suspected witch apparently tripped on her stairs and broke her neck.

Back in the town of Wentworth, our friend Simeon Smith received his own fair share of retribution. It was said that a local boy named Caleb Merrill was struck deaf by the sorcerer. After that, he began acting strangely, running up the sides of the house like a squirrel and writhing in agony.

After some trial and error, Caleb's parents put the perfect combination of ingredients in a witch bottle, a sort of homemade talisman designed to combat sorcery. They buried the bottle beneath their hearth, and soon after, the town was burying Simeon Smith.

These stories of neighborhood witches and the ways in which the good citizens of the towns defeated them were common all across New England. They border on the cruel, and cast these people—often simply the poor or nonreligious among them—in a horrible light. For many people, suspicion was a convenient excuse to hate your neighbor and wish them ill.

In no other place was that attitude more pronounced, more dominant, and more extreme than in the town of Hadley, Massachusetts. In Salem, the townspeople worked within the legal system. In Hadley, however, the people took matters into their own hands. And the results were horrifying.

MARY

When Philip Smith was dying in 1684, the town went looking for answers. It was hard to blame them. Smith was a model citizen and leader in the community. He had been a deacon of the church, a member of the General Court, a county court justice, and a town selectman. He was respected, trusted, and maybe even well loved.

The sole suspect in the crime was an old woman named Mary Webster. She and her husband were poor. They lived in a tiny house in the middle of some pastureland outside of town. Sometimes, when things got tough, they even needed assistance from the town. Colonial-era welfare, so to speak.

It was easy to blame Mary Webster. She and Smith had not been on the best of terms, although few people in town *were* on good terms with her. She was cranky, you see. Accounts of the events include the almost sarcastic comment that her already poor temper had not been helped by poverty. She was a sour and spiteful woman, and she had a tendency to shoot her mouth off. A lot.

Her fierce temper and stinging tongue had earned her a reputation as the town witch. Apparently, she wasn't much of a churchgoer, and that did little to help her case. But the clincher was that she had just gotten back from Boston one year earlier. Why Boston? Well, she'd been on trial there—for witchcraft.

She'd been taken to Boston in chains sometime late April 1683. Mary, an old woman with a foul mouth, had been accused of having congress with the Devil, of bearing his children and suckling them. These children looked like black cats, they said. She had strange markings on her body, they said. It was conclusive and obvious, they said.

There were other stories of Mary Webster. It was said that when teams of cattle were driven toward her property, they would panic and bolt in the opposite direction. They claimed that when this happened, the men would approach the house and threaten to whip her, and only then would she let the animals pass.

Once a load of hay toppled over near her home. The driver of the wagon went to Mary's house—literally went *inside*—and was about to give her a piece of his mind when the cart magically righted itself. Or so they say.

Another story tells how she entered the home of some local parents and when she set eyes on the infant in the cradle, the baby levitated out and touched the ceiling. Not once, but three times.

There's even a story about some people who were inside one evening, boiling water and getting ready for dinner. All of a sudden, a live chicken came down the chimney and landed in the pot, only to escape from the house moments later. The next day, it was discovered that Mary herself had been scalded that night, though she wasn't telling people how it happened.

And so Mary was transported a hundred miles to Boston—along with a sheaf of these eyewitness accounts that had been written by her accusers—and brought before a judge and jury. The jury listened. They read those papers. They looked everything over and did their best as impartial, rational individuals. They discussed it among themselves, and when they returned to the court, they had a verdict: Mary Webster was not guilty.

Maybe this pissed off her neighbors. Maybe they thought they were finally done with her when she was taken away. I can almost imagine their surprise when she rode back into town, a smile on her face and a fire in her belly. She had beaten the odds.

But when Philip Smith, her old adversary in Hadley, took sick just a few months after her return, that newly won freedom looked like it might be in jeopardy.

THE DECLINE OF PHILIP SMITH

The winter after Mary's return from Boston, Philip Smith began to look ill. The people of Hadley didn't know what the cause was at first. What they *did* know was that Smith was in a bad way. He had frequent seizures and seemed delirious most of the time.

The people caring for him—his family and friends and nurses— were all deeply concerned. Whatever it was that he was suffering from, it didn't appear to be normal. In fact, it appeared to be the work of the Devil. What else could possibly cause a man to suffer fits and scream and babble for hours in an unknown language?

When Smith could be understood, he cried out that someone was pricking his arms with nails. Hundreds of them, over and over. Painfully. His nurses looked for the nails but they never found anything that could be causing the pain.

He claimed a woman was in the room with them.

Some of the young men in town had a theory, though. They had been talking about it for a while, and they decided that they needed to give it a test. You see, they thought Mary Webster was behind the man's illness. In their minds, there was only one way to find out.

One of the men stayed with Smith, while the others went to Mary's home. Three or four times, they knocked on her door and bothered her, thinking that if she was indeed casting a spell over Smith, this would break her concentration. When they returned, the man who had been tasked with watching over Smith claimed that the sick man was at ease three or four times while they were gone.

There were other things they noticed. The small pots of medicines that had been laid out for Smith were mysteriously empty, as if someone were stealing their contents. They frequently heard scratching beneath the man's bed. Some of the men claimed to have seen fire on the bed, but when they began to talk about it, it would vanish.

The details of the events surrounding Philip Smith's illness are rife with superstition and fear. These young men even claimed that something as large as a cat would stir under the covers near the sick man, but whenever they tried to capture it, it would slip away. Others said that the bed would shake enough to make their teeth rattle.

All of this was just too much for them. Convinced that they knew who was causing Smith's illness, the group of young men returned to the home of Mary Webster. This time, though, they had more than disturbing her peace on their mind.

They dragged Mary from her home and out into the snow and cold of the New England winter. They beat her. They spat on her. They cursed her in whispers and in shouts. And then they carried her to a nearby tree.

One of the men slung a rope through the branches, while another fashioned a noose. And there, in a snow-covered field outside her own home, Mary Webster was hanged.

When she stopped moving, the men cut her down. They took her body and rolled it in the snow, burying her. And then they left. They walked back into town, back to the home of Philip Smith, back to the others who knew what they had done. And they waited.

They waited for Smith to get better. For the curse to lift and for their lives to return to normal. They waited for safety. For their superstitions and fears to fade away, now that Mary was gone.

But, oh, how wrong they were.

SURVIVOR

The world of the seventeenth century was tensive and harsh, especially for the people trying to carve out an existence in colonial New England. The Protestant Reformation of the century before had left most Europeans with the belief that bad things happened because of the Devil. Everything that went wrong—and I mean *everything*—was caused by something supernatural.

This was a time when misfortune, loss, and even simple illnesses would be blamed on the work of witches and sorcerers. Because of this, everyone in town was on the lookout. If something went wrong, there was always someone to blame. It seems there was a devil in every community.

History is full of people who took things too far. The events that took place in Hadley in the winter of 1685 are just one of countless examples of what superstitious people are capable of when their fear gets the better of them.

Sadly, though, it didn't work. When friends arrived the next day to look in on Philip Smith, he was dead. What they found, though, gave their suspicions new life.

It was said that his body was still warm despite the winter cold. That his face was black and blue, and fresh blood ran down his cheeks. His chest was swollen, and his back was covered in bruises and holes from something like an awl. Or nails.

Now they had more questions than answers. Who had beaten the man overnight? Who had kept his body warm against the creeping chill of winter? And who had put the holes in the flesh of his back while he lay dying in bed?

I imagine the people who visited him that morning were disappointed. He was respected by most of the town. Many people there most likely depended on him for something. They'd done so much to take care of him, even gone so far as to murder another person. And yet it hadn't worked. Philip Smith was dead, and all they had left were questions.

Something else would soon disappoint them. You see, although Philip Smith had died, Mary Webster *hadn't*. Even though she had been beaten and hung from a tree before being buried in the snow and left overnight, Mary had somehow survived. In fact, she went on to live eleven more years before passing away in her seventies.

And it turns out that Mary was also an ancestor of the well-known novelist Margaret Atwood. In 1995, Atwood published a poem entitled "Half-Hanged Mary." It was written in sections, each one covering an hour of her torture, beginning with the hanging and ending with her return from the dead.

The poem, written from Mary's point of view, ends with a line that makes a person wonder: "Before, I was not a witch. But now I am one."

Hole in the Wall

OLKLORE AND SUPERSTITION are fluid, flexible things. There's no set formula for how they're born, no rules or recipes to create them. They just . . . happen. Sometimes folklore is instructive; it comes first and teaches us how to behave. Other times it's reactive; it sprouts up long after a key historical event, like a sapling that grows from an acorn buried by a forgetful squirrel. Either way, it's always been a mirror, showing us who we all really are.

There've been times, though, when people have crafted their own tales, and then set out to convince everyone else of their truth. Counterfeit folklore. Sometimes it's done for money, and sometimes for that drug we all seem to be addicted to: attention.

Take George Hull, for example. In 1868, he purchased a ten-foot-long block of gypsum from a quarry in Iowa. Then he had it shipped to New York, where he paid a sculptor to carve it into the likeness of an enormous human corpse. Finally he transported it to the small New York town of Cardiff, where he buried it on his cousin's farm.

When the cousin, William Newell, hired two men to dig a well about a year later, he pretended to be shocked when they uncovered the stone figure. They pulled it from the ground, and locals quickly decided it was a petrified man. The Cardiff Giant, they called it. Newell built a tent over it and sold tickets to anyone who wanted to see it. He—and cousin George, of course—made a lot of money off the prank.

Before the invention of things like the camera, the Internet, and the telephone, it was a lot easier to pull the wool over people's eyes. That lack of documentable proof helped those hoaxes grow and spread. And most of those fakes were harmless, thankfully.

History contains moments, though, when those lies have come with more serious consequences. Social rejection, legal action, even imprisonment. And on rare occasions those lies have even cost innocent people their *lives*.

All because of a good old-fashioned hoax.

BURN THY NEIGHBOR

In the years between the late sixteenth century and the early eighteenth, a wave of witch trials swept through Western society. Most of us know this. The witch trials of Salem, Massachusetts, in 1692 have become something that few people haven't heard about. And most know, if only anecdotally, that trials just like it happened across Europe and in the European colonies of North America.

Putting witches on trial is something that predates Christianity. In fact, Charlemagne—who ruled much of Europe at the beginning of the ninth century—declared that anyone caught burning a witch would be executed. But religious fervor in the late 1500s began to turn witchcraft into something that was more evil, more feared, and more panic-inducing.

A lot of the beliefs about witches that were common in the Salem trials actually came into the public mind through a trial in England in 1612. The Pendle witches, as they were called, all confessed to have sold their souls to the Devil himself. They took credit for supernatural acts, claiming to have bewitched neighbors. After a short trial, all ten of the suspected witches were hanged.

The Pendle trials happened during a time of strict witchcraft laws that had been passed in England, Wales, and Scotland, designed to outlaw and prosecute anyone who practiced witchcraft as well as those that supported them. The Scottish Witchcraft Act of 1563 declared those crimes to be capital offenses, punishable by death. In England, it's estimated that roughly five hundred people were tried as witches, but in Scotland that number was much higher. Estimates range from four thousand to six thousand suspects brought to trial, and over fifteen hundred of those were executed.

The first major test of the Scottish Witchcraft Act took place in 1590. King James VI had traveled to Europe to marry Princess Anne, sister of the king of Denmark. When a terrible storm prevented their first attempt at a return trip, a Danish admiral made an offhand commend about witches, and that set off a witch hunt in both Denmark and Scotland.

As a result, over a hundred people from North Berwick were arrested and over seventy of those were convicted. Most confessed under torture, although historians are unclear as to how many were actually executed.

Just seven years later, Scotland became caught up in what historians now call the Great Scottish Witch Hunt of 1597. The first case came to light in March of that year with the trial of Janet Wishart in Aberdeen. She was accused of using a cantrip, or spell, and burned for the crime. A month later, though, a key suspect was brought in.

Margaret Aitken from Balwearie was arrested and promptly tortured for information. She struck a deal with her accusers, however, and promised to locate more witches in exchange for her life. But remember, almost all of us would promise anything if it meant that the torture would stop. In a sense, Margaret was helping to build a nesting doll of lies. She would find the fake witches for the people who believed witches were real.

Over four hundred people from across the country were accused of witchcraft. Many of those suspects were identified by Margaret, called out for the simple crime of being noticed by her. It took the authorities over four months to discover that she was a fraud, but at that point it was too late. Over two hundred people had already been executed.

A second Great Witch Hunt took place over the course of a year between 1661 and 1662, and this time nearly seven hundred suspects were arrested. More than half of them were killed. The methods varied, but most were burned, strangled, drowned, or even crushed beneath heavy stones.

I'm telling you all of this so that you can understand the fever that seemed to have spread throughout Scotland. People were afraid. They were afraid that witches might be real things, and that their neighbors might secretly be one. Mostly, though, they were afraid of being accused, because once the judicial system sunk its teeth into them, there was little hope.

That hysteria made an accusation deadly, you see. You could call your neighbor mean, or ugly, or even a thief, but you rarely risked hurting more than feelings. Call them a witch, though, and you could very well spark a wildfire that could consume your entire town.

And in 1697, that's exactly what happened.

Welcome to Paisley

In August 1696, Christian Shaw became sick. She was the eleven-year-old daughter of a wealthy landowner in central Scotland, and thankfully for her, that position afforded her special treatment. Right away, she was taken to nearby Glasgow for medical care, where she was quick to tell the doctors what was wrong with her. According to her, it was simple: she'd been cursed.

Shaw told a story that went something like this. She had walked into the kitchen of her home on August 17 to find one of the servants, Catherine Campbell, drinking from a jug of fresh milk. Shaw might have been eleven, but she knew the rules. She knew how that house functioned. And she understood that the contents of that jug belonged to her father, to her family. To *her*.

Shaw must have been a bold child. Here she was, alone in the kitchen with a grown woman, and she stared Campbell down and told her she intended to report the theft. And that's just what she did. Campbell, according to Shaw, replied with a curse, telling the girl that she wished the Devil would "haul her soul through Hell."

That might have been something she could have forgotten.

Harsh words in a heated moment, you know? But just four days later, Shaw turned a corner and came face-to-face with Agnes Naismith, a local woman rumored to be a witch. *That* made the threat real. If Campbell wanted the Devil to carry her away, it made sense that she'd send Naismith to do it.

And that, she said, was how she ended up in bed, suffering through torment that her doctors couldn't identify or treat. She would twist and writhe with seizures, often crying out in pain. Other times she would pass out and remain unconscious for hours.

She was actually taken to doctors twice, but each time she and her family found no hope of relief. The doctors were just as perplexed as the Shaw family. Sure, this was late seventeenth-century medicine, but it wasn't barbaric. Even still, no one was able to find the cause of her pain and fits.

But that wasn't the worst of it. Back home, Shaw's symptoms started to become more and more unusual. Visitors to her room claimed that she would lean forward from time to time and vomit up objects. Objects, they said, that didn't belong in a little girl. Feathers and pieces of bone. Straw and coal. Hairpins, charred wood, even gravel. All of it was said to have come out of her mouth, and everyone knew that that was impossible. Unless, of course, it was due to a curse.

In a moment of support, old Agnes Naismith actually visited Shaw in her room. Family was there with her, partly for support but also for protection. Naismith was a witch, after all. But the old woman wasn't there to curse the girl further; she said she came to pray. In the days afterward, Shaw claimed that Naismith was no longer tormenting her from a distance. It was as if the old woman had called off her curse and called it quits.

Others, though, weren't off the hook. Along with Catherine Campbell, the servant who had stolen a sip of milk, more names were uttered by Shaw in between her seizures and fits. But when the symptoms failed to disappear or improve, she was taken back to Glasgow for another examination. This time, though, the doctor had new ideas to present to her family.

The doctor was a prominent Glasgow physician named Matthew Brisbane, and he suggested that the girl might actually be wrestling with a demonic force. It was a logical explanation, given the era and circumstances. There was something inside her that was producing mysterious symptoms, and medical care hadn't been able to identify the cause. To him, that left the spiritual realm. Christian Shaw, he believed, was possessed.

Back home, the local church stepped in to do what they could. People fasted. They prayed. They gathered in the meetinghouse. But none of it seemed to help. So as Christian Shaw continued to mutter more and more names of people she claimed were tormenting her, her father wrote them all down.

And then he did what any father might have done in his place at the time. He wasn't a noble, per se, but he *was* the local laird, and that title came with some political pull. Angry, frustrated, and more than a little desperate, he went to the local authorities. He pushed the list of names into their hands, and then he demanded justice.

When that justice arrived, though, it was more than bitter.

MISGUIDED

As a result of Shaw's list, a council was set up to look into the matter. One of the first to be arrested was a woman named Elizabeth Anderson. It's not clear whether she was tortured or just traumatized by the arrest itself, but she quickly confessed to witchcraft, and then started to name others who had done the same. Those others were already on the list, but hearing it from a self-proclaimed witch made it that much easier to go after them.

Anderson's confession earned her lots of company in jail. All told, records show that in January 1697, thirty-five people were arrested and held for trial. Evidence was heard. Neighbors were brought in to speak to the character of the suspects. Stories were told. And these stories weren't nice.

Yes, there was the main issue of Christian Shaw, sick in bed in her father's house, and they covered that. But other items came up. It was as if the town had been given a platform to air their grievances, and they wanted to take full advantage of that. They might not have had buses back then, but they acted like it, throwing people under them with every word they uttered.

The trial stretched on for months. Elizabeth Anderson's elderly father died in jail while waiting for a verdict. Others were released as stories revealed their innocence. In the end, seven suspects remained, including Agnes Naismith. By June of that year—after five months of imprisonment—they were sentenced to death. One of them, John Reid, took his own life in jail before they could carry out his execution.

On June 10, 1697, the final six were hanged in Gallow Green, in the west end of Paisley. After the accused witches had been killed, their bodies were piled together and set aflame. Superstitions of the time told people that even after being hanged, the witches might still be alive, so the fire was a precaution. Even still, they didn't know when to let down their guard.

Local legend says that's just what happened there in Paisley that day. One of the executioners borrowed a cane from someone in the crowd and used it to nudge an arm back into the fire; when he was done, he tried to hand it back, but the villager refused to touch it.

After the flames died down and there was nothing more than a pile of ash, the remains were gathered together and buried. A ring of cobblestones was arranged around the burial site, and a horseshoe—an ancient symbol used to ward off magic and protect specific locations—was placed in the center of the ring.

They did this because of something that happened before the execution. There in the center of town, Agnes Naismith was said to have addressed the crowd that had gathered to watch. She had cursed all of them, and all their descendants after them. She cursed the town of Paisley, the Shaws, the trial, and everything about it. The horseshoe was meant to act as a seal, locking in that curse and preventing it from escaping.

Sadly, it was all a lie. Every last bit of what happened in Paisley was built on a foundation of fraud and make-believe. Naismith knew it—that's why she cursed them, after all—and if it wasn't for the irrational panic that had swept through the community, the villagers might have known it, too.

They knew what we all do: there's no such thing as a witch, who flies on a broomstick and turns neighbors into animals with a word. No one can make a young girl sick, cause her to vomit up feathers and pins. It's not logical or rational. It's not real.

We can see now, looking back, how this mess got out of hand so quickly. Lie upon lie upon lie. The human desire for self-preservation is a powerful weapon, and it was used to justify behavior that wasn't normally acceptable. It always has been. It still is.

I wish I could tell you that this story ended justly, that Shaw was caught in her lie and punished for building such a deadly hoax. But that itself would be a lie. She grew up and eventually pioneered the manufacturing of thread, something that fueled her town's economy for generations. As much as possible, Shaw got away with it all.

But lives were lost. People were tortured and killed. Families were torn apart and forever altered. Shaw had spread lies that hurt others. Then those people told lies that hurt still more. And finally, the rest of the town lied to itself and accepted it all as gospel truth. Because of fear. Because of social pressure.

And because sometimes it's easier to let the current wash you away than it is to swim against it toward the truth.

FULL OF HOLES

No one knows why Christian Shaw did what she did. Maybe she was bored. Maybe she liked the attention. Maybe she truly hated some of the people she accused. In the end, though, those people died, and all because of a hoax.

There are theories. It's possible she suffered from conversion disorder, where anxiety is converted into physical symptoms. It's also been suggested that she might have been exhibiting signs of Munchausen syndrome, a condition where people pretend to have a disease or illness in order to draw attention or sympathy from others. These ideas are certainly true, but it's also possible that she just flat-out lied. People are very good at lying, after all.

If we're honest with ourselves, we're a lot more gullible than we'd like to admit. Spend some time on Facebook and you'll witness the power of a good old-fashioned hoax. Sometimes a lie can fool people because they're blind to reason, or because their prejudice and hatred prevent them from seeing the truth. Sometimes, though, lies persist because superstition feeds the flames.

No matter the reason, people get hurt. Oh, what a tangled web we weave . . . well, you get the idea, right?

In 1839, we came one step closer to understanding the how of what Christian Shaw did in 1696. That year, two researchers were examining the Shaw home and discovered something on the wall where the head of Christian's bed would have been positioned. It was a hole.

The hole was cut at an angle, making it nearly invisible to anyone entering the room from the hallway. But from the bed, it was perfectly positioned for moving small objects through. Objects like feathers, and pins. And don't ignore the other question that this new detail begs us to ask: who passed those items through? Shaw, it seems, had a helper.

In the 1960s, the original horseshoe—the one that marked the grave of the victims of the trial—went missing following some road work. Decades of economic hardship followed, reminding some of the curse uttered by Agnes Naismith. The curse that the old horseshoe was meant to repel. The town placed a new horseshoe over the grave in 2008.

Maybe, like the people caught up in those lies three centuries earlier, we still have a hard time today separating fact from fiction. Maybe we always will.

Familiar

THERE'S A FINE line between belief and obsession. From a distance, that line looks to be a mile wide. After all, no one expects to behave irrationally. But people throughout history have found that line all too easy to cross.

Take William Dowsing. He was a Parliamentarian soldier during the first English Civil War. And he was a believer. Specifically, he was a Puritan—a Protestant Christian who wanted to purge all remaining Catholic elements from the relatively new Church of England. He believed deeply in this cause . . . but as I said before, some people take belief too far.

Dowsing managed to secure a very special assignment from the Earl of Manchester: in August 1643, he was given the authority to travel all over Cambridgeshire and Suffolk literally destroying the physical reminders of old Catholic England. Stained-glass windows, stone carvings, altars, crosses, and anything else that came remotely close.

Dowsing did this for a full year under the self-appointed title of "Iconoclast General," eventually vandalizing over 250 churches. Think about it: a believer so driven by his convictions that he actually destroyed places of worship within his own faith. Like I said, passion shares a very thin, very fragile wall with madness, and it's all too easy to hear its voice on the other side.

Our society is built on the unspoken assumption that everyone will behave rationally. That people will make decisions that are based on common sense and logic, and weighed against their impact on the people around them. It's a noble assumption, but it doesn't take people like William Dowsing into account. And, sadly, he was mild compared to others.

Because given the right mix—that perfect sweet spot between politics, religion, and superstition—one person's irrational obsession can lead to a much darker outcome.

Especially if you're a *witch*.

Permission Granted

King James I had some pretty big shoes to fill. He succeeded Elizabeth I after her long reign of forty-four years, and when he did, he maintained the Protestant England that had flourished under her rule. But where Elizabeth was the voice of reason, James leaned more than a little toward the irrational.

Most historians think it began on his return trip from Denmark in 1589, when a storm forced his ship to take shelter in Norway—a storm that was so unusual and unexpected that it was blamed on the work of witches. The resulting witch trial left quite the impression on King James.

Less than a decade later, he published his own scholarly work, titled *Daemonologie,* where he explored the connections between witchcraft, sorcery, demons, and black magic. His source material was a little sketchy, though, consisting mostly of confessions from accused witches. But one paragraph in particular caused most of the problems to come.

> *The fearful abounding of these detestable slaves of the Devil, the Witches, or enchanters—has moved me . . . to resolve the doubting . . . both that such assaults of Satan are most certainly practiced, and that the instruments thereof merit most severely to be punished.*

Translation: witchcraft is real, and if you find a witch, you should punish them. This was clear, unfiltered permission for violence, straight from the mouth of a powerful ruler. And again, while most people prefer to stay comfortably inside the realm of common sense, there are always a few outsiders. It was just as true then as it is today.

As I mentioned earlier, the Puritans were a sort of activist group within the Church of England who believed that the Church hadn't gone anti-Catholic enough. It needed purifying—hence their name. Puritans were extremists, in a sense, with zero tolerance for anything remotely heretical, and they adored the anti-witchcraft message of their king.

But then their king died, and when King Charles I took the throne in 1625, he began to slowly move the Church of England back toward Roman Catholic elements. For the Puritans, it was their worst nightmare come true. Their worldview had been the law of the land for so long, but now it was under attack.

This is the world that Matthew Hopkins was born into. His father, James, was the Puritan vicar of St. John's in Suffolk, right in the heart of Puritan territory. He was one of six children, and all of them were raised to hate heresy. In fact, it's most likely that they had a copy of *Daemonologie* on hand in their home. That would certainly explain a lot of what was to come.

In 1635, Matthew's father passed away suddenly, leaving the family to support themselves on their own. Matthew stuck around for a while, but in the early 1640s, he took his small inheritance and moved ten miles west to Manningtree, where he purchased a local inn. And it was there, in the early days of the English Civil War, that something life-changing happened to him.

The wife of Richard Edwards, a wealthy landowner and the town's chief constable, had recently given birth, after which she placed their newborn in the care of a wet nurse. But when the baby died unexpectedly after days of unnatural fits, they grew suspicious of Elizabeth Clarke, the eighty-year-old, one-legged woman who lived next door.

Around the same time, some cattle belonging to Edwards were

driven past Clarke's house, and two of them died suddenly, right there on the trail. And that was all the proof the community needed to start whispering. After all, few in town really cared for Elizabeth Clarke, so it was easy to accuse her of using witchcraft to kill the cows and the Edwards child.

On Friday, March 21, 1645, four local women were sent by the magistrates to Clarke's house to inspect her for witch's marks. These were markings that all witches were said to have on their skin, evidence of suckling dark creatures. We don't know whether or not Elizabeth put up a fight, but we do know that when they were done, they claimed to had found not one but three of those marks.

Which gave them the authority to keep her under house arrest while they waited for her to confess. All through the weekend, the women sat with Clarke in silence, waiting for her to speak. But she refused, and the silence went on for days.

On Tuesday, March 24, two men arrived to help. The older of them was John Stearne, a local business owner and a staunch Puritan. With him was young Matthew Hopkins, and together, they set about interrogating Clarke with a more direct and deliberate intent. Finally, after hours of waiting, she gave in and confessed to a whole laundry list of offenses, including a seven-year relationship with the Devil himself.

She also began to call for her familiars—those supernatural creatures who assist witches in their evil efforts—and both men watched as a series of animals entered the room one by one. Elizabeth claimed they were evil spirits, and named them as they came in: Holt, Jarmarah, Newes, Sack and Sugar, and Vinegar Tom.

The men had seen enough. Later, when the local magistrates—Sir Grimston and Sir Bowes—announced that they would be available to hear testimony from anyone willing to share it, Stearne approached them and handed over a transcript of Clarke's confession.

Sir Grimston had a long history of presiding over trials of accused witches, so he was more than a little impressed by the initiative of the two men. As a result, he issued them a warrant, instructing them to go and find the other witches from Clarke's group. Matthew Hopkins, born and raised in a zealously religious home, was in heaven.

They were witch-finders now, and England would never be the same.

License to Kill

Hopkins and Stearne did their job exceedingly well. After conducting an investigation in town, they presented five more names to the magistrates there, including Anne West and her daughter Rebecca—both of whom had been accused of witchcraft in the past but had managed to escape conviction and execution.

Those five women were tortured in the same way Elizabeth Clarke was: by depriving them of sleep and food, and keeping them in isolation until they gave up and handed over names and evidence. Soon the initial group of five grew to a crowd of twenty-three. When the trials were done, eighteen of the women were sentenced to death by hanging. Four others died in prison before their trials even began, and Rebecca West managed to slip out of her sentence because of how helpful she was to the court.

This was the moment the lightbulb flickered on above the head of Matthew Hopkins. With the law on their side, he and Stearne would be able to do this elsewhere. Witch-finders on the road, seeking out anyone who had dealings with the Devil, purging the Church of heresy and sin. It was their calling. It was their duty.

It's important to point out the hypocrisy in Hopkins's actions here. This was a man who proclaimed piety, with a mission to bring the English Church back to its pure, essential roots. Yet his official title, "witch-finder general," was a personal fabrication. He even told towns that he had the backing of the Parliamentary leadership, which was a lie.

Farce or not, though, they had a pretty methodical approach to their mission. He and Stearne traveled with a handful of women, who were there to inspect anyone accused of witchcraft for witch's marks. The accused would be denied food and sleep, and kept isolated until they confessed.

And the craziest part of their operation, I think, is that they charged for this work. It was, in their eyes, a service to the community. Historians estimate that each village paid an average of £20, equivalent to about $5,000 today. Witch-finding was apparently a really good way to get rich, and fast.

When Hopkins and Stearne arrived in the Suffolk village of Brandeston, they found a victim in the most unlikely place: right inside the local church. Villagers came forward to tell them about the unlikable and unsocial nature of their vicar, John Lowes. Worse yet, they said, he was very fond of all those old "high church" rituals that the Catholics were known for.

But Lowes was an eighty-year-old man who had served in his church for over five decades. Of *course* he preferred the old traditions of formal Anglicanism . . . because he'd lived *through* them. Still, in 1645, that was enough to earn you an accusation as a witch, and so Lowes was taken into custody by the witch-finders.

That's when Hopkins pulled out his usual bag of tricks. Lowes wasn't allowed to sleep, and the interrogators kept him moving the entire time, wearing him out physically and mentally. For days, they took shifts torturing the old man with sleep deprivation, until he finally became desperate enough to say anything as long as it ended his suffering.

His crime, according to his own confession, was that he ordered his familiars to sink a ship off the coast of Ipswich. He gave a convincing laugh when he told Hopkins he had made "fourteen widows in a quarter of an hour." And then he named names.

More accused witches were brought in. They were examined by Hopkins's female assistants, and then subjected to the same torture as John Lowes. When *they* confessed, the process was repeated. Over and over, the list of accused grew exponentially, until at the end, between 150 and 200 people were in jail awaiting trial.

But you can't do that sort of thing and not get noticed. Hopkins had walked into town and rounded up hundreds of people, and all of them, he said, were at risk of execution for witchcraft. When Parliament caught wind of what he was doing there in Suffolk, they stepped in and took over the trial process.

A special oyer-and-terminer session—sort of a trial for major crimes—was called for. It would be held in the western county seat of Suffolk, in the town of Bury St. Edmunds. The government felt that Hopkins had generated too many unwilling testimonies and lacked solid, legal evidence. For their trial, things would be run more carefully.

They would no longer allow for confessions received under torture. What they wanted to see was proof of a pact with the Devil, or of working with familiars to carry out their dark magic. It still sounds like fantasy to our modern minds, I know, but it was conservative and reasonable enough that it upset Matthew Hopkins no end.

In August 1645, John Godbolt—a local member of Parliament—served as judge over the trial. Evidence was heard and convictions were handed out. In the end, sixteen women and two men were sentenced to death for involvement in witchcraft.

All of them were imprisoned inside a local barn on the night before their execution. It's said that they came to a unanimous decision to confess nothing but their innocence at the gallows. And then they passed the night in song and in prayer.

On the morning of August 27, all eighteen were hanged, and then the court proceedings stopped. It's easy to think it had ended. The government had stepped in, after all. More common sense had been applied to the panic than Hopkins would ever have allowed himself. But there were still 120 people in jail awaiting trial.

The break, it turns out, was simply a by-product of the ongoing civil war. It was announced that the king's forces were approaching, so the people of Bury St. Edmunds had to stop and tend to military matters. But when that was over three weeks later, the court reconvened, and the remaining accused were brought before the judge.

Of the 120 who remained, sixty more were convicted and sentenced to death by hanging. Among them was the old Brandeston vicar, John Lowes.

FANNING THE FLAMES

Long before the executions in Suffolk, Matthew Hopkins had moved on. He'd done his job, gathering all the evidence he could. He was seen by many in his day as a man of action. He was passionate and driven, and he believed he had more work to do than time to do it.

By August, he was ready to tackle his next challenge, so he headed elsewhere. But his reputation was beginning to travel out ahead of him. Word was spreading about Matthew Hopkins, and of how his arrival in town could signal God's divine justice . . . or the release of a hate-filled mob looking for someone to blame for their own unhappiness. I suppose it's all in the eye of the beholder.

Some towns saw the upside to his work, though. If there was someone in town who caused problems—disrupting the social order or wielding too much power—Hopkins represented an opportunity. Drum up enough false testimony and anyone could be accused of witchcraft. So it's no wonder that almost everywhere he went, villagers eagerly threw neighbors, friends, even *family* under the proverbial bus.

And Hopkins reveled in it. He continued to call himself witch-finder general and claimed that he owned a scroll that contained the names of all the witches in England. The truth was, though, he and John Stearne were just sort of making it up as they went along. But they weren't about to tell anyone *else* that, were they?

When he arrived in Ipswich, the people there told him a story. Mary Lakeland, the wife of a prosperous barber, had apparently conspired with another local woman, Alice Denham. Their purpose, according to town gossip, was to harass a local man named William Lawrence. Mary apparently owed him some money, and rather than paying it back, the two women sent a pair of familiars, in the form of dogs, to attack him.

The trouble was, Mary Lakeland had a spotless reputation. She was known throughout Ipswich as a "professor of religion," someone who was solid in her Christian faith. But this was the 1640s, and no matter how secure someone might have thought they were, all it took was a few suspicious people. Priest or beggar,

any reputation was at risk of evaporating over the heat of all that hatred. Mary Lakeland was not immune to that gossip. And that's when a series of unfortunate events struck the household of William Lawrence: he, his son, and their maidservant all unexpectedly died.

Another rumor said that Mary had been upset at a sailor named Henry Reade, who had pledged to marry her granddaughter but then backed out of the arrangement. Mary confessed to sending her familiars to burn Reade's ship off the coast of Ipswich, but things got worse after that.

Reade developed a series of large tumors and sores that seemed to consume his body from the outside. One of those tumors was said to be on his leg, and had taken a shape that resembled—of all things—a dog, just like Mary's familiars. The pain from that tumor, they say, was so unbearable that he couldn't even walk upright.

But it was one accusation in particular that set Mary apart from all the other witches Matthew Hopkins hunted down. Town gossip said that Mary had tortured and killed her own husband, which in her day was considered treason, and traitors were burned at the stake.

Which was how Mary ended up in custody in the hands of Matthew Hopkins, where she endured the same torture he was known so well for. Days of sleepless nights and growing hunger eventually drove her to fabricate an elaborate tale of taking the Devil to bed. He had then cut her hand with one of his claws and scratched out a covenant with her own blood.

Her confessions led to the arrest of Alice Denham and four others, and all six of them were moved to jail. Denham was later hanged after being paraded through town in front of everyone who cared to see her. Mary, though, was sentenced to death by *fire,* the only witch in Hopkins's entire campaign to be burned alive.

On September 9, a crowd was gathered at the southeast corner of town to watch her execution. Now, when most people think of witch burnings, they think of someone being tied to a tall pole surrounded by a pile of kindling, which is partly true. Mary's burning, though, was slightly different.

When she arrived, the executioner first had her placed inside a barrel of hot pitch, coating her body in flammable black tar. Then, she was pulled out and chained to the post, where her body was surrounded by brush and wood planks. The fire burned hot and black, fueled by that thick tar and Mary's own body.

The following morning, the small pile of ash was carefully cleaned up, because even the smallest fragment of a witch could do irreparable harm. Which, of course, is nonsense, because witches aren't real. They're an excuse. A weapon swung around by angry, bigoted people who allow hate to override their common sense.

Mary Lakeland was no witch, just an innocent woman caught at the intersection of superstition and circumstance. Except . . . well, fate didn't help her reputation much after her death. You see, something happened the very same night her body burned in front of that angry crowd.

Henry Reade, the sailor who had spurned her granddaughter—the man who lay at home in pain, dying from the tumors that were eating him alive—suddenly took a turn for the better. His symptoms vanished, and he quickly returned to health. Mary's death, at least in the eyes of everyone in town, had somehow released the man from her curse.

Coincidence, it seems, might just be the most powerful spell of all.

RIDING THE WAVE

Today we have the benefit of 350 years of distance between Matthew Hopkins and ourselves. We can look back and study the events of his day. We can roll them around in our fingers and feel the rough edges and flaws in a way that maybe his contemporaries were just a bit too personally invested to see.

So it's easy for us to see everything that went on across southeastern England from 1645 to 1647 as pure madness—madness that acted like a wave. And Matthew Hopkins rode it like a pro.

His mission didn't stop in Ipswich, either. After Mary Lakeland's execution, he stopped in at Stowmarket for more of the same. Then he headed to Cambridgeshire, and Northamptonshire after that. As sad as it is, Hopkins got around.

There were sane voices, though, standing firm against that wave of madness. One of them was a minister named John Gaule, from the village of Great Staughton. He held the unpopular opinion that the people involved in these trials were just blaming others for their own misfortunes, and using superstition as an excuse. He even published a pamphlet that politely trashed the young witch-finder general.

When Hopkins read the paper, he sent a letter to Gaule, promising the minister that he'd be visiting him soon to hunt for witches there. I don't know about you, but I'd call that a threat.

For over a year, Matthew Hopkins and John Stearne visited dozens of villages and guided scores of innocent people to the gallows. By some estimates, more than three hundred men and women were charged with the crime, and over one-third of them were convicted and executed. Let's put that in perspective: in just over a year, Hopkins had more people executed for witchcraft than in the entire century before.

Thankfully, he eventually retired. There's a lot that went into the reason for that. Part of it has to do with the expense of it all. When Hopkins entered a town and set the wheels in motion for a trial and execution, those things were expensive to the community. And they were already struggling under the tax burden required to pay for a war.

Then, in the summer of 1646, something else spread across the area: the plague. London was seeing more than two hundred new cases each week, and people were getting very worried. Maybe Hopkins found the villages to be a lot less receptive to his message, or maybe he just decided to stay home and not get sick. I wouldn't blame him if he did.

A year later, he was dead. There's a lot of folklore surrounding that death, too. Some say he was subjected to his own infamous ducking test, where the accused were tied up and tossed into a lake or river. Because witches were said to literally repel Christian baptism, people believed that the guilty would float, while the innocent would drown.

Another legend says that after his death, someone found that mysterious scroll he carried around with him, the one with the names of all the witches in England. They say Hopkins's own name was listed among the guilty.

But there's no evidence that Hopkins was ever tried and convicted as a witch. No evidence that a scroll ever existed. Like so much of his own mission and work, even the stories of his death are filled with lies and hearsay. The truth is a lot less supernatural and a lot more boring: Matthew Hopkins died in August 1647 from tuberculosis.

Look, I get it. It's easy to think that all of this was just primitive behavior, and that we've gotten better in the years since. We've had over three centuries, after all—surely we've evolved. And yes, in some ways we have.

But don't miss the point here: when people are scared enough—when their worldview is threatened and everything they know and believe is put at risk—they lash out and hurt others. Given the chance, people will do *anything* to end the madness . . . even toss their own family into the arms of a murderous zealot. And they'll justify it better than any criminal defense lawyer ever could.

I wish we were better now, I really do, but sadly, very little has changed. Sure, most people no longer believe in witches, but for those who are easily swayed by hatred, there's a whole new list of "others" to focus their obsession on.

The madness, it seems, is all too familiar to us. It's always there, just on the other side of the door, tempting us to step on through. Because in the end, as sad as it seems, there's always another witch to burn, isn't there?

After Sunset

HANNAH HOVEY LOST her husband long before the rumors began. Or maybe it was his death that gave birth to them. You see, Captain Joseph Hovey had been a sailor, but he died on land, under difficult-to-explain circumstances. He was found with a broken neck at the base of a local cliff in their town of Monroe, Connecticut.

Perhaps it was because she lived alone. Perhaps it was the rooster she kept as a pet who had an eerie habit of crowing only at midnight. Or maybe it was just that, like so many women before her who wore the title of witch, she was a cranky, difficult woman.

Up until the 1690s, witchcraft in the American colonies had been a crime punishable by death. Tragedies similar to the Salem witch trials were recorded in countless communities across much of what is now known as New England. But thankfully, the events in Salem brought the issue to a level of attention that warranted changes.

No longer were accused witches executed for their fabricated crimes. Still, that didn't mean that the accused were free from repercussions. Very much like the world we live in today, it was all too easy to hang the noose of social stigma over the heads of anyone who refused to play along. Hannah Hovey was one of those kinds of people.

It was a shame, really. She went out of her way to be helpful when she was needed. You see, Hannah was known throughout town as a witch, not simply because she had a sharp tongue and a quick temper, but because she had certain skills. And when the people of Monroe needed help of a particular type, they reluctantly leaned on her for assistance.

Once a farmer came to her house and begged for her help. The town had been suffering through a drought for weeks, and this man's crops were dying. Naturally, he was desperate for a solution, and that desperation led him to Hannah Hovey.

Hannah agreed to help. She would bring the rain, she told him. But only if the farmer pledged his soul to her, right there in her house. According to the legend, the farmer eagerly fell to the floor and offered her his very soul.

It rained that night. And the next. And many nights after that. And the farmer, whose crop had been withering through the drought, watched as it grew in abundance.

They called her the Wicked Witch of Monroe. They referred to her as Hannah Cranna. It was said, among the people of the town, that her house was guarded by serpents. They whispered to one another about how she would sit atop a tall stone outcropping near Cutler's Farm Road, where she seemed to be surveying the land as if it were her very own kingdom.

Her reputation grew, and Hannah eventually learned to use it to her advantage. It was said that even though she had no income or fortune of her own, she never went hungry or cold because the people of the town gave her what she needed. But they weren't doing that out of generosity. No, these were payments grounded in fear.

Once she visited the home of a local farmer and demanded food from them. The farmer's wife was famous for her pies, but when the woman refused to give one to Hannah, the witch was said to have cursed her. The woman never baked a pie again.

The day soon came when her pet rooster finally died, and the next day Hannah told a neighbor that her time, too, was drawing near. She told the neighbor that she had specific wishes for how her burial would be handled. Specifically, she asked for her coffin to be carried only by foot to the cemetery, not by wagon. She also requested to be buried after sundown.

The following day was white and cold, as a winter storm had blown into town. Almost as if she had predicted it, Hannah Hovey died. By midday, she was given last rites and placed in a coffin, and the community moved to bury her quickly, during the daylight hours.

Unfortunately, the snow made carrying her coffin difficult, so a wagon was brought in to help. But things just got worse. The coffin kept rolling off the wagon, so they strapped it down. After that, the straps broke, sending the wooden box tumbling to the ground. No matter what they tried, the men could not get the coffin to stay on the cart, and after one last spill that sent it sliding back down the hill toward her house, the men decided it might be better to try to carry it.

It was difficult work, to be sure, but the pallbearers eventually moved her coffin safely to the cemetery. Because the work had taken so long, the burial took place just after sundown. Exactly as Hannah had wanted.

After a difficult afternoon, the men returned to town, trudging through the snow and wind, their bodies sore from the exertion. When they got there, though, they found one last bit of resistance from Hannah Cranna: her house had mysteriously caught fire and was blazing out of control.

The fire lasted days, they say. Eventually, though, the embers died down, and the wreckage—what was left of it, anyway—was cleared away, leaving nothing but the wide, stone-lined hole that had been the house's cellar.

It was said that whenever someone visited the remains of that cellar, strange sounds could be heard. Moans and scratching, whispers in the cool night air, even laughter. Even today, people say that similar sounds can still be heard. All you have to do is visit the site of the old home at night.

If you're brave enough, of course.

Peg and Button

IN 1758, THE northeast corner of North America was at war. Two years prior, conflict had broken out between British and French colonists. The French, being vastly outnumbered, leaned heavily on an alliance with the Native American tribes of the region.

Today we call the conflict the French and Indian War, but no matter what you call a war, it's always political, it's always violent, and it always has a way of trickling down and affecting the powerless. So maybe that's why the young men from Gloucester, on the rocky coast of Massachusetts, went out and got drunk the night before they were supposed to ship out to the front lines in the north.

There were five of them—Jack Coas, Job and David Stanwood, Thomas Ayres, and Jim Parsons—all part of a larger battalion of forty men who were about to follow one Captain Byles north into Canada. These men hadn't been conscripted; they'd volunteered, looking forward to the glory and honor of battle.

We don't know why, but these five men did their best to make the most of their last night of freedom. They visited the local tavern and had more than their fill of the local brew. And then, with the night still young, they stumbled out and began looking for trouble. Let's be honest: young, drunk men are always looking for trouble, no matter what century we're talking about, right?

While walking through town, the young soldiers-to-be encountered Peg Wesson. Now, you need to know some details about Peg. First, she was old and widowed. Second, she was tiny. Most records say she was a mere ninety-nine pounds, a number they called a "witch's weight"—because in the 1750s you were apparently a witch if you were tiny. They claimed it helped to be light if you wanted to ride on a broomstick. I know. Don't try to make sense of it all. Just roll with it.

Peg also had a reputation as a troublemaker. She had a quick temper, loved to voice her opinion, and had a tendency to cause trouble in town. Maybe it was the alcohol driving their decisions, or that night-before-deployment feeling of invincibility, but for some reason these young men decided to walk over to Peg's house on Back Street and knock on her door.

When she answered the door, they let themselves in. Then they mocked her while searching the house for her broomstick. It was a horrible invasion of her private space, and most people would feel violated. Peg, however, knew how to fight back. She cursed them.

The legend says that Peg forced all of them out of her home by promising them all a violent death in battle. Specifically, she claimed that the men would meet their ends outside Fort Louisburg in Nova Scotia.

Months later, so the story goes, all of the men from Gloucester, part of a battalion from their home town, found themselves outside the very walls of the fortress Old Peg had mentioned in her curse. They were pinned down by French riflemen who were perched atop the massive walls of the fort, and were doing their best to stay out of sight.

That's when a large crow appeared in the sky. It was larger than any crow they'd ever seen before, and it flew in a large circle around the scene of the battle. Then, without warning, it began to swoop down and attack the young men who had visited Peg's house months before. Each time, the men were forced from their hiding place and put at risk of being shot by the enemy.

Frustrated and frightened, the men fired at the bird. The legend says that some of the shots even struck the bird, but the bullets seemed to glance off it. Convinced the bird was a devil or some supernatural being, these men regrouped and discussed their options. And while doing so, they came to one horrifying conclusion: the crow was not a crow but Old Peg.

Jim Parsons was the son of a minister, and they say he had some knowledge of the supernatural. So he proposed a new idea. Silver was the only metal powerful enough to bring down the devilish bird. So he took the silver buttons off the sleeve of his military uniform and loaded them into his musket. And then they waited for the bird to return.

When it did, Parsons fired, and he struck his target. The bird was stopped in midair and spiraled to the earth many yards away from the men. And that was the end of their trouble. The battle for the fortress was won by the men of Gloucester a short while later, and all of the men soon returned home. They were heroes, and the town welcomed them back.

Their return sparked conversation, though. They told their stories over and over, and as they did, someone in town noticed a detail that no one else did. The date of their battle outside Fort Louisburg—the day they fired the silver button at the ominous crow—was the same day that someone in Gloucester had taken a deadly fall.

Old Peg, it seems, had stumbled just outside her home on Back Street that very same day. When she did, she had apparently injured her leg. Of course, she was an elderly woman, and it's common for older folk to take a fall and hurt themselves. But something was unique about Peg's story.

The people of Gloucester told the soldiers that the fall had actually killed Peg Wesson. And that after she was found and brought to a physician, he examined her leg to see what the cause of the injury was. When he did, he found a curious wound. A wound, they say, that resembled something caused by a gunshot.

When the doctor inspected further, he found a bullet lodged in the bone. He pulled it out of her leg and placed it on the table beside her body, and then grabbed a clean rag to wipe the blood off. When he did, he held his breath.

It wasn't a bullet; it was a silver military button.

High Stakes

THEY SAY HE was a quiet man. In the English countryside, they might say he "kept himself to himself." Maybe he was an introvert, or maybe he was shy. Perhaps he was just more fond of the silence of solitude than the bustle of community.

Being a lover of silence myself, I can relate. But he wasn't a hermit. No, Charles lived with his niece in a small house, and he left every day to work on a number of the local farms. He was sort of a farmhand for hire, moving from place to place helping out as his neighbors needed him.

But at the end of the day, you wouldn't find him at the pub lifting an ale alongside those neighbors. Instead, Charles liked to take jugs of cider home and drink by himself. And maybe that was the behavior that drew the most criticism. It looked antisocial, after all. But once people start whispering, they rarely stop, you know? Rumor is a flame, and the minds of locals tend to be highly flammable.

Charles spent a lot of time alone in the fields, and people had begun to wonder why. He also had a hobby that most people considered strange: rather than raising hounds or normal livestock, Charles bred toads. I know, it seems more like the pastime of a young child, but it was what Charles loved to do.

For all we know, he was running his own genetics experiments, or maybe he just loved the simple beauty of the transformation process from tadpole to adult. Whatever his reason was for the hobby, it was unusual enough to draw attention.

And maybe that explains what happened next.

It had been a cold February day, and his niece had prepared a warm meal and stoked the fire to welcome her uncle home. But twilight turned to darkness, and Charles failed to show up. So the authorities were alerted, and a search party was gathered for the following morning. And it didn't take long.

Out near the field he had been working in, under the wide branches of a willow tree, they found his body lying in the mud and grass. His hedger's slash, sort of a handle with a curved blade, was found buried deep in his chest. It was probably a fatal wound, and would have eventually killed him if it was the only injury— but it *wasn't*.

No, the killing blow was most likely the pitchfork that had been driven through his neck. It had been pushed so hard, in fact, that it went all the way through and pinned Charles to the ground. It's most likely that Charles had first been struck with the hedger's slash, and then the pitchfork was used to finish the deed.

And the authorities looked for the killer for months. They had theories, but they were nothing more than that, and no more valuable than the rumors that had been spread about poor Charles before his death. But those rumors might hold the final clue.

You see, people didn't like the long hours that Charles spent alone in the fields because they believed he was doing something unnatural. Specifically, they thought he was talking with the birds. And those toads in his backyard weren't just pets or the hobby of an introverted man. They were familiars, some said, used to pull a tiny plow and work the fields for him.

Crazy, I know. But whoever killed Charles seemed to believe it. And they believed it enough to walk out to the field on a cold February afternoon and put an end to what they perceived to be a threat. Because if the stories were true, Charles Walton was dangerous. He was the Devil among them, a source of evil power and wicked trickery. Charles, some said, was a witch, and his murder was punishment for that crime.

If true, that makes his murder all the more remarkable. Not

because of the details, or even the fact that it was never solved. No, what makes the murder of a suspected witch so remarkable is the year that it took place, making it the last witchcraft murder in English history.

The year? Nineteen forty-five.

Rise Above

I T'S AMAZING HOW easily people are drawn to simple answers. Complexity just isn't as much fun. Maybe complexity offers us less hope, or perhaps it just reminds us of how small and powerless we are on this giant rock. Simplicity is the opposite of all of that.

When a tsunami crashed against the coast of an island a thousand years ago, it was easy to believe that the gods were angry and punishing its inhabitants. The truth is a lot more complex—tectonic plates, earthquakes, seismic waves, and all that—and therefore a lot less easy to grasp. Simplicity is sexy.

So it should come as no surprise that much of folklore is an engine that runs on the power of simplicity, and no topic represents that more fully than witchcraft. As we've already seen, whenever something odd or unexplainable happened in our community, the conclusion was easy to reach: someone in town was a witch.

That's the world that Grace was born into. She was one of the early settlers of Virginia, the daughter of a Scottish carpenter and his English wife. Unlike her parents, though, she was born in the New World.

In 1680, Grace married a local farmer, James Sherwood. Her father gave them some land as a wedding gift, and the couple settled into life there on their small farm. A year later, her father passed away and left her the rest of his property. Nothing extravagant, but two hundred acres was still something.

The stories say that Grace was unusually beautiful, tall, and full of laughter—the sort of woman who stood out in her Puritan English colony. She turned heads, which probably didn't go a long way toward helping the neighbor ladies like her.

Still, life needed living. She and her husband, James, raised three sons there on the farm, but it was hard work. Everything was hard work in the late 1600s, though. It was hard work to stay healthy, to work the land, to fill the bellies of three hungry, growing boys, and to please everyone around her. Life was hard.

Grace spread herself thin, too. She had all the normal roles that came with being a wife and mother, but she also helped out in the community as a midwife. Part of her garden was even devoted to a large number of medicinal herbs, and she used them often to help others with illness or pain.

Some people didn't care for that. It smacked of dark magic, of someone who was playing with the natural order of things. And it was not a major leap of logic to assume she was fluent in spells, too. So when one of her neighbors, Richard Capps, claimed that Grace had killed his bull with one of those spells, they went to court. Thankfully, the evidence was nonexistent, so the case was dismissed. Grace and James sued Capps for defamation but lost.

A year later, in 1698, it was John Gisburne's turn, only this time it was his pigs and his cotton crop she had bewitched. That case was also dismissed, and Grace lost another lawsuit for the slander. Later that year, it all repeated again when Elizabeth Barnes accused Grace of transforming into a black cat that entered her home through the keyhole. Grace somehow lost that slander case as well.

Each time it happened, she and her husband were forced to pay the court fees, which only served to drive them further into poverty. And then in 1701 James died, leaving her vulnerable to future attacks.

Four years later, it happened again: her neighbor Elizabeth Hill physically attacked her. And maybe it was because of the bruises and scratches on Grace's body, but this time she was able to win her assault case against Hill. She walked away with the equivalent of about $200 in today's currency.

But she also ticked off a few people in the process.

A few months later, Elizabeth Hill returned, blaming her recent miscarriage on Grace, and the women went to court. By March 1706, two separate juries were called to serve in the trial. One was sent to Grace's home to search for evidence of her witchcraft, while the other was tasked with examining Grace's body for witch's marks.

On March 7, Grace was stripped naked by twelve local women, who examined her from head to toe, looking for dark spots or raised parts of her skin. You know, things we might call moles, or skin tags, or freckles. And—surprise, surprise—they found some.

Oh, and the woman in charge of this gang of angry mole-hunters? None other than Elizabeth Barnes, the woman who had failed to get Grace arrested eight years earlier. Someone was holding a grudge, I think.

I won't bore you with court details. There were more trials. There was a bit of controversy, and a clear lack of solid evidence. And yet, the judge felt that something had to be done, and so on July 10 Grace Sherwood was taken to a plantation at the mouth of the Lynnhaven River.

A crowd gathered to watch that day as Grace was stripped naked and examined again by the group of women. This time, though, they were looking for tools Grace might have hidden on her body. Because they were about to do something insane.

They pushed her into a boat with the sheriff, and he rowed it about two hundred yards out into the water. Then, after her hands and feet were bound to each other and a thirteen-pound Bible was tethered to her neck, she was brought to the side of the boat.

Their logic was about as solid as a cloud, and should sound insanely familiar to fans of Monty Python: if she floated, she was a witch. Drowning was the only acceptable proof of her innocence.

Grace Sherwood plunged into the dark waters of the Lynnhaven River around 10:00 a.m. on July 10, 1706. And like so many women before her, this was the end. The delicate balance of life and death hinged on the crazy notion that witches were so immune to Christian baptism that they actually floated.

And so, with a firm shove, into the river she went.

GRACE FLOATS

But Grace was stronger than the fear that filled her community there in Virginia. As her body sank into the depths of the river—as the shock of the cold water on her naked skin and the burn of her lungs overwhelmed her—she fought back. She managed to untie herself and shrug off the weight of that enormous Bible. And then she swam free.

It was a sign of her guilt, though, so she was thrown in jail the very same day. She beat part of the system, only to fall prey to the rest of it. It's twisted and wrong, I know, but to the people of her community, it was simple logic. And simple, as we've seen, is a lot easier to believe.

Grace appears again, roughly eight years later. That's when most historians think she was released from jail. She reclaimed her property, paid her back taxes, and then settled into life alone. Her boys had grown up and moved on, and it seems that the accusations were gone as well. The rest of her life was relatively quiet, and I have to imagine she was glad for that. She passed away in 1740, at the ripe old age of eighty.

I like Grace. She managed to do something that few others had in her era: she faced a test designed to punish the innocent, and she got away.

Yes, our world is still full of dangerously irrational people—people that allow hate and jealously and their own deep insecurities to drive them toward monstrous actions. But maybe that's not the inescapable prison it appears to be.

Maybe, like Grace Sherwood, we can rise above it all and swim to safety.

One can only hope.

Making a Mark

N EW ENGLAND FOLKLORE is rich and deep, and has a sort of magical attraction. One of the biggest reasons for that is because the northeast part of the United States serves as a sort of cultural bridge between the Old World and the New. It was there, more than anywhere else, where the old tales and superstitions first set foot on American soil.

The New England witch hysteria of the late 1600s was a small aftershock of a larger tremor that shook Europe for decades. The American version of the vampire has root in eastern European folktales and legends. Even holidays like Christmas and Halloween were really just Old World injections into the cultural soft tissue of America. And that needle pierced us in New England first—most of the time.

There are other parts of the country that played host to pioneers and adventurers as well. People who risked their lives and loved ones to travel across the cold Atlantic and build a new home here on our shores. And the age of colonization brought more than just settlers and supplies. It brought *lore*.

Settlers up and down the East Coast of what would one day become America came ashore with heads full of superstitions and a propensity to attach meaning to things we might overlook today. Put another way, they brought food for the journey, and the seeds to grow more here.

They came with minds that were perfectly wired to build new folklore on the backs of old tales. New fears, new legends, new hauntings. And we can still find those creations in many places along the Eastern Seaboard. Places like North Carolina. Before the vacation homes and sun-baked tourists crowded along the sandy shores of the Outer Banks, pioneers were attempting to carve out an existence there.

Those that survived left behind more than buildings and descendants, though. Today the Outer Banks is home to tales that still send shivers down the spines of locals and tourists alike. Because folklore, whether it's new or old, has a way of leaving its mark.

Brigands and Beards

Brigand Bay sits on the northern coast of the southern part of Hatteras Island, between the towns of Frisco and Buxton. Hatteras is part of the Outer Banks, which on the map look like nothing more than a thin string of earth and sand a few miles off the coast of North Carolina. Imagine the island as a backward capital L, following the coastline of the Pamlico River.

But don't let that thin strip of sand and state parks fool you; Hatteras, like many of the other islands out there, is still big enough for stories to take root. And that's because it has a long history, longer than most parts of the country, in fact. Near the northern tip of the island, just to the west, is Roanoke Island, the site of England's first settlement in the New World.

Although the colony there disappeared sometime between 1587 and 1590, Europeans didn't stay away long. And it was their constant activity in the region that gave rise to so many of the local stories still told today.

There is a legend in Hatteras of the horrible deeds of one particular captain. According to the story, in 1710, an English ship crossed the Atlantic carrying refugees from Germany. They were known as Palatines and they had originally fled the Middle Rhine area to settle in England, but there were so many that the English decided to help them move to the New World.

When these refugees boarded the ship, they hid their valuables, afraid that they might be stolen by the ship's crew. After a successful journey, the ship entered the waters inside the Outer Banks, heading toward New Bern on the coast. Their new home was in sight, and after such a long journey, it must have been a relief to see it.

Sensing they would soon disembark, the Palatines removed their valuables from hiding and gathered them together for the final leg of their journey. Now, maybe it was the sight of all that treasure—the jewelry and coins and precious heirlooms—that triggered what happened next. Or perhaps the crew had planned it all along. But here was their chance, and they decided to act.

Claiming that the weather wasn't good enough for a landing, they told the passengers to return to their cabins and wait until the morning. During the night, the crew moved systematically through the ship, killing the sleeping refugees and stealing their treasures.

After killing the passengers, the captain and crew set fire to the ship, and headed to shore in lifeboats. But the ship didn't sink. Instead, the legend claims that the flames grew higher and higher, while the ship began to move forward in the calm waters. Fearing for their lives, the crew abandoned the lifeboat and were never seen again.

To this day, locals whisper of a ghost ship that can be seen under the first full moon of September. The ship, orange with flames, passes near the Ocracoke Inlet three times, and then vanishes as quickly as it appeared.

Another prominent local story involves the capture of the legendary pirate Edward Teach, also known as Blackbeard. Teach patrolled the Atlantic and Caribbean in his ship, *Queen Anne's Revenge,* for a little over two years, and in the process became one of the most feared pirates of his day.

As history records, Blackbeard was finally cornered by Lieutenant Robert Maynard and his men in November 1718 just inside the Outer Banks near the southern tip of Hatteras. In a battle that was horribly bloody for both sides, the great Blackbeard suffered no fewer than twenty sword wounds and five gunshots before he was finally brought down.

The English beheaded his corpse and tossed the body into the sea. His head, though, was kept. Maynard hung it from the bowsprit of his ship, and it was turned in later to collect his reward.

Locals there near Ocracoke tell of a spot known as Teach's Hole, where the legendary pirate once anchored his ship. If the stories are to be believed, Blackbeard's ghost haunts the location. There are those who claim to have seen strange lights, both above and below the water, there on the coast. They say it's Blackbeard, swimming through the waters he used to patrol.

Others say you can hear voices there. When storms blow in and waves crash against the shore, locals claim you can hear something besides the rain and thunder. It's the sound of a man crying out in pain, the same words over and over: "Where is my head?"

New Arrivals

Hatteras is still popular with visitors today, though I would assume none of them are pirates. People still build homes there. They have streets and restaurants and parks and trees. Tourists flock there every summer to take in the scenery. But right there, on Snug Harbor Drive near Brigand Bay, is a tree that's called the island home for centuries. In fact, it was most likely ancient when the colonists first arrived hundreds of years before. And although most of the people driving by it are completely unaware, this tree has a story to tell.

According to local legend, it starts with the arrival of a woman near Frisco back in the early 1700s. They say her name was Cora, and she brought a baby along with her. They were always seen together, the child held tight to her chest or strapped into a sling. For an area frequented by sailors, or widows of those who were lost to the sea, that wasn't an unusual sight.

The Brigand Bay area was even more wooded then than it is now, and it's said that she took up shelter in the forest there, rather than in the small community that was forming on the coast. But it wasn't living on the literal outskirts of society that earned her a reputation as an outsider. It was her knack for the unusual.

Some have said that cows she touched would dry up and turn sick. When the fishing got rough and nets were empty, Cora still managed to bring in enough to feed herself and the child. And when a local boy decided to poke fun at the baby, legend says that he got so sick he nearly died.

Naturally, people talked. People always talk when things don't fit the norm. And that talk spread. In an era when it didn't take much more than an unpleasant disposition or off-color comment to earn a woman a reputation as a witch, it seemed Cora was making it a little too easy for the locals to be suspicious.

The legend also tells of how, during Cora's stay there, a ship called the *Susan G.* ran aground off the northern coast of the island. The captain and his crew left the ship and came to town, and from there they made plans to repair it and continue their commercial delivery. It sounds simple, right? Just repair the damage and move on. But doing so meant unloading all of the cargo, piece by piece, and bringing it to shore.

The captain's name, according to local legend, was Eli Blood. That better have been his real name, because come on, how perfect is that, right? Captain Blood. This captain enlisted the help of locals to move the cargo off his grounded ship, and in the process he got to know quite a few of them. Which was good; judging by the repairs, he and his crew from Salem, Massachusetts, were bound to be there for a very long time.

And it was during this long stay that he and his crew heard the stories of Cora and her baby. The heart of the rumors pointed to one single, sensational conclusion: Cora was a witch, and the child she brought with her was her familiar, her supernatural pet. And as it turned out, Captain Blood was probably the last person on earth that this mysterious Cora wanted to draw the suspicion of.

The captain, it seems, was not *just* a sailor from Salem. He claimed to know Cotton Mather, the Puritan minister who was a passionate voice in support of the Salem witch trials. He had read Mather's books. He had studied them. He was a student of

Mather's methods, and apparently shared the man's intense hatred for the dark arts.

So much so, in fact, that he considered himself a white witch, someone trained in combating the forces of darkness with their own brand of magic. He claimed to have his own familiars, which he fed with drops of blood. And those familiars acted like spies for him, informing him of black magic nearby. Captain Eli Blood considered himself a witch-hunter.

I realize this sounds incredibly hypocritical—which it *is*, of course—but back then it was heroic. It gave the people of the area a feeling of safety. At last, they might have said, we have someone here who can deal with Cora the witch if she gets out of hand.

And that's when the body of a man washed up on the beach.

THE BODY AND THE BURNING

The body wasn't one of Captain Blood's men, but it drew his concern nonetheless. It was the body of a young man from town, and although no marks could be found that pointed to the cause of his death, there were a number of other clues.

Local legend tells of how the man's face was twisted into a horrible expression of fear. His hands, they say, were clasped together, as if he had been kneeling before someone powerful, begging for his life. The man even had the number 666 carved into his forehead. The most damning evidence of all, however, were the footprints in the sand near his body. They were smaller than a man's, and they moved away from the body in a clear, definable direction: the woods.

Someone needed to investigate the man's death, they said. And who better to do it than the witch-hunter himself, Captain Eli Blood? He had little else to do while he waited for the ship's owner to send help and supplies. This sounded like the perfect job for his idle mind. Captain Blood, for his part, agreed.

He gathered his men—mostly slaves from Barbados, who had a healthy cultural fear of black magic—and together they went in search of Cora's shack in the woods. When they found her, she was inside making breakfast for herself and her child, and the men seized them both and brought them back to town.

They accused Cora of witchcraft and murder, of course. How could they not, in a society governed by deep superstition and intense fear of people who failed to fit in? But before you write them off as barbaric, remember that this is a flaw we have yet to overcome. We still fear those who are different from us. Maybe it's genetic, or maybe it's culturally ingrained. And that fear is like a snake hiding in the bushes, always ready to strike.

It struck hard for Cora. Captain Blood had her bound, left hand to right ankle, right hand to left ankle, and then carried to the shore. There he ordered her to be thrown into the water. It was a test, he said. If she floated, she was a witch. And seeing as how the tide was low and the waves were calm, of course she didn't sink. How could she?

Satisfied with the results, the captain moved on to his second test. Pulling his knife free, the man tried to cut a handful of Cora's hair, but the blade failed to do its job. More proof, he declared, that she was a witch. Or at least proof that he needed to sharpen his knife, but hey, I'm no witch-hunter.

The final test was the creepiest and most ambiguous of them all. Taking a bowl of sea water, the Captain asked each of his crew to cut their fingertip and drip blood into the bowl. When they had all done so, he stirred this mixture with his knife until it foamed and swirled. And then he chanted words that no one else understood while staring hard into the bowl, and then raised his face in triumph.

"She's a witch!" he exclaimed. And then, as if needing a second opinion, he passed the bowl around to the others. Each of them, according to the legend, saw two things in the bowl: the Devil and the face of Cora.

That was all the proof they needed. Cora was a witch, pure and simple. Now her execution would be carried out. The captain had his men gather firewood and branches and pile them at the base of a large oak tree near the bay. And then Cora and her child were tied to the tree, ready to be burned alive.

Now, what happened next will sound unusual. That's the fingerprint of an old story. They sometimes take on a patina of oddities and otherworldliness. But sometimes the patina adds texture, even value, to an antique. I'll let you be the judge.

According to the locals who tell the tale to this day, Captain Blood approached the tree with a lit torch in his hand, ready to set fire to the wood and burn the witch and her familiar alive. But another captain, a local man named John Smith, held him back, asking instead for Cora's trial to go through the proper legal channels. Smith, being a sane man, wanted to do things right.

But as the men argued, two things happened. First, the child in Cora's arms twisted and writhed as it transformed into a large black cat with shimmering green eyes. Second, a dark, ominous cloud began to gather overhead in an otherwise cloudless sky.

Both men cried out in horror, and then Captain Blood lunged forward with the torch to ignite the kindling. It was at that very moment that the cloud overhead rumbled, and a lightning bolt flashed down, striking the tree and blinding everyone around it.

When the smoke cleared, the tree was empty. The ropes were still there, as was the pile of branches and firewood. But the woman and the cat were gone without a trace. Well, that's not true. There was *one* clue, but it was difficult to believe.

Etched by lightning into the bark of the old oak tree were four clear letters, which spelled out one single word: C-O-R-A.

SIGNS AND TRAILS

The Outer Banks is just like any other place in the world on many levels. It has a history, and over the centuries that constitute that history, stories have been told. In a lot of ways, story is one of our greatest legacies. Wherever we've been, we've left story in our wake, like footprints in the mud.

Some stories are true and act like time capsules. Some are exaggerations of the truth and are meant to entertain later generations more than anything else. Some, though, serve to fill in the blanks, to answer those lingering questions, or to explain the things we can't wrap our minds around.

Are there really fiery ghost ships and headless pirates haunting the Outer Banks? Was the word on the Cora tree—a word that you can still go see for yourself, if you want—really carved into the bark by lightning? The chances are pretty good that it's all just a collection of old, entertaining folktales. But sometimes stories do both: beneath their decorative paint and fantastical flourishes, they conceal a grain of truth deep in their core.

The most famous local legend in the Outer Banks, by a mile, is the story of the lost colony of Roanoke. The island is located off the west coast of Hatteras Island, and when the English settled it in 1585, they knew they were on the edge of the world. Building a settlement there took a lot of guts, and it came with a lot of risk and danger.

When John White and a hundred new settlers landed in July 1587, the first settlement was gone, so they stayed to investigate. They set up their own fort there, and also worked to establish relations with the local Native American tribes: the Croatoan on what is now Hatteras, and the Coree on the mainland.

White left for England one year later to get more supplies, but didn't return for three years. When he *did* come back, no sign of the second group of English settlers could be found. He'd left them with a plan, though. If they were forced to leave, they'd been told to carve a cross into a nearby tree so White would know they'd been attacked. And he *did* find a carving, but it wasn't a cross. It was a single word: "Croatoan."

This was good news, because it meant they'd departed peacefully. But where did they go? White wanted to search Hatteras immediately, but when a terrible storm blew in, his men refused to stay. However painful it might have been—after all, White's own granddaughter was among the missing—they left the very next day.

It's interesting to note that the Croatoan lived in southern Hatteras, in the area between modern-day Buxton and Frisco. Right by the Cora tree. And if it wasn't really lightning that carved those letters, perhaps it was an actual human being. Sure, it could be nothing more than a centuries-old prank, or just a bit of lover's graffiti. Anything's possible, right?

Or maybe, like a myth with a grain of truth at its heart, this tree is the last hint in a chain of clues that point to the final destination of the settlers from Roanoke. You see, the Cree tribe on the mainland went by a few other names. Some called them the Cores, or the Coranine. Or, interestingly enough, the Cora.

A LITTLE PECULIAR

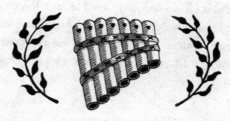

A Stranger Among Us

OLKLORE IS A living thing. In many ways, the stories we tell and the lessons we pass on are like a tree. There are branches that reach out into generations and cultures, sometimes in obvious ways, and other times reaching surprising new places.

One good example of this would be the folklore surrounding small fairy people that we've discussed before.* Puckwudgies, trolls, goblins, pooka, and dozens of similar variations are scattered around the world with amazing consistency and reach. How or why is something we'll probably never know. But it shows us how folklore can spread, how it can migrate, and how it can build upon the past.

At the same time, though, folklore also has roots, and those roots run deeper than we might expect. Some stories that we still whisper about in the dark today have crossed the lips of people for centuries, and in some cases millennia. When I hear a story for the first time, or discover a new collection of tales that have been widely distributed, I often stop and ask myself the same questions: Where did it come from? What lies at the bottom of the narrative? What are its roots?

Outside of Halloween, there is no other time of the year—at least for European cultures—where folklore rushes to the fore-

* In the first volume in this series, *The World of Lore: Monstrous Creatures.*

front of everyone's lives with such significance, such power, and such ease as the Christmas season. And rightly so. There is so much there to unpack and explore.

The tree. The gifts. The food. And the nocturnal visit from a stranger, one who has seemingly stalked our lives all year long, and yet whom we blindly welcome into our home. And if there's one lesson that folklore has taught us over the centuries, it's to beware of strangers. They aren't always who they seem to be.

OLD STRANGERS

When we think of coal in our stockings, and food and drink left out for a visitor, we rarely pair those ideas with the image of a woman flying through the air on a broomstick. But in Italy, there are those who still tell the story of La Befana.

La Befana's story has been told since at least the thirteenth century, originally connected with the Christian Feast of the Epiphany. But while many people have never heard of her, the details of her story are eerily familiar. During her visit, La Befana was said to enter homes through the chimney. She is typically depicted carrying a basket or bag full of gifts, but is also known to leave behind a lump of coal or a single stick for children who failed to behave during the year.

Before leaving each home, La Befana would sweep the floor with her broom—something scholars see as a metaphor for sweeping away the deeds of the previous year—and then she would eat the food left out for her, oftentimes sausage and broccoli. (Side note: cookies and milk sound *so* much better, don't they?)

Interestingly enough, La Befana is not the only Christmas legend with a passing resemblance to a witch. In the German Alps, there have been stories of another female figure dating back to the tenth century. Some call her Perchta, or Berchta, and later Bertha.

Jacob Grimm, while researching his *Deutsche Mythologie,* theorized that she was one of the ancient Germanic mother goddesses. She and her sisters were said to have taught humanity the arts of agriculture, spinning wool, and cooking. Over time, though, her legend began to integrate with parts of the Christmas season.

Because of her role in teaching humanity the basics of home management, Perchta's meaning began to shift over the centuries, turning her into the punisher of those who worked during the holidays and failed to feast properly; much later, she became known for hunting down the lazy. And what better time for her to conduct an end-of-year review, so to speak, than Christmas?

Just how did Perchta dish out her punishment on the people of Germany? Well, a hint can be found in her other popular title: the Belly-Slitter. During the Twelve Days of Christmas, she would travel through the towns and inspect the people's behavior. If they had followed the rules and done right in her eyes, they were rewarded.

If they had not been good, though, she was known to have a very nasty side. Anyone disobedient enough to warrant punishment—adult or child alike—would have their stomachs ripped open. Perchta would scoop out whatever might still be inside, pull out the full length of their intestines, and then stuff the victim's belly with garbage, straw, and rocks.

While a stomach full of refuse might seem a little over the top, that distinction actually goes to another ancient female in folklore. While stories of Gryla, the mythical giant goddess, are far outside the common narrative of Christmas for many of us, for the people of Iceland she is still a whispered source of dread among children.

One of the earliest mentions of Gryla dates back to the thirteenth-century collection of Icelandic mythology known as the Edda, written by Snorri Sturluson. According to the many stories told about her over the centuries, Gryla possesses the ability to locate disobedient children. She can do this year-round, so they say, and because of that, she was often used as a parental tool to coerce children into doing what they were told.

It was in the Christmas season, though, that Gryla became even more monstrous. That was when she was said to climb out of her home in the mountain and make her way toward the towns. She would hunt far and wide for all the naughty children, and then

take them back to her cave. There she would cut them up, place them in her stew, and devour them.

According to the legend, she never ran out of food.

The Punishers

There have been other stories of strangers told throughout the centuries, but not all have happy endings. In fact, there is often more loss than gain when it comes to the visits of some of these legends.

In the northern Alps, stories have been told for generations about the traveling stranger known as Belsnickel. Considered to be one of the helpers of St. Nicholas, Belsnickel travels ahead of the big red man and dispenses his own form of Christmas cheer—with physical abuse.

Descriptions of Belsnickel liken him to the wild men of old, with torn and dirty clothes fashioned from animal skins and furs, and a face that is covered in a snarled, filthy beard. Some stories report that he wears a mask with a long tongue protruding from the mouth.

According to the legend, which spans centuries in both Germany and the American state of Pennsylvania, Belsnickel would enter the home of a family and scatter nuts and sweets on the floor for the children to collect. And then, when they had their backs to him, he would lash out with a switch made of hazel or birch, whipping their backs and leaving red marks.

And Belsnickel isn't alone. Another traveling stranger from the same region, one who has seen a rise in popularity around the globe, is the creature known only as Krampus. At first blush, Krampus sounds similar to many of the other strangers in folklore around Europe. But what sets him apart is truly frightening.

It is said that Krampus visits the homes of children during the Christmas season. But he doesn't have a dual nature. There's no reward or special treat when Krampus comes to town. No, his sole purpose and passion in life is to dole out punishment to children who have failed to obey and do their work.

Like Belsnickel, he too carries a switch, but in most stories there is more than one. Apparently, he beats so many children that he needs a few spare branches, so he carries them in a bundle. In addition, he is often depicted wearing chains and dragging some form of large sack or cart. Because ultimately, Krampus isn't as interested in beating children as he is in taking them.

When he arrives in each legend, we are greeted by the appearance of a wild, demonic creature with long horns, cloven feet, and a twisted face. After beating the disobedient children, Krampus chains them up and tosses them into his sack before vanishing as quickly as he came, taking the children with him back to hell.

The origins of Krampus are still unclear, but some scholars think that the legend predates Christianity. Instead, they believe that the story has roots in an ancient Alpine myth of a horned god of the witches. Even the switch, his weapon of choice, might have been a carryover from the initiation rites of witches, where the novices were beaten.

These legends are far from forgotten; festivals are held throughout Europe to this day that feature many of them. Events like Krampusnacht in Germany and the Befana festival in Urbania attract tens of thousands who dress in masks and dance and celebrate. Like Halloween, these are instances where monsters and strangers have been embraced and elevated to something of a children's story.

Which is ironic, when you understand the roots. Stripping away the detail, Krampus has, from a 30,000-foot view, more than a passing resemblance to Pan, the Greek horned god of nature, shepherds, flocks, and mountains. Along with his musical flute, Pan was widely known for robbing the innocence from people, usually through sexual means. In a culture that saw the threshold between childhood and adulthood as the loss of virginity, Pan figuratively stole people's children.

And when you think of it that way, it's more than easy to see similarities, not only between Krampus and Pan but also between Pan and a character that Disney has helped us all fall in love with: Peter Pan. While he might be able to fly, has no horns, and is missing the cloven feet that Pan sports in every image and statue, Peter

Pan fulfills the role perfectly. He arrives at night, carries a flute, and lures our children away to another place.

It's a modern story with a familiar ending, but it was far from the first of its kind. That honor, according to some, falls to a small German village in 1284. You might already know the story, but the truth beneath it is far worse than you'd ever expect.

An Infestation and a Solution

In 1284, the German village of Hamelin was struggling with an infestation of rats. Now, I've only seen a few rats myself over the years, but I also don't live in a densely populated urban area like New York City or London. But in medieval Europe, from what I can gather, rats were as abundant as squirrels, only bigger. And more disease-ridden.

It's hard to imagine the impact that an infestation of rats could have on a town today. If we found a bag of flour in the cupboard that had been half-eaten by rats, there's a grocery store down the street where we can get more, year-round. But in the Middle Ages, food was grown locally and stored up to be used throughout the year. If rats ate and ruined the food supplies, there was little a town could do. Rats meant death in many instances.

According to the story that has been passed down through the centuries since then, a stranger entered Hamlin in the spring of 1284. He was dressed in colorful clothing, possessed what we might today call a silver tongue, and claimed to have a very unusual—and also very *timely*—skill: he was a rat-catcher.

As a profession, rat-catching dates back centuries, but it's rarely been a safe and sanitary job. The risk of being bitten or contracting some disease carried by the rats has always been a hazard of the job. And while the exact nature of rats' involvement in the spread of plague has been up for debate for decades, most scholars agree that they have been key players, particularly during the Black Death of the fourteenth century.

And there were few truly effective tools at their disposal, which made the job that much more difficult. Some rat-catchers used a special breed of terrier, while others made use of traps. But the most effective tool for centuries was the most minimal and inexpensive of them all: bare hands. And seeing as how most rats preferred to stay hidden inside dark places, this was a risky technique.

The motivation, though, was the meritocracy of it all. The more you caught, the more you earned. And while there's no documented proof of this rumor, it has been whispered for centuries that rat-catchers would sometimes raise their own rats in captivity and then turn them in as part of a job, inflating their numbers. This allowed them to pad their paychecks when business was slow, but it also earned them a shady reputation.

As a side note, one of the most famous rat-catchers in London's history was a man named Jack Black, who claimed that his black-and-tan terrier was the father of all the black-and-tan terriers in London, and who pioneered the art of breeding rats and keeping them as pets. He even wore an outfit made entirely of scarlet cloth, with a big, wide sash across his chest that had two cast-iron rats on it. He was probably also a riot at parties, but I can't confirm that. Just a hunch.

The man who walked into Hamelin that June wasn't any less of a character, if the legends are to be believed. He wore an outrageous outfit, although his was reportedly one of multicolored fabric that was known back then as "pied," which was typically a sort of blotchy pattern. And he carried a tool that no other rat-catcher claimed to use: a flute.

And the mayor of Hamelin trusted the man. Maybe it was the not-so-subtle allusion his appearance made to the ancient stories of the god Pan, a deity who tended flocks of animals and played a flute. Maybe it was the man's marketing ability, that silver tongue and outrageous outfit. Perhaps he overpromised, winning the mayor's approval. Whatever the reason, this stranger was said to have struck a deal.

He would catch all the rats in town, he told the mayor. He would lead them out of town and away from their lives. And he would do this with his musical instrument, a pipe that he claimed would lure them away.

Now, I don't know about you, but I would have been skeptical. The mayor, though, was desperate. Sure, they haggled over the price, but in the end the stranger won. The exact amount of money differs from version to version of the story, but in all of them it's an exorbitant sum. And that's the point: Hamelin was so desperate, they were willing to overpay for a solution.

And then he got to work. According to all the stories, and even the children's tales we were raised on, the piper picked up his flute and began to play. As if driven by some magical force, all of the rats in Hamelin scuttled out of their hiding places and began to crowd around him. Streams of them. Thousands of them, all writhing in a mass at his feet.

Then, when it seemed like they had all come out, he marched out of town and down to the Weser River. The stories say that he was beyond successful. Most accounts say that all but one of the rats drowned in the river that day. Hamelin's troubles were over. For a while.

You see, the piper returned later to collect his money. He had done the job they'd hired him to perform. The rats were gone. But for some unknown reason, the mayor refused to pay him. The stories don't say why, but we can speculate. Maybe it was because the stranger didn't return with any bodies to show for his work, as was the custom for rat-catchers. How could the town pay him per head when there were no heads to count?

At any rate, the mayor turned the stranger away, and the man stormed out of the village. But not before turning to face the people of Hamelin and proclaiming a curse on them. He would return one day, he said. And when he did, he would have his revenge.

Remember, this is a story that's been passed down for over eight hundred years. Most of what we know about the real events is pure legend, based loosely on scattered reports of a stained-glass window in the church there in Hamelin. The window itself was lost in 1660, but there are drawings of it that predate the destruction, as far back as the fourteenth century. And the earliest mention of these events is a 1384 entry in the Hamelin town chronicles.

The events were recorded, of course, because the stranger did return. According to the story, though, he changed clothing, trading in his colorful robes for the uniform of a hunter. Gone was the salesman; the stranger was returning for vengeance.

While the adults were all in church on June 26, the stranger strode into town and began to play his flute again. This time, rather than crowds of writhing rats, it was the children who clambered out of the houses. They flooded the streets, gathering around the strange visitor. And then, when they were all present, he marched them out of town, never to be seen again.

There are, of course, a number of morals to this story, but one that has stuck with us for centuries remains ever true: never trust a stranger.

THE DEVIL YOU KNOW

Folklore is full of strangers. In many stories, it's flat-out amazing just how much freedom people have given them in their lives. Even stories of someone as benign as Santa Claus have an element of danger when you view them from outside the cultural fishbowl. Here's the story of a strange man who stalks our children year-round, noting their behavior and secret desires, and who then breaks into our homes, eats our food, and leaves a few presents to prove he was there.

For the people of Hamelin, though, that stranger cost them far more than a plate of cookies. Their ill-treatment of the man who came to town led to the loss of their children. And as difficult as it is to believe, the story of Hamelin is true. Part of it, at least.

Scholars are in agreement that the rats were a later addition to the tale, showing up about three hundred years after the events were said to have taken place. But as far back as the records go, there has always been a stranger, a visitor from the outside, who leaves with the children.

And although it's taken a very long time to figure out why, some historians think they have the answer.

To understand the truth, they say, we first have to understand the political culture that Hamelin found itself in. In 1227, about fifty years prior to the events in Hamelin, a battle took place on the border between what was then the Holy Roman Empire and Denmark, pushing the Danish border north of modern-day Germany. As a result, a whole new territory opened up that needed colonists.

Men called "locators" were assigned to travel the land and find volunteers to populate this new territory. They often wore colorful clothing. They were eloquent speakers. They were, in a sense, a lot like today's door-to-door salespeople.

The empire needed farmers, craftsmen, and soldiers to protect these new lands. But it was hard to find people willing to uproot their lives and travel north, especially when that new land was alongside a contested, military-heavy border. It was a hard sell.

And so when the locators came knocking, rather than shipping off a handful of adult volunteers, the townsfolk would sometimes get creative. Instead of paying with their own lives, they would sell their children to these men.

The proof, it turns out, is in the phone book and on Google Maps. Many town names along a line between Hamelin and Poland bear a striking resemblance to town names from medieval Germany, oftentimes even showing up more than once. More compelling, surnames from the 1284 Hamelin town records still show up in phone books in Pomerania, a region of Poland along the Baltic Sea.

The folklore, you see, tells a colorful story, one that's as easy for children to swallow as a spoonful of honey. But the truth that the story hides turns out to be far less palatable: an entire town, desperate for a solution to their economic and social challenges, actually sold their children off to recruiters hoping to colonize new lands.

It's a plot reminiscent of M. Night Shyamalan's *The Village,* in that these people constructed a fantasy around certain events and then passed that lie on to later generations in order to justify their actions and avoid questions.

In the end, an outsider did indeed come to Hamelin that day, but he wasn't the one who took the children. No, it turns out that the true monsters were already there, living in the house next door, shopping in the market, farming the fields.

The most dangerous stranger, it seems, isn't the outsider; it's the one who hides among us.

First Impressions

DOROTHY FORD STOOD next to William Streat inside his own church while a visiting priest performed their marriage rites. It was November 27, 1667, in South Pool—a village in Devon, England—and the church was packed. Most people hadn't actually expected the wedding to take place, so they'd all come out to witness the miracle.

Their doubts hadn't been because William Streat was the rector of their own parish. They hadn't doubted the couple's love for each other. Nor did their doubts stem from the fact that Streat was sixty-six years old. And they certainly hadn't doubted it because the original wedding date had been postponed.

They doubted it because William Streat had died a year and a half earlier in a riding accident. His funeral had been followed by a series of community dreams. Multiple people in South Pool began to have nightmares, and all of them were eerily similar: in each, Streat himself would appear and tell them that he couldn't find peace. Only his wedding could do that.

After months of this, with dozens of people reporting the same dream-like demands from the dead clergyman, the village relented. The church was decorated for a wedding, Streat's coffin was exhumed, and Dorothy stood beside it while the priest married them. Afterward, Streat was reburied and the visions stopped.

Dreams are a funny thing, aren't they? We don't always remember them when we wake up, but when we do, they often leave us feeling entertained and informed. We see them as signs of things to come, of glimpses into treasured memories. They often seem real enough that we hope for dreams of lost loved ones. In our dreams we might fly, or travel the world, or run as if we're waist-deep in a pool of water.

But they aren't always a source of completion and peace. No, dreams can often leave us feeling uneasy, sometimes even frightened. Sometimes, you see, our dreams can turn into nightmares.

I Was Only Sleeping

Dreams have held deep cultural meaning since the earliest days of humanity, and that meaning has always varied. Depending on when and where in history you pick, dreams have been viewed as either a blessing or a curse. They've revealed unknown truths to rulers, and warned others of impending danger. Or . . . you know . . . so they thought.

In ancient Egypt, if you had vivid dreams, you were considered special. How they proved that, I have no idea, but they were so obsessed with it that they built special sleeping rooms where people could go to help them dream better. Practice makes perfect, I suppose.

The Greco-Roman world was full of dream interpretation. They even had a god devoted entirely to dreams, named Morpheus. The ancient Hindu scriptures known as the Veda divide our existence into three distinct states: the waking, the sleeping, and the dreaming.

But even without the attachment of religion, dreams have commonly been seen as a predictor of things to come. Whether we call them premonitions or dark omens, the things we see in our sleep have long been viewed by some as a preview of what's about to happen, and history is full of stories that claim to be true-life examples.

John Brodie Innes was a clergyman and close friend of Charles

Darwin. In 1919, he recorded a story from his time in Germany decades earlier, about two friends who had fallen into an argument over the love of a young woman.

One friend was an American, and the other was a Hungarian nobleman, and when the American felt slighted, he challenged the Hungarian to a duel. The two men set a date, and the Hungarian was given his pick of weapons. When he picked cavalry sabers, the message was clear: this would be a fight to the death. Now all they had to do was wait.

A week before the duel, John was called to the American's quarters to see something. The man claimed to have had a vivid dream the night before, a dream in which he was wounded in the face before killing the Hungarian. John wrote that the American stood before him with a large red welt on his face, a product—so he claimed—of his dream.

That same morning, John was summoned to the Hungarian's home, where he heard something even more fascinating. The nobleman told John that he'd also had an odd dream that night. In his, he claimed, the American struck him down and killed him. The dream frightened the man so much that he issued what John called a "handsome apology" to the American, and the duel was called off. Both men were happy with that.

This idea—that the things we experience in our dreams can somehow have a physical effect on us after we wake up—is an old one. And it's not just about premonitions and visions of the future. Dreams, it's been said, have the ability to manifest, to take shape and walk among us.

Take the story of a young woman from Scotland in the early 1800s. She was unmarried, but in late 1816 she became pregnant. Seeking to make things right, she reached out to the courts for help. The woman was asked who the father was, and she identified him as one John Woods, a respectable local gentleman.

After hearing the woman's claims, and being called to court over them, Woods adamantly denied them. He said, in fact, that he wouldn't believe he was the father unless his own name was written across the child's face. The young woman was devastated, and rightly so, and the tragedy weighed on her constantly, more and more as the baby inside her grew. And then, in 1817, the woman gave birth to a healthy son.

Healthy, except for some markings on the baby's eyes. It confounded the doctors, and so the mother and child were sent to Edinburgh for a more educated inspection. Professors, faculty, and experts in other fields were all brought in, and each of them left the room completely astonished. There, written on the boy's right eye in tiny letters, was the name "John Woods." On his left, it simply said, "Born 1817."

John Woods, to his credit, had been waiting and watching. When he caught word of what the doctors had discovered, he bolted. No one ever saw him in town again.

One last story: Joseph Merrick was born in England in 1862. In his early childhood, he started to develop growths on his skin. His face was enlarged and covered with lumps that led to him eventually being known as the Elephant Man. For years, he toured England and Europe with human novelty exhibitions. Today we call them freak shows.

During his lifetime, the accepted theory about the cause of his condition was that Merrick's mother had been frightened by an elephant while she was pregnant. Somehow that traumatic event had embedded itself so firmly in her mind that the image manifested itself in her son.

As fantastical as it might sound for a pregnant mother's thoughts to have a real, physical effect on her unborn child, it wasn't an idea limited to popular rumor or the musings of university professors. In fact, in the eighteenth century, something happened that left the medical world—and everyone else—completely baffled.

SEEDS SOWN

They had a term for it, like so many other mysteries in life. Centuries ago, it was referred to as "maternal impression," and it was a way of explaining the unexplainable. According to the theory, strong emotional events in the life of a pregnant woman could have a lasting impact on her unborn child.

It was a backward approach to things that were outside the scope of our understanding, though. They looked at the evidence after birth and made assumptions about what caused it. Joseph Merrick is a perfect example of that logic. Why did his body begin to deform and twist? Well, it must have begun in the womb. And this logic was applied to things like birthmarks, depression, and congenital diseases. If a baby seemed to be born with it, they chased the cause back to the life of the pregnant mother.

Pregnancy is something that Mary and Joshua knew all too well. They were a young, poor couple from Godalming, a village in Surrey, England. They rented a small home on a farm that they both were required to work, although Mary was in the field much more than Joshua, who also worked as a clothier.

Now, that might make his occupation sound fancy, but it wasn't, believe me. Joshua's family, the Tofts, had lived in the area for well over a century, and for a long time had been prominent, successful clothiers. Apprentice records from the mid-1600s always listed Toft family members among the masters in their trade, and of course with all that prominence came wealth. It's easy to imagine that they grew very used to a certain standard of living.

And then manufacturing pushed its way onto the scene. Records started to show signs of that wealth and prominence slipping. When master clothiers were listed as dying inside workhouses, the signs were pretty obvious. And this was the generation that Joshua was born into. Raised on tales of former glory, Joshua and his family now lived as peasants. At the risk of projecting, it probably stung a bit.

The couple married young, and within five years Mary had given birth to three children. Then, at the age of twenty-three, she became pregnant again. Remember, though: if you were poor and working in the fields to pay your rent in 1726, pregnancy wasn't enough to get you pulled off the job. So, like everyone around her, Mary worked. She worked long and hard, and she did it day after day after day, well into her pregnancy.

One day she and another woman were in the field. There's no date for the story, but a safe guess would be sometime in late May 1726. And while they worked, they talked. At some point, though, the other woman pointed over to the edge of the field, and Mary followed the gesture. There, nibbling on some weeds, was a rabbit. Or, as they would have called it three centuries ago, a good home-cooked meal.

The women tried to catch it, but they failed. A few days later they saw it again and, like the first attempt, failed to get their hands on it. And that must have been frustrating. So it's no wonder that Mary had a dream that night. She described it months later, and even then, it was still vivid in her mind. In it, she was sitting down in the field, her skirts piled up in her lap. And there, curled up in the folds of the fabric, was not one rabbit but two. They were finally hers.

It wasn't long after the dream that she started to have complications with her pregnancy. For a while the couple thought that perhaps she'd even miscarried, but by early September she was still pregnant and growing. So she continued to work in the fields, continued to hope, and continued to have weird dreams about rabbits.

On the twenty-seventh of September, Mary went into early labor. She sent word to her mother-in-law, Ann Toft, to help her. Ann, who was an experienced midwife, arrived later that day, and by the evening Mary was in the final moments of the birth. But something was wrong.

Something was so wrong, in fact, that Ann—a woman who had delivered eight children of her own, as well as dozens of others in the village—felt out of her league. So she called for John Howard, the physician in nearby Guilford. Maybe he would know what to do, she thought.

When Dr. Howard arrived, he asked Ann to bring him up to speed on the delivery so far, and then examined the situation for himself. And then, like Ann, he stared in disbelief at what lay on the sheets in front of them. It defied logic, but it was right there for his eyes to see, still wet and still covered with blood.

Mary Toft, you see, had not given birth to a baby at all. Something had come out of her body, but it wasn't what anyone had expected. It was a large handful of pieces of an animal. Each piece was hairless, as if it'd been skinned, but despite that, it was still easy enough to recognize what the creature had been.

It was a rabbit.

Dr. Howard was understandably horrified, but also skeptical. He told the others in the room that night that he wouldn't believe it to be true until he delivered the head. And for a while, that seemed like it wasn't going to happen. The labor stopped, and Mary rested. For days, it seemed as if the events of that night were going to fade into memory and be written off as a medical oddity and nothing more.

But one week later, Mary went into labor again. This time, Dr. Howard was present, and it appears that he got his wish: Mary delivered the rabbit's head. At this point, Howard decided that Mary needed more observation, so he had her moved from her home to his own.

Maybe it was just the action of a concerned physician, but it also could have been an attempt to discover if the unnatural births were really just a hoax. Surely, he thought, Mary wouldn't be able to keep up the act if she was right under his roof. But the mystery continued.

In the days that followed, Mary proceeded to give birth to more and more rabbits. Sometimes they came days apart, and sometimes closer together. And each time, Dr. Howard was right there, a thirty-year veteran of childbirth, to help her through the ordeal. He reported that he would often place his hand on her belly and feel movement, as if whatever was inside of her wanted out.

This went on long enough that Howard even gave Mary some money to make up for the work she was missing out on. I think that's also a good sign that Howard was fascinated. How could he not be, though? He was delivering rabbits. From a human.

By early November, according to the doctor's own count, Mary had given birth to a total of nine rabbits. They were all dead, all hairless, and all young. It was mind-boggling, and defied all logic and reason.

Mary, however, was just getting started.

After delivering nine rabbits personally, Dr. Howard decided it was time to bring in more experts, so he sent word to Nathaniel St. André, physician to the royal household. St. André brought a friend with him named Samuel Molyneux, who worked as secretary to the Prince of Wales.

The men arrived and found that Howard had amassed a collection of the delivered animals, all arranged in glass jars filled with a clear liquid. They set to work examining the samples, studying their color and features. And then the men opened the jars and took the pieces out.

When I was in college we dissected pigs in my biology class. Thanks to that experience, I have images in my head of metal trays containing dead animals, with pins holding back flaps of gray skin. I'm sure it wasn't pretty, but it was a good way for them to see things that Dr. Howard might have missed. These men were trying to be scientific and analytical. After all, if these births were fake, then there must be a clue hidden somewhere in the animals themselves.

According to a later report, the lungs floated in water, which suggested that the animals had breathed air at one time. But while that information was persuasive, both men were present at a number of new births, each producing the same result: more dead rabbits. And the longer they stayed there in Dr. Howard's house, the more difficult it was becoming to not accept what their eyes were seeing.

After the fifteenth rabbit was born, news was sent back to King George, who responded by sending his personal surgeon, Cyriacus Ahlers, to investigate. Ahlers arrived just in time to witness the sixteenth, but right away, he noticed some odd circumstances.

First, prior to the birth, Mary seemed to walk to the bed with her knees held tightly together. It was as if, he suggested, she was afraid something might fall out. Second, Dr. Howard eagerly suggested that Ahlers deliver the first rabbit, but after it was done, he wasn't allowed to examine her further.

The final oddity was something he kept to himself that day.

After helping with the birth of the first piece of dead rabbit, Ahlers was ushered out of the room by Howard, but he managed to smuggle the partial rabbit with him. In a private room, Ahlers set about dissecting it, and discovered something remarkable: its bowels were full of pellets. Pellets that contained corn and hay.

Ahlers made an excuse and left Guilford early, heading back to London to report his findings to the King. Once King George was up to speed, he ordered St. André and Molyneux to return as well. When they arrived, they brought news that Mary Toft had given birth to yet another rabbit—her nineteenth, in fact.

That was it for the king, apparently. He wanted to properly get to the bottom of the matter, so he ordered her to be brought to London for examination there. And at this point, word was spreading about Mary and her miraculous deliveries, so she was discreetly put up in an out-of-the-way, low-cost boardinghouse—without Dr. Howard, mind you—and St. André was assigned to keep a watchful eye on her. And then something amazing happened.

The births . . . stopped.

For Ahlers, who'd already been suspicious up to this point, that was the final straw. He had a judge sent to the boardinghouse to question Mary and get the truth out of her. But the judge was met with silence. Mary didn't want to talk about it, and he left empty-handed. So Ahlers dug around for the truth in other places. And struck gold.

First, Dr. Howard approached him after Mary's arrival and asked for help. Mary had been out of work for a long time now, he told Ahlers. Considering how much of a medical marvel she was, he suggested that perhaps the king might grant her a pension. Howard asked Ahlers to make that request, and Ahlers, being a smart man, saw through it.

Second, Mary's sister Margaret was caught smuggling a rabbit into the boardinghouse. She claimed it was a meal for Mary, but, well, that'd be a pretty tough sell, given the circumstances. Then it came to light that Mary's husband, Joshua, had been pretty busy over the previous weeks, buying all of the rabbits he could find. The younger the better, apparently.

Finally, when word got out that Mary herself had tried to pay the porter of the boardinghouse to go out and buy her a rabbit, the authorities had all the evidence they needed. She was taken into custody in early December 1726 and immediately questioned about the mysterious births. How, they asked her, did you pull off such a hoax?

Mary denied the hoax entirely. She claimed she'd asked the porter to buy her the animal because she was hungry. She insisted she was currently pregnant with more rabbits, and despite all the questions that were thrown at her, she refused to budge from that declaration. That is, until she received an offer she couldn't refuse.

One of the men questioning her, a Sir Richard Manningham, was a prominent physician in London. He was brought in as an expert in the field, having specialized in pregnancy and birth for much of his career. On December 6 he looked at Mary from across the room and told her that if she didn't confess, he would "perform very painful operations and experiments on you to discover your secret."

Mary took just one night to think it over. She confessed to the hoax the next morning.

WHAT DREAMS MAY COME

Historians are a bit torn about what Mary's motivation really was. Some view her as a woman caught up in something bigger than herself. They think that she was the victim of a mother-in-law with a hunger for fame and fortune, and a local doctor with his eye set on moving up the medical ladder.

Others, though, see her as a shrewd and careful individual. She planned every last detail, they say, and orchestrated all of the events—from chasing the rabbit with a neighbor woman to the purchase of rabbits—all without anyone noticing. Maybe no one thought she was capable of it. Certainly no one would have expected a woman to skin and cut up a bunch of young rabbits and then insert them . . . well, I think you get the idea.

It's hard to know for sure whether Mary believed, in some strange, detached way, that her dreams and emotions were truly creating the rabbits inside of her. It is clear, though, that enough of the world around her believed it was possible. For a couple of months, at least, it appeared that all of London was falling for it, hook, line, and sinker.

Either way, Mary's adventure seems to have been a chase for glory. She wanted the fame and all that came with it: the attention, the money, the renown. She'd married into a family that had once been prominent and important, so perhaps she just wanted to do her part in restoring them to that position.

But after her confession, that house of lies came crashing down, and it took a lot of the key players with it. Two years after Mary's trial, Samuel Molyneux became sick and collapsed while on the floor of the House of Commons. His old friend St. André was there to treat him, but he died a few weeks later.

St. André somehow managed to retain his position as the royal physician for a while, although the king took away his salary for the services. Interestingly, on the same night as Molyneux's death, St. André eloped with Molyneux's wife. Or widow. You get the point. And naturally that aroused suspicions. Molyneux's cousin accused St. André of murder.

St. André's career was never the same. His new wife lost her position in the court of the queen, and the couple retired to an estate outside of London. He died at the ripe old age of ninety-six.

On January 7, 1727, after carrying on their hoax for months, and then undergoing weeks of questioning, Mary Toft and Dr. John Howard were brought before the judge's bench. Howard was fined the equivalent of $140,000 in modern currency, and then released. He went home and continued to practice medicine for another three decades.

Mary, though, was charged with "being an abominable cheat and imposter in pretending to be delivered of several monstrous births." She was sent to Tothill Fields Prison for . . . well, they weren't really sure. Being deceitful? Tricking a lot of people? Cruelty to animals? Mary's story was complicated, after all.

She was released in April, just a few months after arriving. To be honest, the court wasn't sure what charge she could be held on. They didn't have an official sentence for pretending to give birth to rabbits. Plus, crowds were gathering outside the prison each day to catch a glimpse of her. It was annoying. Better to just let her go home, they figured. I can't blame them.

Mary went back to her home and her family, and back to work in the fields. Within weeks she was pregnant again. In February 1728 she went into labor and gave birth.

It was a baby girl.

Seeing Double

THOMAS HARVEY WANTED to give his mother's home a bit of a cleaning. She'd lived in the house for forty years, but little had changed in the decades leading up to 1960. If you'd asked around the neighborhood there in the Welsh town of Rhyl, every single person would have said that Sarah Harvey deserved that gift. She was kind and quiet, if unremarkable. And she'd been living alone ever since her husband passed away in 1938. Well, that's not entirely true.

For a handful of years, beginning in 1940, Sarah Harvey played host to a lodger. Mrs. Knight was an older woman who had recently separated from her husband. She wasn't well, and so Sarah had looked after her while she stayed there. But when World War II ended, Mrs. Knight moved out of town.

Fifteen years is a long time for someone to live alone. Which is why her son Thomas wanted to freshen up the house before she returned home from a stay in the hospital. On May 5, 1960, he was standing on the landing of his mother's stairs, looking at a large storage cupboard. Maybe he thought it contained cleaning supplies, or perhaps boxes of old decorations. I have no clue, really. Whatever the reason was, though, he reached up and opened it wide.

And found a body. The petrified, mummified body of a woman. Insects had eaten away most of the face and hair, and there was a thick layer of dust on the skin, but that didn't stop the police from identifying it. It was Mrs. Knight. Harvey had apparently strangled the woman in 1940, and then continued to collect her pension illegally.

We think we know our neighbors, but do we really? No one would have suspected Mrs. Harvey of murder, after all, if it wasn't for her curious son. Whether they're a respected public figure or a quiet elderly widow, it's impossible to know the whole story.

It seems that some people quite literally have skeletons in their closet.

OLD TOWN, MEET NEW TOWN

Edinburgh is a complex city that deserves a bit more attention before we move forward. Today we know it as the beautiful, ancient capital of Scotland, but that wasn't always the case. People have lived in the area for over ten thousand years, but it wasn't until the end of the seventh century that they started to gather into anything resembling a community. A Celtic fortress was built there in 638, and that's where the city as we know it today began.

Sure, it had the usual outlying village, but it wasn't until the Scottish king David I established an official royal settlement there in the twelfth century that things really started to take off. Within two centuries, writers across Europe began to refer to the city as the capital of Scotland. But that expansion came with some growing pains.

Up until the end of the sixteenth century, every bit of the city was still wrapped up in the tender embrace of the defensive walls that surrounded the community. So rather than growing outward, buildings were starting to climb higher. Some of them even reached a height of eleven stories. Not too bad for the pre-skyscraper era.

But all those people living in such a confined space was creating a problem. For a long time, Edinburgh was known as one of the filthiest and most overpopulated urban centers in all of Europe. Those high-rise tenement buildings were packed with people, and beneath them were countless vaults, like an ancient hybrid between a dungeon and a basement. And as the city attracted more and more immigrants, they tended to find themselves down there, in the shadows.

Thankfully, that was about to change. In the 1760s the city reinvented itself. It's a long story, involving a competition to find the best architect, so I won't dig into the finer points. But the end result was going to be a brand-new part of the city (referred to as "New Town") situated north of the older portion (logically known as "Old Town").

The planning committee had a clean slate, so a grid of streets was laid out north of Nor Loch. As construction went on over the coming years, the loch—which had originally just been a dumping site for sewage—was filled in with earth, and today it's known as the Mound. All those gorgeous buildings—the National Gallery, the General Assembly Hall, the Museum—all of it, you see, was built on the human waste of Old Town.

And New Town was gorgeous, there's no doubt about it. It was modern and beautiful, and perfectly matched to the enlightened minds that were flocking to the city. Before long, Edinburgh was known as the "Athens of the North." And all that knowledge and advancement, along with the available space for new construction, attracted a wave of elite and wealthy landowners.

This new setting created a demand for luxury products. Those fancy Georgian townhouses practically begged for beautiful new custom furniture, right? And those wide, clean streets? Well, they were the perfect place to drive your brand-new carriage. A whole new set of industries, from ironwork to cabinetry, began to blossom.

New Town, whether it was intentional or not, quickly became Rich Town. And because it was situated at a higher elevation than the rest of the city, a very real, physical separation was formed between the wealthy and the poor. If you lived on the southern side of New Town, you could, quite literally, step outside and look down on the poor.

But no city can engineer away all of its social problems. As the eighteenth century gave way to the nineteenth, Old Town continued to suffer in the shadow of New Town. Between 1750 and 1850, the population of the city tripled from 60,000 to nearly 180,000. Most of those newcomers settled in the poor areas of the city, and with them came rampant crime, deep poverty, and increasing waves of illnesses like cholera.

In a very real sense, Edinburgh had become a city with a split personality. To the south, there was darkness and danger and filth. The north, in contrast, represented hope and a bright future. But few people ever saw both sides of the city. If you were born in the slums of Old Town, you were more than likely going to live there, work there, and die there.

The wealthy to the north put themselves into a similar situation. They were isolated from the lower class. They'd left their problems behind, in a way. New Town was a place of wealth and progress and knowledge. The elite who lived there were, at least in their own eyes, better because of that.

But Edinburgh wasn't unique in its dual nature. Sometimes people are capable of double lives as well.

A LIFE OF CRIME

William's first real crime could be viewed as an act of mercy, if you squint really hard and ignore all the illegal bits, I suppose. He had a friend, you see, and that friend had a problem that needed to be solved. So the man asked William for help.

The friend, a Mr. Hay, who worked as a stabler in Grassmarket down in Old Town, was mourning the loss of his son. The boy was barely a teenager, but he had been charged with a crime, and it looked as if all the evidence pointed to his guilt. As a result, the boy was set to hang in just a few days. So on the eve of the execution, both men approached the Old Tolbooth—a building that was sort of a mixture of a jail and a courthouse—and made their way to the jailkeeper.

They'd brought along a large quantity of alcohol, and while Mr. Hay made sure the jailer drank as much of it as he could, as quickly as he could, William slipped over to the cell holding Hay's son and picked the lock. Then he smuggled the boy out and into the darkness. But he needed a hiding place where the boy could stay until he could be safely removed from the city, and that's where William proved how bright he was.

He took the boy to the cemetery known as Greyfriars Kirkyard, and then made his way to the tomb of Sir George Mackenzie, known throughout town as "Bloody Mackenzie." William broke into the crypt and hid the boy in there. And the plan worked.

In August 1786, William stepped up his life of crime. He managed to use a counterfeit key to break into a locked desk drawer in the offices of Johnston and Smith, bankers in the Royal Exchange. He stole a pile of sterling banknotes valued at about $125,000 in modern U.S. currency. Business, it seems, was good for William.

But you need to spend money to make money, right? So a short time later, he hired a handful of associates to become a sort of heist team. He needed more hands, more faces, and more players if he was going to be able to take on bigger jobs with higher pay-offs. And that's how Andrew Ainslie, George Smith, and John Brown ended up working for William.

On Christmas Eve of that year, they assembled for their first job as a team, breaking into a jeweler's shop called Bruce Brothers. They walked away with about $50,000 worth of precious stones, watches, and rings. Satisfied that the team had worked well together, William and his crew began a string of thefts that spanned nearly ten months.

In late October 1787 they somehow managed to gain access to the room at the University of Edinburgh where the old ceremonial mace was kept. This object was a symbol of the university's authority, as well as being a priceless antique. And the men made off with it as easily as if it'd been left out on the back steps.

The rumors were rampant. The city was plagued by a thief, or thieves, who could not be caught. Shopkeepers were terrified of being the next victim, and some people even whispered about the supernatural nature of the thief. Whoever it was, they said, he seemed to be able to walk through walls.

But of course they weren't going to catch him, because they were looking in the wrong place. They assumed, as anyone would have in late-eighteenth-century Edinburgh, that the thief was a poor, desperate tenant of the slums of Old Town. But he wasn't. Instead, he was a member of the Town Council—the same people who were charged with investigating the theft of the mace and finding a replacement.

William, you see, was the deacon of the Incorporation of Wrights and Masons—sort of the president of the organization, if you will. He was, in fact, one of the most prominent cabinetmakers in the city, a trade he'd inherited from his father, Francis.

He'd inherited a lot, actually: four houses, the cabinetry business, and a bank account worth about $1.6 million in today's American currency. He fit right in up the hill in New Town. He was upstanding, respected, admired, and emulated. William Brodie was a rising star.

And it was all that prominence, as well as his position on the Town Council, that had actually aided his life of crime. Whenever the council needed someone to handle the city's carpentry jobs, they called on him. Things like repairing security mechanisms and installing locks. He frequently installed the front doors on local shops, and all of this work gave him access to their keys.

By night, though, he had this alter ego that felt ripped from the pages of modern comic books. He would step into a hidden area of his home and literally suit up for criminal activity. He had a disguise, a vast collection of tools, and even strapped on two pistols . . . for those tricky situations, I'm sure.

But you can only keep a secret for so long, you know? At some point, the world was going to find out.

A REAL-LIFE DRAMA

Brodie wasn't always criminally inclined. Most historians actually think that the source of his shift was a bit of pop culture. You see, as a teen, Brodie was obsessed with a play called *The Beggar's*

Opera, which was a huge hit at the time. Written in 1728 by John Gay, the show set a record for the most consecutive performances of any play in Scotland or England up to that point. Even after the streak ended, it was still performed consistently for decades.

The story centers around the world of thieves and the upper-class women who love them. One of the main characters is the dashing, charismatic leader of an entire gang of criminals, and yet he somehow managed to find time for not just one but two mistresses. The glamour of that lifestyle, according to many historians, must have appealed to young William, because as he grew into adulthood, he took on more and more of that persona.

William loved to gamble as well. He belonged to an exclusive men's club known as The Cape, and he spent a good part of his time at a tavern called the Dice-Box. But all of that gambling had also led to a good amount of debt. And even with all of this on his plate—a full-time job, his city appointments, the gambling addiction, all of it—he still managed to father five children by two separate mistresses. And all without either of the women knowing that the other existed.

Sometimes, it seems, life truly does imitate art.

As you might guess, paying for this lifestyle wasn't easy. And that's where the nighttime career as a thief came in. But as good a thief as he was, Brodie never seems to have stopped. Maybe his gambling debt was just too large to ever go away, or perhaps he just fell in love with the thrill that came with each successful heist. It's hard to say for sure, but what we do know is that even after a theft as high-profile as the university mace, he stayed active.

In early 1788, he began planning the biggest heist of his career. It would be an armed burglary of His Majesty's Excise Office, the building where all of the tax revenue of Scotland was kept locked up. So he assembled his team, and they set their plan in motion. This time, though, they had no key, and Brodie insisted that the whole team be armed with pistols.

The events of that night are a bit fuzzy, but we do know that they managed to gain access to the building. At some point, though, it seems that Brodie stayed outside the door to act as look-

WICKED MORTALS

213

Seeing Double

out while the others made their way to the loot. While he was there, an excise official randomly returned to the building, and when Brodie saw the man, he bolted into the night.

Abandoned and exposed, the rest of the gang did their best to escape. The men walked away with about £4 in their pockets—nothing like the fortune that Brodie had promised them—and as a result, they were more than a bit disgruntled.

Later that same night, one of the men, John Brown, decided it would be more profitable to turn Brodie in. There was a price on the man's head, and so he reported the whole crew to the authorities in exchange for £150 and a king's pardon. Ainslie and Smith were arrested immediately, but William Brodie was nowhere to be found.

That's because he'd fled the country, making his way to Amsterdam. While he was away, the story broke, and Brodie's careful public image shattered instantly. The city was shocked. He'd been one of the bright ones, the elite, a hero . . . but he had turned out to be nothing more than a fraud.

Brodie was taken into custody and then brought back to Edinburgh, where a trial was set for August of that year. It went on for over two days with very few breaks, and in the end, Ainslie managed to escape charges. Smith and Brodie, though, were found guilty of theft. The penalty? Death by hanging.

A crowd of over forty thousand curious onlookers gathered to watch their executions on October 1, 1788. They'd come to see a hanging. They'd come to see one of the New Town elite get strung up like an Old Town pickpocket. They'd come for justice.

Despite all this, Brodie was in good cheer that day. He wore a splendid black suit and powdered wig, as if he were dressing up for a celebration, and climbed up the ladder with a spring in his step. He requested that his hands be left untied, and then helped the hangman adjust the noose to get it just right before pulling the hood over his own head. His last act was to pull a handkerchief free from his pocket and drop it into the crowd.

There's a legend that, as a carpenter for the city, Brodie actually built the gallows, but there's little evidence that the rumor is true.

If anything, he helped draw up the plans for them, but that's about it. Another legend claims that he somehow inserted a metal pipe into his throat to prevent his neck from breaking, and that afterward a French doctor revived him and spirited him away to safety. None of it, sadly, is true.

One thing that is true, though, is that Brodie's execution took place at the Old Tolbooth. The very building, if you remember, where he'd committed his first crime years earlier by freeing a prisoner who'd been sentenced to death.

Irony is a wonderful thing sometimes, isn't it?

HYDE AND SEEK

The idea of double lives certainly has its appeal. If historians are correct, that attraction is what got William Brodie into trouble in the first place. For him it was a necessary evil that provided a solution to his personal problems. For others, maybe it's the desire to live out secret fantasies, or to express themselves in ways that their public life won't allow.

Most people have a secret. Some people yell at their kids behind closed doors, or drink a bit too much. Some, apparently, live secret lives as criminal masterminds and take their final bow from atop the gallows.

The old cliché says that the real you is the person you are in private. For Brodie, that couldn't have been more true. He was a womanizer, a cheat, and a criminal. But you wouldn't have known it by looking at him. It certainly begs the honest question: deep down, beneath all the polish and public make-believe, who are any of us, really?

It's a question that another Edinburgh native tried to answer nearly a century later. He was a writer, and in his youth he'd written a play about William Brodie that he called *The Double Life.* Sadly, it was a commercial flop.

He took that failure personally, too, because he felt like he had a real connection to Brodie. Growing up, his parents owned furniture hand-crafted by the man, so as far as this writer was concerned, it was as if he'd been raised in the same household as the legendary thief.

There was something about the tale that always stuck with him, even as he pushed further into his writing career. In 1885, he was sick in bed, struggling to recover from a lung infection, when his sleep became fevered and broken. Then, one night, he awoke from a dream with the plot perfectly formed in his mind. Surely, he told his wife, this would satisfy his publisher's demand for a cheap new thriller, what he liked to refer to as a "shilling shocker."

Today, that novel is one of the finest psychological thrillers in all of British literature. It's been adapted more times than *Frankenstein* or *Dracula* and has inspired countless storytellers over the years. And if it wasn't for the influence—and duplicity—of William Brodie, we wouldn't have the book at all.

So let's all be glad for what Robert Louis Stevenson ended up writing: a little novel that he called *The Strange Case of Dr. Jekyll and Mr. Hyde.*

Labor Pains

THEY WERE STARING at a paradox. It was a stone tool, chipped away to form a sharp edge, with all the characteristic marks of something handmade. It was, in fact, a perfect example of an early stone hand tool. And yet . . . well, there was a problem.

You see, the scientists who uncovered this tool in Kenya back in early 2015 believe that it was created 3.3 million years ago. Which is about half a million years further back on the evolutionary scale than the earliest humans known to date. We don't know who they were, but we know this: like us, they used tools.

Clearly, technology has always been intoxicating to us, however far back we go in time. Tools for hunting and food prep later gave way to instruments of war and writing. Complex machines powered by gears, or steam, or electricity. It's our heritage, and it's evidence of a deep passion for *making* things.

It's actually a great way to view human behavior, when you think about it. If a tool was created, it usually points to a major interest or passion from that era. Inventions are, in a sense, a cultural fingerprint.

Study the history of firearms, and you'll see the transformation of ballistics and chemistry into military hardware. But it's also a revealing glimpse into the violence of human nature. The history of navigational science is also the history of our passion for exploration. Who we are drives what we make.

Some inventions have gone further, though. They've tapped into a deep longing that most people have felt, but few were willing to admit. That there was a world beyond our own. The otherworld. The afterlife. Heaven. Whatever we called it, it was a world populated by divine beings.

And there were people who wanted to control it.

Speaking Up

People have always wanted to talk with spirits, and for just as long, we've crafted tools to help us do it. Nearly one thousand years ago in China, mediums used a device called a talking board. They're part of the ancient tradition known as automatic writing, the modern Ouija board being a newer interpretation of that old idea. But all of them share a common purpose: they were tools for speaking with the dead.

As we moved into the middle of the nineteenth century, new devices rose to prominence. Like the planchette, that heart-shaped piece of wood that mediums would set their fingers on so the spirits could guide them. Those were originally made with a hole in the tip for a pencil, allowing the spirits to write messages from beyond the veil. And mediums loved it.

Mediums, if you remember, are individuals who claim to stand between the living and the dead in order to pass communication between them. And while they've been around for thousands of years in one shape or another, it wasn't until the mid-1800s that mediums really began to gain attention.

In 1849, three sisters from Rochester, New York, became overnight superstars. The Fox sisters toured America and performed séances in front of packed audiences. In the process, they kicked off a wave of Spiritualism that transformed the way people thought about how this world was connected to the next.

Another New Yorker, Andrew Jackson Davis, was making his own contributions to the movement. He was a self-taught expert in mesmerism who traveled all over and lectured about topics from his many books. Books, according to his own account, that he wrote by falling into a trance and dictating them to a secretary. It was a claim that earned him a nickname: the "Seer of Pough-keepsie."

In 1853, a Universalist minister named John Murray Spear published a book of his own, a series of messages from his hero and namesake, John Murray. It was a collection of messages that wasn't so revolutionary in their content as it was in their premise. You see, Murray had been dead for nearly forty years.

We don't know a lot about John Murray Spear's early life, but we do know he was born in 1804 in Boston. His father died when he and his brother Charles were still young, forcing him to leave school and find work in a local cotton factory.

He managed to make the most of it, though. A kind factory clerk took the time to teach him to read and write, which, looking back, most likely saved his life. Without those skills, he might never have left that factory. Reading was a tool that allowed him to move on, to grow, to become his own man.

And by 1830, he'd made it. He was married, the father of five children, and fully ordained for ministry in the Universalist Church. But John also had a passion for social justice, which he spoke about frequently. Issues like labor reform, women's rights, and the abolition of slavery.

In 1844, he traveled to Portland, Maine, to participate in an anti-slavery rally. While he was speaking, an angry pro-slavery mob dragged him off the stage and beat him senseless, leaving him horribly injured. His wife, along with a friend named Oliver Dennett, cared for John over the following months, slowly nursing him back to health.

But the attack only served to deepen his commitment to the cause. After recovering, he began to organize public events of his own. Anti-slavery conventions, speeches, local rallies. He even became a leader in the Boston portion of the Underground Railroad.

But when his friend Oliver Dennett died unexpectedly, John's focus began to shift. Maybe he was already on the edge emotionally. Or perhaps it was the country's growing obsession with the spiritual world. Whatever the reason, John left the church in

March 1852 and the following year published the book of letters from his long-dead hero, entitled *Messages from the Superior State*. And in it, he made some pretty strong assertions.

He claimed that God was asking him to communicate with the spirit world. John saw this as his new calling, and he threw himself into it with the same passion as he had with social issues. And it was at some point in his practice of mediumship that he learned he could fall into a trance and become a mouthpiece for forces beyond the veil.

While he was in that state, John was said to dictate medical advice for sick friends. And although he wasn't a physician, his recommendations actually worked. John was helping people get better. And while he was proud of that, he refused to take all the credit.

Everything he was doing, he said, was made possible by his spirit guide, none other than his old friend Oliver Dennett. But Dennett wasn't the only spirit sending important messages to John. According to him, there were others, all lined up and waiting on the other side of the veil, eager to share their messages as well. And John said they had a mission for him.

Just what the spirits were asking him to do, though, would turn out to be one of the most ambitious undertakings of the nineteenth century.

THE PLANNING COMMITTEE

The various spirits that John claimed to be hearing from resembled a who's who of important dead personalities. Benjamin Franklin and Thomas Jefferson are just two examples, but there were so many others. John's guides included prominent minds from the fields of philosophy, medicine, science, agriculture, politics, and education.

He called them the Association of Beneficence and said that they were a collection of spirits, all grouped into specialized categories, whose goal was to help advance humanity. Through their connection with him, he claimed to be gifted with insight into a number of unusual topics.

For example, John claimed that one of the spirits told him that women shouldn't curl the hair on the backs of their heads because it interfered with memory. And while that one is pretty laughable, other claims were a lot harder to disprove. Like the accurate and comprehensive twelve-part lecture on geology that he gave at Hamilton College in New York—a topic that John had absolutely no training in.

More spectacular were the devices that these spirits requested him to build. I can't find evidence that he actually followed through on any of these projects, but he was given plans for electric airships, for devices he called "thinking machines," even for an entire circular city. It was Jules Verne on a whole new level.

But John said that these benefactors had one particular task in mind for him. They wanted him to help give birth to what they called the New Messiah, the second coming of Christ. But this Messiah wouldn't be a flesh-and-blood person. No, it would be a machine, a mechanical being built by John's own hands. But to do it, he would need help.

So he began gathering a group of followers. There weren't many of them, but some of the prominent members included a pair of editors of popular spiritualist publications, Simon Hewitt (who had helped John publish his book the previous year) and Alonzo Newton. Both men brought clout to the project, and their own small cadre of supporters.

John said that the spirits told him to build the New Messiah in the town of Lynn, just north of Boston. There was a hill there called High Rock that was said to hold deep spiritual power. And conveniently enough, the hill already had a building on it, owned by a music group called the Hutchinson Family Singers. Think of them as a mid-nineteenth-century version of the Osmond Family, traveling the country as a variety show that combined song, comedy, and dramatic performances. But with a hint of politics, including anti-slavery songs. Which is most likely how John Murray Spear first met and befriended them.

The Hutchinsons handed over the keys to their building there on the top of the hill, and John moved in to set up shop. In October 1853, John lay down on a bed and fell into a trace, giving control of his body to the scientific group of spirits he referred to as the "Band of Electricizers."

He spoke while others took dictation. The plans were drawn out, and all of the important steps were written down. Their goal was to build what John kept calling the "New Motive Power" or, even more mysteriously, the "Infant Motor"—a device that would become home to the spirit of the New Messiah. But don't picture a little robot, ready to get up and walk around; this thing was completely unique.

There are no pictures of the device. Nothing exists today that can allow us a better glimpse of the vision that John was given. No notes or drawings or schematics. And the construction was said to have been completed in a manner reminiscent of modern remote surgery. John would literally just place his hands on the parts and tools and let his spirit guides do the work.

Over time, the machine was given limbs, a respiratory system, and a central motor—all of which were fastened to the top of a small table. Each part was hand-crafted from either copper or zinc, neither of which was cheap. Estimates put the cost at around $2,000, nearly $60,000 in modern American currency.

So here's where things get really bizarre. You see, while this mechanical Messiah was being built, two other things were taking place. First, only the most carefully selected individuals were allowed into the machine's presence. John said it was to introduce the Infant Motor to what he called "positive vibration levels."

Second, and more important, a woman was chosen to be the new Mary. Through her, somehow, the spirit of the New Messiah would be born and passed over to the device.

Yeah. I know. But stay with me.

On June 28, 1854—nine months after the construction began, for anyone looking for more birth symbolism—Mary went into labor. In response, Spear was said to have climbed inside some sort of copper armor, complete with gemstones and batteries, and then slipped into a trance.

Witnesses reported seeing a glowing, transparent umbilical cord appear between the machine and Mary. Or maybe it was John—the events aren't really clear. But after two hours of labor, Mary was said to have reached out her hand and touched the Infant Motor.

What happened next? An article in the spiritualist magazine called the *Boston New Era* tells us everything we need to know:

> *It is with no ordinary feelings of satisfaction that we now announce to our readers for the first time the result of some peculiar labors under spirit direction. . . . Now, after about nine months of almost incessant labor, often times under the greatest difficulties, we are prepared to announce to the world . . . the thing moves.*

HUMPTY DUMPTY

John Murray Spear was the proud father of a mechanical Messiah. Or, at least, that was the idea. He'd allowed himself to be used by the spirit world in order to help create a new life, a life that was meant to usher humanity into a better age. An age of enlightenment and power and salvation.

In an earlier article in his *Boston New Era* publication, Hewitt said that this new "God Machine" was built as "an exact correspondence of the human body, at least, in so far as involuntary motion is concerned." It was designed to be a living being, with a divine soul and earthly parents. And everyone wanted to see it.

Spear's collection of spiritualist followers there on High Rock were soon given access to the device, to see for themselves this new, world-changing power. And as word spread, more and more people flocked to Lynn to see it with their own eyes. But the vast majority of them walked away severely disappointed.

The trouble was, no one was seeing the movement that had so boldly been proclaimed. I mean, a living creature moves around, right? This thing . . . well, contemporary accounts say it basically just had balls. Dozens of metal balls, hanging from its chassis like Christmas tree ornaments. And if you watched it long enough, and stared at just the right places—sometimes, *maybe*—you might see one of them move.

Perhaps.

It was all enough to attract a constant stream of criticism. Spear's experiment was a hoax, they said. A fraud. Or, at the very least, an experiment in misguided thinking. Remember Andrew Jackson Davis, the "Seer of Poughkeepsie"? He didn't go as far as to declare it a hoax, but he was pretty sure that the spirits had played a practical joke on their earthly representative.

Not everyone was as accepting of the notion of spirit guides, though. Well-known nineteenth-century medium Daniel Home later called Spear's machine "the strangest shadow which ever darkened spiritualism." Home, by the way, built his reputation on the claim that he could levitate into the air during his séances. To get a man like that to call something bogus is, admittedly, quite the achievement.

In fact, just a few decades after Spears made his first claims, another medium by the name of E. W. Wallis wrote a popular book called *A Guide to Mediumship and Psychic Unfoldment* and took a moment within it to trash the whole idea. A spirit guide, he suggested, was an easy cop-out. If a medium turned out to be wrong, oh, look, it was the *spirit guide*'s fault. Wallis found that to be all too convenient in a field that already had a steep uphill climb toward credibility. And maybe the events that unfolded in John Murray Spear's life simply highlighted that flaw.

As the days and weeks went on, John encouraged Mary to spend more and more time with their mechanical child. Maybe it needed maternal attention. Maybe it needed her around to grow and develop. But instead, the God Machine seemed to grow weaker and weaker.

There was also a storm brewing. Enough of the public had heard about the machine and found the purpose behind it so offensive and heretical that it was actually inspiring anger and resentment. People were upset at John and his followers, and they were becoming restless. Given enough time, that anger was bound to spill over into violence of some kind.

Conveniently, John heard from his spirit guides once again, his Band of Electricizers, and they told him that the device needed to be moved to a better location to thrive. They directed him to move everything to Randolph, New York, where a tall hill was located that spiritualists had long believed was electrically conductive.

The move happened in late 1854. It's not clear how many followers joined him, but Spear and a few of the others managed to transport their God Machine to its new home in Randolph, in a small structure on top of the hill.

Then, later that fall, tragedy struck. In Spear's own words, "under the cover of night, [a] mob entered, tore out the heart of the mechanism, trampled it beneath their feet, and scattered it to the four winds." No one discovered who had done the deed, but the rumor was that a local Baptist congregation was to blame.

John later wrote that a good number of his friends had sacrificed everything for the project—their time, their energy, their wealth—and he knew they were mourning the loss with him. Regardless of whether the world viewed it as a success or a failure, their great experiment had finally come to an end.

According to everyone who knew him, the loss utterly destroyed John Murray Spear. Like the death of his friend Oliver Dennett, which had sparked this crazy adventure in the first place, the death of the Infant Motor flipped the switch the other direction. John seems to have walked away from divinely appointed mechanical projects and his Band of Electricizers.

Life after that was much less unusual but still had its rocky points. He left his wife in 1863 for another woman, and they married a short while later. The couple spent six years touring England, trying to promote John's spiritualism to a new audience, but his message fell on deaf ears.

In the end, they gave up and returned to America, settling in Philadelphia. In 1872, the spirits reportedly told John to retire. He died five years later at the age of eighty-three.

The old cliché says that we are what we eat, but I think it's more accurate to say that we are what we build. Our creations reflect out true nature. The history of invention, if viewed the right way, can also be an insightful journey into the human psyche.

We're prone to exploration, to risk, and to uncovering the answers beneath the mysteries of this world, and so we, for millennia, have been explorers. Our craving for stability and safety transformed us from nomadic tribes to city dwellers, literally building nests around our lives. And proof of our fear of death is just around the corner in your local graveyard.

What we make says a lot about who we are.

Maybe that means John Murray Spear was a lunatic. I wouldn't fault anyone for jumping to that conclusion. But it could also mean that he, and the dozens of people who followed and supported his experiment, were really just deeply interested in knowing more. To get a glimpse behind the curtain.

In that sense, their intentions were good. They meant well, even if most of the general public found the journey to be more than a bit insane. Still, there are some who wonder . . . what if it actually *did* work?

John was already intimately familiar with mob mentality. Getting dragged off that stage and beaten senseless in Portland almost a decade earlier had taught him just how violent people can be when they disagree with something strongly enough. It was only a matter of time before the crowds brought their hate to his workshop door. Only this time, their violence would destroy something else.

So John knew it was coming. There's no way he couldn't have. But if that's true, then why move the device and broadcast the location of its new home? It was like taking out an advertisement specifically targeting the people he most wanted to avoid. What history says took place should never have happened at all.

Unless it didn't. What if the device didn't go to New York? Some believe that the proof is in the press—or in the absence of it. There was no newspaper coverage of their arrival in Randolph, no reports of visitors and this bold new attraction in town. At the height of the Spiritualist movement, Spear claims he brought the centerpiece of that movement to a new location. But no one there wrote about it.

Even more telling, there are no local reports of the destruction of the device. That dark night in early 1855, when the Baptist mob was said to have crept up to the top of the hill and destroyed the New Messiah . . . not a single newspaper mentioned it. The only reason we know it happened is because Spear himself told us, over a year after it was said to have happened.

So what options are we left with? I'm not sure. But those who believe the move and destruction were a hoax also believe something else about the device. They think it actually worked. It was small and weak, for sure—even Spear himself called it nothing more than an embryo—but it was the beginning of something bigger to come.

The God Machine, they say, was hidden away. To protect it from the angry mobs. To give it time to learn and mature and grow in power. It was a newborn, after all. The Infant Motor. But given enough time, it will come back, throw the modern world to the ground, and usher in a new era of humanity.

I suppose if that's true, we'll all eventually find out, won't we?

Sideshow

THE TWO MEN who walked into Joseph Johnson's place of business in early 1912, Aver and Wayne, claimed to be brothers, and they were interested in buying a popular prop that Johnson had standing in the corner. Now, most of it was true. They *did* in fact want to buy the thing, and they *were* brothers, but their names were actually James and Charles Patterson.

The Patterson brothers owned and operated a traveling entertainment business, the Great Patterson Carnival Show. And the prop, they said, would be the perfect addition to their exhibition of creepy things. It was a lifelike figure of a dead man, and they were banking on the notion that people would pay to see it. People, they assumed, loved creepy things. And they were right.

When the Patterson brothers sold their operations a few years later, the prop went with it, and the new owner quickly included it in an exhibit he created called the Museum of Crime. It was full of statues, some of which were wax figures of prominent criminals. Men like Bill Doolin and Jesse James. Patterson's prop fit right in.

In 1933, a Hollywood director used the prop in the promotional efforts of his new film, *Narcotic*. It was literally moved from theater to theater and placed in the lobbies as a dead drug addict. And it looked the part, all wasted and leathery. The director, Dwain Esper, even claimed that it was a real body and he had killed the drug addict himself. It was all a lie, of course, but the public loved it.

When the owner of the prop died in 1949, it went into storage in Los Angeles. But it was still in demand for films, and in 1964 it was rented out for a film called *She Freak.* Then it was sold in a batch of wax figures to the owner of the Hollywood Wax Museum. The prop wasn't made of wax, but that didn't stop the new owner from using it in an exhibit anyway. It looked too real *not* to, after all.

And then it just sort of disappeared.

In December 1976, a production crew was preparing to film a scene for the hit TV show *The Six Million Dollar Man,* an episode that happened to be set in an amusement park in Long Beach, California. They were filming in the spooky funhouse exhibit, which featured an ax murderer, multiple ghosts, frightening sounds, and the corpse of a man hanging from a noose. It was exactly the setting they were looking for.

While preparing the set for the scene, the crew began to rearrange some of the objects in the exhibit. All part of the production process, of course. Everything needed to be in the right place. And that included the hanging corpse. But when one of the crew grabbed the figure's arm, it broke off. It felt like papier-mâché, and the shock of it caused everyone to chuckle. But that's when they noticed something odd.

The inside of the figure's arm was more than lifelike. Human bone and muscle tissue could be seen where it had separated from the torso. I can imagine there was a very long, pregnant pause in the laughter where the man holding the arm was doing the math and processing what he could see.

In the end, a coroner was brought in and quickly confirmed that the figure wasn't a prop at all, but the mummified corpse of a man. A man, it turned out, who was actually an Oklahoma outlaw named Elmer McCurdy, who was killed in late 1911. How McCurdy's body made the sixty-five-year journey from the Midwest to California, though, is less macabre than the reason it all started in the first place.

McCurdy, you see, had died in a shootout with police in

Pawhuska, Oklahoma, before being moved to the local funeral home, owned by none other than Mr. Joseph Johnson. After embalming the man's corpse, Johnson had settled in to wait for a relative to come claim the body and pay for his services.

But the wait dragged on and on, and at some point it became clear to him that no one was coming. Either Elmer McCurdy had no family or they simply weren't brave enough to associate themselves with him, even in death.

So Johnson got creative. He dressed McCurdy's body and propped him up on a stand in the lobby. And then he did what every business owner could only dream of: he put a dead client to work paying off his outstanding debt. Elmer McCurdy, it turns out, was the ultimate deadbeat.

In a Pickle

WHEN ANDREW HARRADEN set sail on April 14, 1724, he had fish on his mind. He was just twenty-two years old, and his vessel, the *Squirrel,* was brand-new. Naturally, Harraden was eager to put it through its paces. He and his crew set sail that day out of Annisquam Harbor in Gloucester, where his family had lived since the mid-1600s. And from the beginning, Annisquam had been a fishing village.

The *Squirrel* headed north, up toward Canada, and after a while they spotted another ship headed in their direction. This was long before the telephone and satellite navigation, though, so Harraden and his men knew nothing about the crew piloting the oncoming ship. It wasn't until they were within shouting distance that the newcomers raised a black flag up high. The kind of black flag that made sailors all across the Atlantic shudder.

Pirates.

What happened next was a whirlwind. Lines were cast and the ships were drawn together. The older one was in rough shape, but her crew proudly called her the *Revenge.* And once Harraden and his men were gathered together and held on the deck, the captain of the *Revenge* stepped over.

His name, it turned out, was John Phillips, and Phillips had a pedigree. In the world of pirates, pedigree meant a lot. Who had trained you? Who had trained them? How powerful and fearsome were they? And Phillips brought a lot of that to the table.

He had once been a carpenter, but after being captured by a pirate named Thomas Anstis, he converted to a life of crime. Anstis, by the way, trained under Bartholomew Roberts, who was known to sailors all across the Atlantic as Black Bart. He was also, incidentally, the inspiration behind the character of the Dread Pirate Roberts from *The Princess Bride*.

Phillips fell in love with the *Squirrel* and decided that he would take her for his own. He put all of Harraden's crew on the *Revenge* and left them to fend for themselves, but he kept Harraden on hand. Maybe he wanted someone who knew the ship. Maybe he saw potential in the younger captain to someday inherit his own crown. Whatever the reason, Phillips set sail with Harraden as his prisoner.

But Andrew Harraden had no desire to stay on John Phillips's stolen ship. He wanted to go home. He had a girl back home, and he planned to marry her. And there was fishing to be done. So Andrew Harraden began to plot his escape, and he knew right away that in order to succeed he would need help.

Thankfully, a good portion of the pirate crew was in much the same position as he was. In fact, when push came to shove, there were fewer than ten men who were actually loyal to John Phillips. The rest of the men, though, were ripe for dissension, and so Harraden set about making plans.

One of his main recruits was the ship's carpenter, a hulking man named Edward Cheeseman, and together they distributed some of the carpenter's tools around the top deck, making them available for the right moment.

On April 17—just three days after the *Squirrel* had left Gloucester—that moment arrived. When Cheeseman found himself alone on the deck with Phillips's largest and most intimidating follower—a man named John Nutt—Cheeseman seized the opportunity, literally, and picked the brute up and tossed him overboard.

Nearby, another friend of Harraden's took action. This man, John Fillmore, threw a hand ax at the boatswain, reportedly splitting his head in two. Another loyalist was thrown overboard just as Phillips himself was entering the deck to see what the commotion was all about.

Harraden was waiting, though, and he smashed the pirate captain's head with a hand ax. And just like that, the *Squirrel* was his again. All the remaining men who had been loyal to Phillips—men who had willingly committed crimes as pirates—were gathered and placed below. And then Harraden set sail for Boston.

The prisoners were tried in Boston, and four of them were convicted and sentenced to death. Each man made an elaborate speech about his actions and repentance, and for two of them it resulted in a reprieve for one year. For the other two, though, it was too little, too late. They were hung in June 1724 at Charlestown Ferry, and then their bodies were suspended from gibbets—almost like one-armed crosses—where they served as a warning to others.

Andrew Harraden did in fact marry his sweetheart. He and Mary Davis were wed later that autumn, on September 17, in their hometown of Gloucester, Massachusetts. He never served with pirates again.

Edward Cheeseman was awarded £42 for his bravery and contribution to the capture of the pirates. After that, he disappeared from the pages of history.

And John Fillmore, the ax-throwing sailor, went on to settle down and have a family. In fact, his great-grandson would be named Millard, and Millard Fillmore would grow up to become the thirteenth president of the United States.

But whatever happened to John Phillips? Sure, the notorious pirate was killed in the mutiny that took place that day in April 1724, but this was the era of bounties and literal prices on the heads of criminals. So it's no surprise that around the same time the other pirates were being sentenced to death in Boston, the magistrates there took delivery of a package from Andrew Harraden.

It was a small barrel. And inside, floating in brine, was the pickled head of the pirate himself.

MAGIC TRICKS

From Within

I N 1987, IN a small village in northwestern India, a young widow stood beside the funeral pyre that held the body of her husband. She was just eighteen, and he twenty-four. As the flames climbed higher and cremated his body, she stepped forward and threw herself onto him. Right there, in front of thousands who had gathered for the funeral, she burned alive.

And the people responded . . . by building her a shrine. What she did, as horrible as it sounds to our modern sensibilities, was a tragic yet common act in her culture. It's an ancient Hindu funeral ritual known as *sati,* and by practicing it, this young widow became one more participant in a very old tradition.

Sati as a practice dates back at least two thousand years. It wasn't an obscure practice, either; in the last fifteen years prior to its ban in 1829, it's estimated that over eight thousand women committed suicide through *sati.* And although it's illegal today, it still occasionally happens in remote villages that have yet to leave the old ways behind.

Maybe that's because it's a ritual that taps into a deep, ancient attraction we all seem to have toward fire. For a very long time, fire was a thing of power, a thing of *mystery.* Our ancestors' torches were used to frighten off predators, and were then brought indoors to keep them warm on cold winter nights. While humans might not have always understood it, we quickly learned that it was a tool we could use.

Ever since, fire has been something we've played with and harnessed. As in the practice of *sati,* humans have worked fire into countless religious and civic practices over the centuries. Maybe that's why we tend to think that we're the boss, that *we*—and not the flames—are in control. It's just a tool, after all; we're the masters.

But that's a dangerous assumption, because fire has one other inescapable, undeniable quality: whether we want it to or not, fire burns.

ETERNAL FLAME

Throughout the long, elaborate, complex history of humankind, there is a small handful of recurring themes. They're universal, crossing the borders of culture and chronology, and they never seem to go out of style. Power, death, love, money: these are ever-present ideals that play out time and again, like main characters in an epic novel. And with them through it all, from the beginning of civilization up to the present, was fire.

The ancient myths built stories to explain why we even had something as dangerous and helpful as fire. The Greek story of Prometheus tells of how he defied Zeus and stole fire from Mount Olympus, bringing it to humanity as a source of power and civilization. And that idea—the notion of a deity or supernatural hero who steals fire from the realm of the gods—is present in dozens of cultures around the world.

Across the Atlantic and centuries later, the Cherokee would speak of Grandmother Spider and how she entered the land of light and brought fire back in a clay pot. Hebrew mythology tells of a fallen angel named Azazel who brings knowledge of how to use fire and grants it to humanity. One of the Hindu sacred texts, known as the Rig Veda, carries the same theme, with fire locked away from humanity until a brave hero retrieves it.

In all of the stories, fire is a possession of the divine, and when humanity gets hold of it, they grow and advance and change for the better. It's not difficult to see, then, how the idea of fire evolved over time to become a sort of symbol of the divine. Fire blesses us, in a sense. It makes life better.

As a result, we've worked fire into every aspect of our lives. It's the cornerstone of technology, enabling us to evolve from cave paintings to cellphones. Think about it: the earliest examples of writing were on clay tablets. If those clay tablets couldn't be fired, they would have fallen apart and vanished long ago. Fire, in a literal sense, made it possible to pass knowledge down to the next generation.

Early on, we also discovered another place in our lives for fire: our funerals. Evidence for cremation dates back at least twenty thousand years, and although it was never the sole method of burial, it was vastly more common that it is today. The speed bump was Christianity. When belief in the resurrection of the body spread across Europe and the New World, a distaste for cremation came with it. In some places and times, it was even outlawed, carrying the death penalty.

Cremation is a mixture of science and symbolism. In one sense, our bodies are just reduced to their basic elements, returning them to the earth as part of a greater chemical cycle. In another, the afterlife—in the form of fire—consumes us. Either way you view it, at the core of the act is that ever-present force: fire.

Cremation is a powerful process, too. Even at temperatures in excess of 1,500 degrees Fahrenheit, it still takes the average human body almost three hours to burn completely. When it's over, though, all that remains is just a few pounds of bone fragments, which are then crushed and moved to an urn.

True to much of human history, though, cremation is something we've managed to twist and bend to our own nature. As far back as four thousand years ago, the Babylonians used death by burning as a punishment for certain crimes. That practice was echoed in ancient Egypt, and carried on later in the Roman empire.

By the thirteenth century, many European kingdoms had begun to make burning a legally required method of execution for certain crimes. Wielded by Christian emperors, that punishment quickly became focused on people accused of heresy, for straying from the accepted religious norms of the time. That's why, by the early 1500s, witchcraft and burning at the stake had become as synonymous as chocolate and peanut butter. Just, you know, a lot less enjoyable.

If there's anything to learn here, it's that humans have a long history of burning one another. We burn our dead, and sometimes we even burn the living. The key to both scenarios, though, is that we're in control and we know the reasons why, whether they're honorable or horrific. In every case, fire has been a tool in our hands.

There have been rare and unexpected moments in history, though, when that hasn't been the case. When someone has been consumed by fire, and despite all attempts to explain why, we're left with nothing but mystery.

And it's happened enough that we've even given it a name: spontaneous human combustion.

WE DIDN'T START THE FIRE

We didn't always have a name for it. The term "spontaneous human combustion" first appeared in print in 1746, but there were stories told long before that fit the description. One of the first, as far as I can tell, was written down in 1641 by Danish physician Thomas Bartholin.

According to him, there was an Italian knight in the fifteenth century named Polonus Vorstius. The story goes that the knight was at home in Milan in 1470, eating and drinking with friends and family. And he apparently had a great love of strong wine, which he drank a lot of that night. Bartholin describes how the knight, fully intoxicated and stinking of alcohol, belched fire. It probably surprised him as much as his parents, who were right there with him at the table. And then, without a source of ignition, he burst into flames and died before their eyes.

More than a century later, a professor of philosophy named

John Christopher Sturmius recorded a similar tale. In one of his books, he tells a brief story of three men who apparently liked to party. After encouraging each other to get absolutely blitzed on wine, two of the men died. Their cause of death was that they had been "scorched and suffocated by a flame forcing itself from the stomach."

This idea that alcohol was to blame, and specifically the excessive ingestion of it, was one of the most common explanations tossed around in the early days of these tales. On one level, it was pretty logical: alcohol is a flammable substance, so if someone was found mysteriously burned alive and they were a known alcoholic . . . well, the story sort of wrote itself.

On the other hand, though, there was little science to support these claims. Most of the stories about these events speak of the wrath of God, and how the sin of these alcoholics brought judgment by fire. It was a convenient theory, but it didn't hold water. Especially when you take the story of Contessa Cornelia di Bandi into consideration.

Di Bandi was an Italian countess in the city of Cesena back in the early part of the eighteenth century. In an account from 1731, her story was recorded in detail. According to the tale, at the age of sixty-two, the countess ended her evening one night with a long conversation with her maid, and then retired to bed.

The following morning, when the maid entered the countess's bedroom, she discovered nothing more than two legs and a pile of ash. The legs, by the way, were still wearing stockings. And unlike other stories of spontaneous human combustion, this woman wasn't a heavy drinker. In fact, she was known to abstain from alcohol entirely.

Most tales of events like this remain in the realm of speculation and whispered rumor, and rightly so. Every now and then, though, our superstitions sneak into more formal locations. Like the courtroom. That's what happened in 1725.

Jean and Nicole Millet were innkeepers in France, and they had quite the reputation. Nicole, so the story goes, was almost always drunk. And she was verbally abusive, and difficult to work with, and maybe that's why Jean was rumored to be sleeping with one of the young servants there at their inn. They were an imperfect couple with a lot of issues to work through, apparently.

In late February 1725, a surgeon named Claude-Nicholas Le Cat was passing through the area and booked a room at the inn. According to his account, the following morning, a small pile of human remains was found in the inn's kitchen, about two feet from the hearth. It was Nicole, and all that remained of her were her unburned feet, her skull, and a few pieces of her spine.

Almost immediately, her husband, Jean, was arrested and charged with the murder by fire of his wife. But he protested the charges. He told the court that his wife had gone to bed with him at 8:00 p.m. the previous night, but a short while later had told him she couldn't sleep, left the bed, and exited the room. He assumed she had gone off to drink somewhere by herself, and so he went back to sleep.

Considering all the rumors about their unhappy marriage, the judge was slow to believe the innkeeper. It was too convenient, honestly, and they were ready to convict. And that's when the traveling surgeon, Le Cat, stepped in. He spoke to the judge. He told him that there were many documented examples of unexplainable burnings like this, and that there were scientific, logical causes behind them. As a medical expert, he supported the idea.

Whatever the true cause of Nicole's death might have been, Le Cat told the court that her death seemed more like punishment from God for her heavy drinking and bitter attitude. And with no physical evidence to support the charge of murder, they should let her husband off the hook.

It worked. Jean Millet was released, a free man thanks to a surgeon who was well-read and open-minded. Or thanks to a judge who was gullible; I'll let you decide. That's a luxury we have when we're talking about stories that are three centuries old, after all. That distance, that age . . . it gives us a bit of freedom in our interpretation.

When the story is just a few decades old—from the age of photography, forensic science, and modern medicine—it gets trickier. Not because it's harder to believe, though. Quite the opposite.

Sometimes the evidence is so overwhelming, so documented, and yet so bizarre that it takes on a life—and death—of its own.

CRAZY MARY

Mary had two visitors on July 1, 1951. Her son, Dr. Richard Reeser, had been to her apartment that evening, and they'd been joined by Mary's landlady, Mrs. Pansy Carpenter. Mary was sixty-seven years old, and she lived alone there in her apartment in St. Petersburg, Florida, so it was probably a friendly social call.

Mary's guests left at about nine o'clock that evening. She stayed in her recliner in the living room and they let themselves out. And that was that. Except for waking up at five in the morning to the smell of something burning, Mrs. Carpenter had a lovely night of sleep.

There was a knock on the landlady's door at eight that morning, and she opened it to find a telegraph boy standing there. This was the 1950s, well before personal computers and cellphones, so this was basically the midcentury equivalent of a text message. Except this message was for Mary Reeser. The landlady signed for it and then walked up to Mary's apartment to deliver it personally.

She knocked a few times and waited, but no one answered, so she figured that Mary was either asleep or already out. She figured she would just set it on her kitchen table and remind her later, so she grabbed the doorknob—and then pulled away.

The metal knob was hot to the touch. Not only did it hurt, but it set off an alarm in her head. What if there was a fire? So she dashed back downstairs, where two house painters were at work in another of the apartment units, and asked for their help. They followed her up and quickly forced the door open.

A wave of heat rolled out through the door, and the apartment inside showed signs of fire. Well, sort of. Really, it was just a corner of the living room, centered around the recliner that Mary loved to sit in. But the chair wasn't there anymore. All of the wood and fabric had burned away, leaving just a few springs in a blackened pile on the floor.

And Mary had been in the chair when it burned. We know this because when the police and firemen arrived, they found her unburned foot lying nearby. Other than the burn marks around the ankle, the foot and the fabric of the slipper it was inside of were both unharmed.

They found a few other pieces of Mary in the pile of ash. Her liver was there, charred and fused to some vertebrae. And her skull was still intact, or at least nearly intact. You see, it had somehow been shrunken. Some anecdotal reports say it was the size of a teacup, but the official medical examiner's report just says that it was much smaller than it should have been.

An FBI forensic team was called in. They took over and started to really examine the apartment. As a result, things became even more confusing and mysterious—if that's even possible. They determined that Mary had been smoking, and that she'd been sedated with a sleeping pill—something her son confirmed was part of her evening routine. But they also determined that, in order for her body to incinerate so completely, a fire of at least 3,000 degrees would have had to burn for over three hours. And that's a lot of heat.

So you'd expect the apartment to show signs of a fire like that. There were some, but it was mostly heat-related, and all of the visible damage was located about four feet off the ground and higher. Above that invisible line, candles had melted into puddles of wax, a mirror had cracked from the heat, the plastic light switches had melted, and a greasy soot covered the walls.

The grease, they said, was from Mary's body. She'd weighed about 170 pounds at the time of her death, and the idea was that perhaps a cigarette ignited her clothing or bathrobe. Then her body would have burned like a candle wick, using her fat as a fuel source. Some scientists think it's possible, but it would still produce an intense amount of heat. And that presented some problems for the investigators.

Because, yes, there was heat damage higher up the walls, and that greasy residue. But right beside the spot where the recliner had once stood there was a pile of newspapers that remained untouched by flames. The investigators were baffled. How could a human being burn so thoroughly that only a handful of bones remained and not ignite everything else in the apartment?

Toward the end of the investigation, the police brought in a physical anthropologist named Dr. Wilton Krogman. Due to his research, he had a wealth of experience with the physical elements of events like Mary Reeser's death. Later, he would write that he could not "conceive of such complete cremation without more burning of the apartment."

As for the skull, that too left Krogman utterly baffled. In a newspaper interview shortly after the investigation, he told a reporter: "I have participated in the investigation of some 30 fire deaths in the past 20 years. Never have I seen a human skull shrink by intense heat. In fact, the opposite has always been true."

Years later Dr. Krogman said that the case still haunted him. It was the inexplicable nature of it all. The mystery. The clues and physical evidence that just didn't seem to line up. He later wrote: "The apartment and everything in it should have been consumed. . . . I regard it as the most amazing thing I have ever seen. As I review it, the short hairs on my neck bristle with vague fear. Were I living in the Middle Ages, I'd mutter something about black magic."

BURNT ENDS

There's a dance that we do with topics like spontaneous human combustion. We want to unravel the truth, to untie the knot and make sense of it all. That's very human of us, very logical and rational. I fully support that kind of behavior.

On the other hand, though, we cling to mysteries like a beloved childhood toy. Don't kill the mood, don't shatter the dream. Just let me revel for a little bit longer inside this warm, cozy blanket of unexplainable conundrum. If that's you, I'm right there with you, trust me.

We love knowing and we hate knowing. And these stories—of

knights and countesses and widows and drunks who all have burst into flames and been reduced to a handful of ash—well, they do something to us, don't they? That's why authors like Herman Melville, Mark Twain, and Charles Dickens all used spontaneous human combustion to kill off characters in their novels.

Maybe science will one day point to the true source of these events. Maybe someone in a lab somewhere will be able to reproduce the circumstances and results and brush every last bit of mystery off the box we use to store these tales. Or maybe not. Because sometimes we just never find the answers.

These stories are full of the unexplainable, though, and that pushes us toward wonder. Whether we tell ourselves that some natural external source caused the fire or that it came from within, we're still left with too many questions. Why these people? Why was there so little damage outside the location of the body? Why weren't the houses or apartments burnt down around them?

And like all of the unexplainable tales that tickle at the back of our minds, we know we'll never get all the answers. Thankfully, though, the world sometimes tosses new stories our way. To remind us that these things still happen, and that, love it or hate it, we still don't know the answers.

In 2011 in Ireland, the fire department entered the home of an elderly man named Michael Flaherty. They were responding to a smoke alarm there, and when they entered, they found a small pile of human ash on the floor. Other than some heat damage close to the ash and above it on the ceiling, there were no other signs of a fire. The coroner listed the cause of death as spontaneous human combustion.

Back in 1966, another elderly man, Dr. John Bentley from Pennsylvania, suffered a similar fate in his bathroom. His cremated remains were found beside the toilet in his home. His walker had toppled into the fire, but the rubber grips were completely untouched.

In 1986, Kendall Mott was worried about his retired father, George, who hadn't called him that day. So he went over to check on him. He arrived to find the doorknob hot to the touch and the windows coated in a dark soot. Worried, he let himself in.

George had died in bed while watching television, but there wasn't much of him left to examine. The pile of ash was contained to the mattress and nowhere else. Forensic investigators determined that a fire of nearly 3,000 degrees had incinerated the man over the span of hours. Which explains the ash, of course.

But it doesn't explain the box of matches on the bedside table that were unburnt and perfectly intact. Or the fact that George Mott wasn't a smoker. Yes, the TV melted, but the rest of the house was untouched by the fire that had to have taken place.

As I said a moment ago, the only thing left of George Mott was a small pile of ash. And a leg. And a skull. A skull that hadn't exploded or fallen apart, mind you.

It had shrunk.

Teacher's Pet

Maria Arana was a Franciscan abbess who lived and worked in Spain during the first half of the seventeenth century. Later in life she would become a prolific author, and everywhere she went she wore the blue garments of her order. But in 1620, when she was just eighteen, she started reporting odd experiences.

María claimed that she was having incredibly real visions. Visions, she said, of being in a foreign land far away from Spain. In these dreams, she encountered a tribe of people known as the Jumano. But Mary considered these to be more than just *dreams*. She said that angels were literally transporting her spirit to another place.

For over three years, María spoke with the Jumano people, telling them of her work in the Church, and teaching them as best she could. And then, in 1623, her visions stopped.

Six years later, a group of Native Americans from the western region of modern Texas approached the local Spanish authorities there and asked for a missionary to be sent to their village. Before agreeing to do so, the local priest asked why. The men said that they had been visited by a beautiful young woman dressed in blue, and that she had taught them many things.

Those Native Americans, it turns out, were members of a tribe known as the Jumano. And their arrival in 1629, along with their mysterious connection to a young abbess thousands of miles away, sparked questions that are still impossible to answer, even now.

In a world as enormous and enticing as our own, it's easy to see how people would dream of being somewhere else. We long for tropical vacations, or a chance to visit our ancestral home. Right now you might be in an office, or classroom, or sitting in traffic, and at the same time, your mind might be on a beach somewhere else entirely. But that's nothing more than a daydream.

No one can be in two places at once. Or can they?

SNOWFLAKES

There are nearly 8.5 million people living in New York City at this moment. Los Angeles is home to another 4 million—half of whom are probably sitting in their cars on the 101 right now—and there are another 3 million souls in Chicago. Cities can be crowded places, no doubt about it.

And it's not an American problem, either. London is home to nearly 9 million human lives. Tokyo has over 13 million, and Shanghai clocks in at over 24 million. Everywhere we go, there's a crowd, and as our cities fill up faster and faster, it's no wonder some people feel a little lost. When there are 5 or 10 or 20 million other humans buzzing through our streets, how can anyone feel truly *unique*?

How many other people on the subway with you are wearing the same color? Or the same jacket, or sunglasses, or headphones? How many other redheads work in your office? How many other guys in your dorm have a beard? The more of us we cram into a small space, the more our uniqueness becomes typical and common.

Which is why we always step back and smile when we see someone who looks a lot like someone else, isn't it? They're an example of extreme odds, I know. The genetic roll of the dice that results in your cousin looking just like Brad Pitt, or Adrian Brody having more than a passing resemblance to the seventeenth-century philosopher John Locke. Trust me, just look it up. It's crazy.

But there's a huge difference between the genetic probability that someone somewhere else in the world might look like us and the belief that a Spanish nun could somehow transport herself around the globe through her dreams. *That* fantastical feat is what some writers call bilocation, which literally means "two locations at once."

There are stories involving bilocation sprinkled throughout history. Centuries ago, claiming to be present in two places at once was seen as an act of witchcraft. In fact, María Arana herself was investigated by the Inquisition, sort of a fanatical police force inside the Catholic Church that chased down heresy.

In the end, though, they didn't pursue her case. Some historians think that was because her bilocation resulted in true, fruitful missionary work, while others believe it was because she happened to be a good friend of the king of Spain. Either way, her stories were believed. For others, the results weren't so positive.

One of the common pieces of evidence brought up during the Salem witch trials was, in fact, bilocation. Many of the witnesses who claimed witchcraft had been used against them also claimed they saw the witches themselves, in spectral form, inside their homes. And while the events of the Salem trials are now looked at as a horrific case of mass hysteria and social prejudice, those who lived through it firmly believed these things were possible, and therefore *punishable*.

In more modern times, bilocation has been viewed less as an act of witchcraft and more as a mystical ability, however *fringe* it might seem. Examples are found in Christianity, Judaism, Hinduism, and the occult. Famous occultist Aleister Crowley was known to appear in person in front of many of his friends, while actually being far away in another location.

In some cultures, these mystical duplicates are referred to as changelings, and their source is more sinister. While we've already seen that folklore in action in Ireland, similar stories of changelings appear in the folklore of Wales, Sweden, Poland, and many other places. And in all of them, the common thread is very dark, and very terrifying, to parents.

Fairies from the dangerous world outside the home will, upon occasion, sneak inside and steal children. Sometimes they replace the stolen child with an enchanted wooden dummy called a *stock*. Other times, they leave their own fairy child in its place. And because humans aren't skilled in caring for fairy babies, or, you know, magical blocks of wood, these replacements would always fail to thrive.

These tales were often used to warn mothers of the importance of watching their children closely. But when people felt that a loved one had undergone an inexplicable, dramatic shift in personality, this folklore became the logical explanation: "No, your husband hasn't become an angry, abusive monster overnight; he's just been replaced by a changeling."

Today, psychologists think those stories have roots in a disorder known as Capgras delusion, where a person believes someone close to them has been replaced with a look-alike imposter. Rather than being the work of elves, though, it's a neurological disorder caused by lesions on the brain.

Yet one more example of how science can take the magic out of folklore and replace it with something even more depressing and horrible.

But there are other stories that are much harder to explain. Stories where more than one copy of a person has been witnessed, oftentimes by people of strong reputation or those who can prove their claims. And while those stories have taken place in many different countries, most of them feature a term that we can trace back to one language in particular: German.

And that word? *Doppelgänger.*

DOUBLE FEATURE

The term *doppelgänger* is one of those misused words, slapped on a whole slew of stories in a way that dilutes the true meaning. Do a Google search for "celebrity doppelgängers" and you'll find a lot of examples of that genetic game of chance I mentioned earlier. But strangers who look eerily like other strangers aren't doppelgängers, in the true sense of the word.

"Doppelgänger" is from the German and means "double-walker," which admittedly isn't very specific. But in historical context, it's a term that's full of magical connotation. Another term used interchangeably with doppelgänger is the Irish *fetch*. The core idea for both words, though, is this sense of seeing the ghost of someone who's still alive. An apparition, or spectral copy.

But the key characteristic of doppelgängers isn't what they are; it's what they *mean*. Because seeing a doppelgänger or a fetch—the literal act of seeing one with your own eyes—can have powerful consequences. In fact, one common interpretation is that doppelgängers represent our true desires brought to life.

Secondhand stories tell of individuals seeing the very things they wish would happen, or their spectral doubles participating in activities they long for. One story tells of a farmer who worked so long each day that he was never able to come home and see his family. On multiple occasions his neighbors saw him walk up to the house in the afternoon and enter through the front door, all while the farmer claimed he had still been working in the fields.

Sir Frederic Rasch was a British military figure from the mid-1800s, and he served as a member of Parliament for over twenty years. In March 1905, though, he was sick at home with influenza and wasn't able to travel to London to participate in a debate. He'd spent months preparing for this key political moment and was, understandably, full of regret and frustration.

During the debate in London, though, another member of Parliament—Gilbert Parker—turned in his seat and noticed Rasch sitting toward the back of the room, near the door. Parker later said that Rasch looked "pallid, steely, and grim," but after turning away for a moment and then looking back, Parker saw that Rasch was gone.

Parker later spoke with others in the room, including Sir Arthur Hayter and future prime minister Henry Campbell-Bannerman, and both men confirmed what Parker had witnessed. Rasch, they all confirmed, had been in the room. Except he hadn't. He was still at home, sick in bed, and had never left. He *wanted* to be there, of course, and *that,* according to some, was enough to send a copy of himself.

Some people, however, interpret doppelgängers as a sign or portent that something dark is about to happen. They're a visual premonition, if you will . . . a prediction acted out in spectral form right before our eyes. According to one story, English poet John Donne was privy to just such a vision.

Donne and his wife, Anne, had twelve children over the span of their sixteen-year marriage. In 1612, while his wife was due to give birth to their eighth child, he traveled with a friend to Paris on business. And it was while he was there that he experienced a most unusual vision.

One afternoon his friend, Sir Robert Drury, entered their apartment to find Donne in a state of shock. He was pale, almost vacant, and this worried the man. When Drury pressed him for an explanation, Donne told an amazing story.

He'd been in his room earlier that day when his wife appeared before him. But it hadn't been a happy vision. Anne, he said, had been weeping. And in her arms she held a dead child. Later, upon returning home to England, Donne learned that his wife had given birth to a stillborn baby on the very morning he had witnessed her doppelgänger.

In other situations, seeing a doppelgänger of yourself is viewed as an omen of your *own* impending death. That's what happened to another writer in early 1822, according to his own account. Friends reported seeing him numerous times, only to discover that he was actually elsewhere, verifiable by other witnesses.

One friend, Jane Williams, lived near the writer on a dead-end street. One day she looked through her window to see him pass by, headed in the direction of the dead end, but though she waited for a few minutes, he never walked back. She checked the street and couldn't find a sign of him.

More significantly, though, he claimed to have seen himself on multiple occasions, which he reported later to his wife. Once, he claimed, he was walking alone on a terrace when a man approached from the shadows. When the figure's face came into view, the writer was shocked to see that it was his own. And it spoke.

"How long do you mean to be content?" it asked him.

On July 8, 1822, he was sailing across the Gulf of Spezia in Italy when a severe storm caused his boat to sink. All three men aboard were drowned, and their bodies washed to shore later that day. It seems that seeing your own doppelgänger can, in some case, truly end in death.

The writer's name, by the way, was Percy Bysshe Shelley. He was a famous poet, a respected novelist, and a close friend of Lord Byron. But most remember him today as the husband of Mary Shelley, author of the classic horror novel *Frankenstein*.

SUBSTITUTE TEACHER

From the early twelfth century until a hundred years or so ago, the region of northern Europe on the coast of the Baltic Sea was known as Livonia. It's an ancient name that held on for a very long time, but today that area has become the three separate countries of Estonia, Lithuania, and Latvia. The Latvian town of Valmiera is an important industrial center today, but two centuries ago it was home to a prestigious finishing school for girls.

This school, known as Pensionnat Neuwelcke, was run by the Moravians, and was highly sought after. If you were the daughter of a noble Livonia family, the odds were good that you would be sent there for your education. And in 1845, under the care of Principal Buch, there were forty-two young women in residence at the school.

One of those young girls was Julie, the daughter of the Baron of Guldenstubbé, who was thirteen years old at the time. Years later, Julie sat down with the American writer Robert Dale Owens and told him her story, which he reprinted in one of his books. It's a story that is, to say the least, peculiar.

In 1845, the school welcomed a new teacher. She was in her early thirties and described as slim, with pale blue eyes and chestnut hair. She'd traveled all the way from her home in Dijon, in eastern France, although she appears to have had family there in Valmiera. Her name, according to Julie, was Mademoiselle Emélie Sagée.

A few weeks after she arrived, the students began to whisper about odd happenings. One of the girls walked into a room and asked if anyone knew where Mademoiselle Sagée was. One friend replied that she had just seen the teacher in a particular location moments before. Another girl said *she* had just spotted her in a *different* room. It struck the girls as odd.

Weeks later, Mademoiselle Sagée was teaching a class of a dozen or so students and was using the blackboard to illustrate her lesson. While her back was to the class, the girls looked up to see a *second* Mademoiselle Sagée, standing behind the first. They looked alike, they were dressed alike, they even moved with the same gestures. And then, after a few moments, the duplicate vanished.

The entire class of girls witnessed it, though, and that made it impossible for them to forget. Which made for a tense moment a few days later when Mademoiselle Sagée offered to help one of the students, Antonie, clasp a difficult hook on the back of her dress. While standing in front of the mirror, Antonie looked into the glass to see not one but *two* Mademoiselle Sagées behind her. The girl, frightened by what she saw, fainted instantly.

Months went by, and more and more encounters were reported by the girls. Sometimes two of her would appear at the dinner table, side by side. But only one of the figures would be holding silverware, while the other would not. And then, just before the holiday season, the strangest event of all took place.

All forty-two of the students at the school had gathered in one room and were seated together at a long table. They were there to practice their embroidery, and were being supervised by one of the teachers. One wall of the room, though, was a series of tall glass windows that looked out onto the school's garden, and through them, all of the girls could see Mademoiselle Sagée outside, slowly gathering flowers into a basket.

At some point in the lesson, their teacher stood and excused herself. The girls had run out of blue silk, and she knew where to find more, so she went to retrieve it. A moment later, some of the girls gasped: Mademoiselle Sagée had silently appeared in the vacant chair. She didn't speak or move, but all forty-two of the girls saw her.

The trouble was, when they turned back to the windows, they could still see her in the garden, gathering flowers. Two of the students were brave enough to approach the seated figure, and even tried to touch her. They later compared the sensation to pressing your fingertips into loose fabric. There was resistance, but very little of it.

When the school let out for the holidays that year, all of the girls went home and told their parents about the unusual events. And true to form, most of the parents were furious. How dare the school subject their daughters to such a bad influence? When school resumed weeks later, Principal Buch was shocked when only twelve of the original forty-two students returned.

Worried for the financial security and the reputation of the school, the principal had no choice but to fire Emélie Sagée. Julie Guldenstubbé was one of the few who had returned, and she claimed to have heard the teacher exclaim something to the effect of, "Not again!" When Julie asked her about this, Sagée replied that this wasn't the first time this had happened. Or even the second.

According to her, it had happened to her eighteen times before.

Julie also noted that Emélie Sagée had remained in town for a few months after being fired. Apparently her sister-in-law lived there, and Sagée had moved in and tried to find work in town. Julie knew this because she'd actually gone to visit her there.

When Julie arrived at the house, she claims she was greeted by several young children. According to her, when she asked them where she might find Emélie Sagée, the children shook their heads. They didn't know, but they told her that it was never difficult to find her.

With expressions of wonder, they said that they often saw "*two* Aunt Emélies."

DOUBLE VISION

Maybe we look for similarities because it helps us fight loneliness in a crowded world. Maybe we need those moments when we see someone else who looks a lot like someone we know, or a celebrity, or that college roommate we haven't seen in years.

When we're all so very different, those similarities are like footholds, giving us a place to stand, to feel safe, to find comfort. There's a little bit of a rush when you see someone else wearing the same concert T-shirt you've got on, or reading the same book as you in the café. That's one of the paradoxes of being human: we strive for individuality, and yet we long for inclusion.

So it's no wonder that for centuries people have claimed to see their body double, or a duplicate of a friend or family member. On some level, it's just more of that same grasping for familiarity, isn't it?

But how can over forty students all have the same delusions? How can events repeat themselves, month after month, and all be explained away as just figments of the imagination? Where do we draw the line between those who can't be taken at their word and those who *must*?

One last story. In November 1860, a man found himself at the end of a very long, very exhausting day. Thankful to finally be home, he wandered into his bedroom and sat down on a lounge. Think of it as a sort of couch with no back, and maybe a headrest on one end. But after a long day on his feet, even a wooden bench would have felt amazing, I'm sure.

He closed his eyes and felt exhaustion rush over him, and then slowly lowered himself to lie down. Just a moment, he thought. That's all I need. Just a little bit of rest. And then he opened his eyes again.

Straight ahead, just a few feet away, was a dresser with a mirror on top, the sort that can be pivoted to point up or down, as your needs required. And the mirror appeared to have been tilted down enough that he could see himself stretched out there on the couch. But when he saw his face, he caught his breath: there were two faces, not one.

He sat up in horror and looked at the mirror again, but the duplicate was gone. He shook his head, probably mumbled something about being too tired to see straight, and lowered himself back down. And there, in the mirror, he saw it again. Two copies of his own face looking back at him.

He later told a friend that the faces were slightly different from each other. One of them, he said, seemed normal and what he would expect from any mirror. The other, though, seemed much paler, sicklier. Almost dead, in fact.

He shook it off for a while, but later that evening he told his wife about it, and she didn't like what she heard. Now, maybe it was her Irish and English heritage, or perhaps it was just something she'd learned later in life, but the man's wife called it an omen, and not a good one.

As much as it pained her to say it, the sign was clear: her husband was fated to die unexpectedly, sooner rather than later. The doppelgänger lore is pretty clear about it, after all. Seeing his double could only end tragically. And it did. Less than five years later, a stranger held a gun to his head and shot him. And just who was that man in the mirror?

The sixteenth president of the United States, Abraham Lincoln.

Where There's Smoke

ONE OF MY favorite Stephen King novels is *Firestarter*, which, without giving away too much, is the powerful story of a little girl with a supernatural gift. King refers to it as pyrokinesis, the ability to control fire with the mind, and that's a frightening thought. But at the root of the concept is the idea of control. Fire serves the person directing it.

But what if that control were gone? What if the flames seemed to take on a mind of their own, and all of those tragic, terrible characteristics suddenly became unpredictable and possible? Fire under control is a powerful, life-giving tool. On its own, though, it can destroy everything in its path.

That's exactly what happened in central London way back in September 1666. Over the course of four days, fire engulfed building after building, ultimately destroying the homes of over seventy thousand people. Two centuries later and a continent away, another fire swept through the American city of Chicago. After three days of burning, over a hundred thousand people were left homeless.

These were both accidents, of course. The London fire is thought to have started in a bakery, while the Chicago fire has traditionally been blamed on a cow kicking over a lantern in the O'Leary barn. But accidents happen, especially when it comes to fire. Sometimes it's minor, while other times it leads to horrible destruction.

As a result, we fear fire. I've said it before, but it certainly bears repeating here: fire is a dangerous tool. It benefits us as a society, but it also poses a great risk to our well-being. So we hide the matches from our children, build safety systems into our homes, and maintain teams of brave men and women who stand ready to fight back when fire breaks out.

But what would we do if all that power fell into the hands of something out of our reach, invisible and unpredictable? Something with clear malicious intent and zero regard for human life.

Something, perhaps, that's *supernatural*.

THE COTTAGE

It was the dream that unsettled her. They always seem to have a way of doing that, don't they? In her dream, she'd been at home in the small cottage she shared with far too many other members of her family when an angry bull appeared outside.

The bull was black as night, with eyes that glowed an icy blue. And after a tense moment of silence, it began crashing into the side of the cottage, threatening to knock the little house to the ground. And then she awoke.

Daily life for Esther might sound like a bad dream as well. She lived in a small cottage that belonged to her sister Olive and Olive's husband, Daniel, along with their two small boys. Her brother William also lived in the house, as did her other sister, Jane, with whom Esther shared a bed. And as if that wasn't enough, Daniel's brother John stayed there as well. Add it all up, and Esther had seven roommates.

She was also just eighteen years old, that age when we're all still trying to figure out exactly who we are. But Esther was having to do that in the middle of a packed, noisy house. I realize this is most likely me projecting my social preferences on her, but it must have been maddening.

So while the dream of the blue-eyed bull and the falling cottage might have left her feeling unsettled, daily life most likely washed over her like a tidal wave. She moved on, and by the time evening arrived, it was all but forgotten. And I think Bob McNeal had something to do with that.

McNeal was her gentleman caller, a local young man she'd taken an interest in. He was good-looking, charming, and maybe a bit "wild" and rough around the edges, something Esther didn't mind at all. But her family did. They weren't a fan of Bob McNeal, and told her so every chance they had. Bob McNeal, they told her, was dangerous.

But that didn't stop Esther from climbing into his carriage that night. He wanted to take her for a ride. It was late August 1878, and the countryside around Amherst, their little town in Nova Scotia, was beautiful, even in the dimming light. But there's always darkness just around the corner, isn't there?

When they reached a wooded area, McNeal pulled the carriage over and got out, and then he asked Esther to do the same. She sensed something was wrong and shook her head. No, she said, I'll stay here. But McNeal insisted, and he pulled a revolver out of his pocket to show her how serious he was.

Esther was about to scream, or maybe cave in and get out of the carriage, but instead a noise from somewhere in the shadows startled both of them. Another carriage was approaching. McNeal quickly shoved the pistol back into his coat, then jumped into his seat and urged the horses to move.

Their journey back to Esther's home was tense. He sped the entire way, and at some point it began to rain, leaving her drenched and cold. By the time she climbed out of the carriage, she was crying uncontrollably from the entire ordeal. Of course her family noticed—how could they not in a household so small and confining?—but they just assumed the couple had had an argument. But they never asked, and Esther never stopped to talk; she just headed straight to bed.

Days went by. Life was unremarkable and uneventful for everyone in the cottage. And then, on September 4, Esther awoke in the middle of the night screaming. When Jane asked her what was wrong, Esther told her that there was a mouse in the bed. She could feel it, and soon enough, so could Jane. Except they couldn't see it.

In the end, they both just went back to sleep, assuming the mouse was now inside their mattress. But the next night it happened again. This time, though, the sounds were coming from a different location. It was almost as if the mouse had moved into a box beneath the bed. So the young women pulled the box out.

Before either of them could open it and expose the mouse, the box jumped straight up into the air—at least a foot, they said—and landed on its side. Their screams caught the attention of Daniel—their sister Olive's husband—who came rushing in, but after hearing their story, he just told them to go back to bed.

Whatever had happened seemed to sit on that fine line between unbelievable and unremarkable. The type of event that's frightening enough to shock you, but not powerful enough to be provable, or worth obsessing over. But the following night, new events crossed that line.

Jane awoke to the sound of Esther thrashing around in bed, and found her sister having some sort of seizure or fit. Her eyes were wide open, and she was grinding her teeth and shaking. Jane screamed for help, and after a few moments, all six of the other people in the house were standing beside their bed.

But before anyone could do anything to help Esther, the room shook with three massive, powerful sounds. It was as if explosives had been detonated, or—if your imagination was really creative—as if something large were crashing against the side of the cottage. Like a bull.

When the sounds stopped, everyone turned back to Esther, but she no longer needed their help. She was fast asleep.

House Calls

It would be another two nights before anything new happened. Daily life was smooth and uneventful for everyone, it seems. But it wouldn't last; their short break was nothing more than the calm before the storm.

On September 8, just a couple of hours after everyone had gone to bed, screams came from Esther's room, waking everyone up. When they arrived, they found her having another seizure, jaw clenched and hands balled up in fists at her side.

That's when things started to fly—literally. First it was a sheet from the bed, and then another. Then a pillow flew up and hit Daniel in the face. No one saw who was throwing the items, but they could clearly see it happening. It was like a brief, awkward, supernatural pillow fight. It all stopped, however, when three more loud booms shook the room, after which they found Esther peacefully sleeping once more.

Daniel said he'd had enough. The following morning, he called on the local physician, Dr. Carritte, to come and check on Esther. Something was wrong with her, he said. She needed help. All of them did. So when Carritte walked through the cottage door, most of them probably sighed with relief.

After his examination was complete, the doctor declared that Esther was suffering from some sort of "nervous excitement." It was his opinion that something significant had happened to shock her, and the anxiety from that event was still haunting her.

And that's when the pillow beneath her head somehow flew out and onto the floor. Someone put it back, but it happened again. Daniel's brother John tried to hold the pillow down, but it continued to fly out and away from the bed.

Dr. Carritte was astonished. He'd never seen anything like it in all his years of practice. Before he could examine her further and try to find a rational explanation for such an unusual thing, the room shook from the sound of more massive booms. This time, though, it didn't stop with three. It kept going on and on, leaving all of them confused and afraid.

Which made it all the more frightening when writing began to appear on the wall over the head of Esther's bed. It was as if an invisible finger were scratching words into the plaster. As each letter appeared, more and more plaster would crumble to the floor, but one of the larger chunks actually levitated upward before flying directly toward the doctor's face.

When the invisible message was complete, everyone stared at it, eyes wide and mouths open. The words were chilling: "Esther Cox, you are mine to kill."

And then it was over. The booming stopped, as did Esther's seizure. Oddest of all, though, was how the writing slowly began to fade away, almost as if it were evaporating, vanishing back into the realm it had come from. But things were far from over.

The following day, Carritte returned to check on Esther, but found that the same violent activity was still occurring. The booming noises were still happening from time to time, but as much as the family searched the house, they just couldn't seem to find a cause.

Daniel was increasingly frustrated. Once, standing in Esther's room with a handful of others, he shouted out for the thing to tell him how many people were standing in the room. Everyone heard the response: five slow knocks, one for each person present.

Chairs and other small pieces of furniture would be seen sliding across the floor, or sometimes levitating up and into the air. On one of the doctor's visits, a handful of potatoes appeared from nowhere, aimed straight at his head. No one admitted to throwing them.

It was Esther who suffered the most, though. Her seizures and fits refused to go away. But she was also talking in her sleep. One afternoon Olive walked in to find Esther mumbling quietly. When she stooped down to listen, she heard her sister describe the terrifying evening she'd spent with Bob McNeal on the night of August 28.

So Olive began asking around. Maybe McNeal was somehow responsible for all of this. His behavior certainly fit the description of the traumatic event that Dr. Carritte had originally blamed. But every person she asked in town gave her the same puzzled look. McNeal, they all told her, had gone missing days before. The night of August 28, in fact.

That wasn't the only thing the community was whispering about, though. Esther and her strange, invisible assailant had become *the* talk of the town. So much so that neighbors and strangers began to knock on the cottage door, hoping for a chance to experience the odd events for themselves. And they were never disappointed.

All signs pointed to something bigger than a neighborhood prank. With McNeal nowhere to be found, a growing list of eyewitnesses to the events, and the seemingly supernatural nature of it all, it was becoming more and more obvious that something darker was at work. The clues were there. Everyone could see them, like smoke on the horizon.

But as everyone knows, where there's smoke, there's fire.

Catching Fire

The family decided that a new plan was in order. If the invisible attacker would not leave Esther alone, perhaps Esther should try to escape it. So she and Jane were moved to a different room in the house. If it worked, the spirit might actually give up and leave.

The very first night they slept in the new room, however, their invisible assailant followed them, waking Esther up in the middle of the night with a loud, otherworldly voice. It told her that it planned to burn the house down. Jane, however, never heard a sound.

More voices followed the second night. The spirit told Esther that it had once been a living person, but that had been many years before. Excited by this new revelation, Esther called out for the others to come and listen, but just like Jane, they were all deaf to the voice.

That's when the fire appeared. It was a lit match that seemed to spark into existence high above them, against the ceiling, before falling to the floor. Jane rushed over and stomped her foot on it to put it out, but almost immediately a dozen more burning matches appeared in the air and fell to the floor like a rain of fire.

This time everyone helped put them out, but as the collection of little flames was extinguished, one more landed on the dress that Esther had left on a chair. The fabric caught fire, and at the same time, something invisible moved the dress onto the floor and then pushed it under Esther's bed.

For one frightening moment, it looked as if the spirit or ghost or whatever it was just might have its way and burn Esther alive. But at the last moment Daniel reached under the bed, pulled the dress back out, and stomped on it.

And then it was over. No more flames that night. No more falling matches. No more burning dresses. But it left everyone feeling very afraid, because what if, right? What if one of those matches had fallen in a room no one was in? What if one had landed on something more flammable than the floor or dress?

Three days later, that's just what happened. While most of the family was out of the house, fire broke out in the cellar. It was just by chance that Olive and Esther noticed the smoke, and when they rushed down to see what had happened, they found a barrel of wood shavings absolutely erupting with fire. Olive ran back up for a bucket of water but spilled most of it in the panicked rush to get back downstairs.

Esther ran out into the street, where she found a stranger passing through town and begged him to come help. His assistance is what saved the house that day.

A few nights later, Esther claimed to actually see the spirit that had been haunting her. She said it was a gray man with bright, evil eyes. And this gray man told her to leave the house, or else he would burn everything she loved to the ground.

So she did. She packed up and went to a neighbor's house, but the spirit followed her. And that became normal life for her for months. She moved from place to place in town, staying with friends and neighbors, and at each stop, the spirit would manifest in some frightening way, eventually driving her on to a new home.

Sometimes it was the fire. Other times it was the loud voices or unexplainable booms. More furniture moved, and more objects levitated. Once she was stabbed in the back with a knife that belonged to a boy in the shop where she worked. The knife had been in his pocket but had somehow flown out and pierced her skin not once but twice.

In June 1879 she finally tried moving home, but almost immediately the fires began all over again. Daniel and Olive's landlord was finally forced to threaten the family: either the fires go, or you do. And although it pained everyone to do it, they agreed that Esther had to leave for good. In late July, at the age of nineteen, she hugged her family goodbye and left town.

She eventually found her way to a nearby farm, where she found lodging and employment. It was close enough to Amherst that she could visit her family from time to time, but far enough away that everyone felt safe.

I wish I could say that Esther's story ends there. That after this she disappeared from public record because her life returned to normal. But it didn't. Not long after settling in at the farm, the barn burned to the ground, and the owner accused Esther of arson. After a short trial, she was sentenced to four months in prison.

She was released just one month later.

On and On

Esther's story is a complex one. I can see how, at least on the surface, her tale sounds a lot like so many other haunted house or poltergeist stories, with the invisible entity and deadly occurrences. Been there, done that, right?

And yet . . . well, it's hard to escape the notion that every story is worth telling, that every story holds a unique quality or element that makes it worth passing on. The common elements give us a baseline for understanding the plot, and the nuances add flavor and character. And the story of Esther Cox gives us all of that and more.

In the end, it's impossible to say what the real source of the disturbances was, no matter how skeptical or open we might be. Perhaps it was the trauma of that evening attack in the woods. Bob McNeal seemed to step out of the story rather quickly, but so much of her emotional distress and suffering could easily be blamed on his assault.

Or maybe it was the trauma of living in that house with so many other people. As an introvert who craves silence more than anything else, I can attest to the maddening nature of community. But then again, the benefits of having people around you, supporting you, caring for you . . . all of that more than makes up for the madness. And Esther experienced that side of it as well.

Oftentimes the clues are found in the aftermath. The public eye has a way of wandering on in search of some new shiny thing long before the story has stopped kicking on the floor like a dying bug. We can learn a lot from those last twitches.

After being released from prison a month after her conviction for arson, an actor named Walter Hubbell reached out to her with a proposition. He had been one of the countless "supernatural tourists" who had traveled to Amherst to witness the events of the year before, and he had written the experience up in a book he called *The Great Amherst Mystery*.

His new idea was to travel the country and promote the story with Esther at his side every step of the way. She agreed, and for a while they worked together to tell her story throughout Canada and America. But when an angry mob scene broke out at one of these events, Esther refused to do another, so she packed up and left.

Hubbell went on to make a fortune from his book. Esther, though, stayed on the move. After two sons by two husbands, she finally settled in Brockton, Massachusetts, where she passed away in 1912 at the age of fifty-five.

Whether it was paranormal and otherworldly, or just a manifestation of a flammable personality, the fire of Esther's youth is gone, pulled apart by the wind of time, like a fragile wisp of smoke.

Iced

I N 1991, TWO German hikers were walking a path between two mountains in the Alps. When they moved off the trail and onto the glacial ice, they saw something that stopped them in their tracks. It was a body.

They were more than ten thousand feet above sea level, and like a lot of experienced hikers, they assumed that what they were looking at were the remains of another mountaineer, someone who had fallen or become injured on their hike and then died before help could come.

It turns out they were very wrong. They had, in fact, stumbled upon the mummified body of a man who had died over five thousand years ago. And over the next three days, the corpse was extracted from the ice and moved to the University of Innsbruck, where scientists quickly got to work on learning everything they could about him.

They named him Oetzi. They examined his belongings and pieced together the man's story. He had been a hunter, but in the end, someone else had hunted him. It's believed that he had been shot with an arrow and then clubbed on the head, breaking his skull. He was probably mugged, or whatever it would have been called in 3300 BCE, and then left for dead.

That's the story that the textbooks tell: the story of an archaeological marvel, the story of the oldest natural human mummy in

Europe, the story of one ancient man's murder and the literal cold case that followed. But the textbooks usually leave out a few details.

The year after Oetzi's discovery, the forensic pathologist who had lifted the mummy with his bare hands and placed it in a body bag—a man named Rainer Henn—was killed in an auto accident. He had been on his way to speak at a conference about the mummy.

Shortly after Henn's death, the mountain guide who had escorted him to the iceman's body, Kurt Fritz, was killed in an avalanche. Fritz had been an experienced mountaineer, and yet he somehow managed to be the only member of his hiking party who was crushed by falling rocks.

That same year, tragedy struck another person who had been present on the day of Oetzi's extraction from the ice. Rainer Hölz, an Austrian journalist who had filmed the removal of the mummy from the ice, died of a brain tumor. With his death came rumors: perhaps the mummy was cursed. Perhaps, like some ancient artifact from a forgotten age, Oetzi's body carried some supernatural marker, dooming all of those connected with its recovery.

It sounds too exotic to believe, but what happened next did nothing to dispel the whispers and theories. While hiking in the Alps in 2004, Helmut Simon—one of the original German hikers who found the mummy—fell more than three hundred feet to his death. His body was found less than a hundred miles from where Oetzi's had been discovered.

Dieter Warnecke was part of the rescue team who eventually found Helmut's body. He was a fit, experienced mountain man, and knew the Simons well enough to even attend Helmut's funeral. One hour after the funeral ended, Warnecke died of a sudden heart attack.

Members of the media approached Konrad Spindler, an Austrian archaeologist who was a leading expert on the iceman, and asked him about the curse. Spindler laughed off the idea, saying, "I think it's a load of rubbish. It's all a media hype. The next thing you will be saying is that I will be next."

Perhaps Spindler was right. Maybe a curse is nothing more than rubbish, or primitive mankind's way of finding their place in a world where they have little control. According to him, if there really *was* a curse, he would in danger of meeting the same fate, something that seemed very unlikely to him. Unfortunately—and coincidentally, perhaps—he died in 2004, just six months after he dismissed the curse to the media.

A year after the death of Spindler, another of the scientists working on the Oetzi case passed away. His name was Tom Loy. He was the molecular archaeologist who had discovered human blood on the mummy's clothes and weapons.

The official cause of Loy's death was a blood disease that caused clots to form. It was a natural death—natural, at least, in the sense that there was no accident to blame. And while his loss was grieved by family and friends, it would be hard to pin that death on the iceman.

Except for one odd detail. This blood disease, the disease that ended his life in 2005, had been diagnosed thirteen years before, in 1992, the very same year he met the iceman.

The Handkerchief

IN OCTOBER 1776, the Declaration of Independence was already three months old, and Benedict Arnold was fighting the Battle of Valcour Island for the American colonies. He lost horribly, but the fight managed to stall the British long enough to give New York time to prep their defenses.

Across the Atlantic, though, in the Italian city of Florence, a surgeon named Joseph Battaglia was trying to save a patient. Like Benedict Arnold, his patient was fighting a losing a battle. Still, Battaglia tried.

The patient was a priest named Don Gio Maria Bertholi. He'd been traveling on foot through the area and, rather than walking the long distance back home, decided to see if his sister and her husband would put him up for the night. The records tell of how the priest, upon entering their house, requested a handkerchief before going to his guest room to take part in his evening prayers.

The handkerchief might sound like a weird request unless you understand that the most devout priests in those days would have worn rough undergarments that irritated their skin. It was a way of staying aware of their humanity and suffering. It doesn't fit our modern sensibilities, I know, but in context, this was a perfectly logical request. Placing that small bit of silk inside his shirt, just between his shoulder blades, would have been a like an oasis in a desert. Sweet, beautiful relief.

He'd only been in his room for a few minutes when his family heard a sharp, loud noise, and then a cry of pain. They ran to see what the trouble was, and found the man lying on the floor—and covered in pale blue flames. As they approached to help him, the flames seemed to fade away on their own. What was left, though, was a badly burned priest.

Miraculously, he was still alive, so Dr. Battaglia was called in the following morning. It didn't look promising, though. Bertholi had been burned severely from the top of his shoulders all the way down to his knees. His right arm was especially bad; it had been so severely burned that the flesh had begun to fall off the muscle, and the hand seemed the worst.

Despite all of this pain and suffering, Bertholi was still able to speak, which is how Battaglia came to know the man's story. The priest explained how, in the middle of his evening prayers, he felt a pain in his right hand. He said it felt as if someone had struck him with a club. Almost at once, flames sprouted from that hand and ignited the rest of his body. The results, of course, were devastating.

And Dr. Battaglia was having trouble repairing and healing that devastation. Over the course of four days, Father Bertholi grew worse and worse. The man reeked of burnt flesh, and it had become impossible to wash away the smell. The priest vomited continuously, and his body seemed to be full of acidic bile and rotten fluids. Even the poor man's fingernails had fallen off.

Worst of all were the worms, though. Dr. Battaglia recorded that he actually watched as worms slowly pushed through the man's charred skin and climbed out and onto the sheets of the cot. It was as if he was decomposing from the inside out—all while still alive.

In the end, Bertholi died a painful, horrible death. And it was a death that no one could explain. No one had witnessed the accident, but at the same time, no one could find clues to help explain it. How, they wondered, did this man end up burning to death on the floor of his room?

The clues they could see weren't very helpful, honestly. It had been a clear night with no storms or lightning. There'd been a lamp on the table, but all the oil was gone and the wick had been blackened. His shirt had burned away completely, which, obviously, makes sense given the fire and all, right? But then why were his trousers untouched by the flames? Heck, even though his cap had been incinerated, not a hair beneath had been scorched.

More mysterious than any of that, though, was what they found when they rolled him over. There, stuck to the raw, burned flesh of his upper back, and exposed when the shirt burned off completely, was the handkerchief.

It was still white, and clean, and completely untouched.

Christmas Mourn

I T WAS CHRISTMAS EVE in 1885. The Rooneys owned a farm just
outside of Ottawa, Illinois. Today Ottawa straddles I-80 as it
cuts across the state just south of Chicago, but in 1885 it was
farms as far as you could see.

Patrick Rooney and his wife were celebrating the holiday with
a very small gathering. Besides Mr. and Mrs. Rooney, they were
joined by their son John, who owned a neighboring farm about a
mile away. There was a fourth—their farmhand John Larson—
and together all four of them sat around the kitchen table.

They were celebrating Christmas. It would be safe to assume
there were stories and laughter. I can even imagine good food and
treats they wouldn't have eaten at any other time during the year.
We know for certain, though, that Mr. Rooney had a jug of whis-
key that he had picked up in town earlier in the week. And they
were all thirsty.

But life on a farm doesn't come with days off. There are always
things to do. So at some point in the evening, their farmhand John
Larson staggered up to bed to get some rest. A short while later,
the Rooneys' son John said his goodbyes and left to go home to his
own farm and his own responsibilities. Which left Mr. and Mrs.
Rooney alone in the kitchen to clean up the mess.

Typical, right? Moms and dads always get stuck with the
cleanup.

Early in the morning, Larson dragged himself out of bed and down to the kitchen. Yes, it was Christmas morning, but he had daily chores to do. It was pitch-black in the kitchen, though, so he pulled out a match and struck it against the stove so he could see what he was doing.

The match, though, refused to light. He felt it. The tip hadn't broken off, but it was covered in grease. He didn't remember the stove being that filthy the night before, but he shrugged and grabbed a clean match. This one, he struck on his thumbnail, and a flame sparked to life.

But he nearly dropped it. Not because it was hot, or he was clumsy. Because sitting in the same chair he'd been in the night before was Mr. Rooney, eyes closed, head hung low. Larson must have had a heart attack, but he quickly recovered and said good morning to his employer. Mr. Rooney, though, didn't reply.

He didn't reply, you see, because he was dead. Larson looked briefly around the room but didn't see Mrs. Rooney, so he bolted out the kitchen door, saddled his horse, and rode hard toward young John Rooney's farm. After he found him, the pair rode back.

John Rooney brought a lamp, and the two men stepped back into the kitchen. John was heartbroken to find his father's body in the chair, but equally concerned for his mother. He stepped around the table to walk toward the door to the stairs—she could very well still be in bed, after all—and that's how he found the hole in the floor.

I mean it. There was a hole in the wooden floor of their kitchen. It was big, too, maybe three feet by four feet. And the edges were blackened, as if they'd been scorched. Hanging his lantern over the opening, John gasped. There, just a couple of feet down, was Mrs. Rooney.

Well, sort of. There wasn't a lot left of her, to be honest. A skull, one foot, some vertebrae, and a lot of ash. And that was it. It was clear from her remains and the scorch marks on the floor that she'd burned to death, but there was no clue anywhere in the room as to *how*.

That's what the police were for, at least in theory. And they almost immediately blamed the only person who survived in the house that morning: John Larson. His employers had died, and he hadn't. So that made him a suspect, and as a result, the man was put on trial.

Almost immediately, though, new evidence cleared Larson's name. Solid, irrefutable proof that Larson had been asleep while Mrs. Rooney had burned alive. According to the police, so much soot had filled the kitchen as a result of the fire that it actually drifted upstairs. Then it settled on everything. Furniture. Decorations. Shelves.

Even, it seems, John Larson. Because when the police examined his bed, there was a clean, white silhouette of his body on the sheets. While Larson slept, you see, Mrs. Rooney's ashes had rained down over him like snow.

The coroner told the jury it had been a case of spontaneous human combustion, but that didn't give an immediate answer to the cause of *Mr.* Rooney's death. Yes, she had burned to death; the evidence was pretty clear on that. But what about her husband?

That, the coroner said, was another simple matter. Mr. Rooney, it seems, had been killed by his wife, but not intentionally. He had died of asphyxiation . . . suffocating to death on the fumes of his wife's burning corpse.

The U~Turn

GEORGE WAS A military man from a military family. He was the third of four sons, and each of the brothers had served the Crown in battle. But unlike his three brothers who had served on land, George was at home on the open sea.

He was posted to HMS *Wellesley* by the age of sixteen, and began a steady climb up the ranks. He built a career as a naval officer, and was known to be sharp, consistent, and a stickler for details. If there was ever any sort of training exercise or military operation to be prepped for, George Tryon was the man they wanted in charge.

Much of his career was spent in the Mediterranean, and when he was finally promoted to vice admiral, that's where he remained. And then, in June 1893, he began to prepare for another training exercise. It's what he was good at, and something he loved. He loved the challenge of pushing his crew, and the task of planning the maneuvers that each massive battleship would repeat.

The mission this time was actually pretty simple. George Tryon was in command of the HMS *Victoria*—the flagship of the entire Mediterranean fleet—and was joined by another, the HMS *Camperdown*. Together, they were supposed to travel parallel to each other away from the shore, turn toward each other to make simultaneous U-turns, and then travel back.

A crowd had gathered to watch the two battleships there off the coast. These battleships were modern marvels, and to see them move so nimbly was a treat. Then Tryon gave the orders, and the ships began their maneuver.

Like I said, this was a simple exercise, but it did have some requirements. The biggest was space. For both ships to turn toward each other in the middle of their U-turns, they needed to be at least fifteen hundred meters apart. But as they moved into position for the turn, it was clear that they weren't. In fact, the distance between the ships was barely two-thirds of that.

Still, the maneuver continued unchecked. Part of the reason was Tryon's confidence in his planning, but another element was his approach to the mission. He kept all of the details secret from his crew, because he wanted to see how they would perform on the spot, with no time to prepare. Real combat, he knew, never went exactly according to plan.

So the ships turned. As they did, the crew noticed right away that there wasn't enough room. The captain of the *Camperdown* hesitated, but Tryon ordered him to continue as planned. Reluctantly, the man did.

By the time Tryon admitted that the ships were too close together, it was too late. The *Camperdown* slammed nose-first into the side of the *Victoria,* and then her engines reversed and they pulled apart, leaving a massive hole in the side of Tryon's battleship.

The *Camperdown* would later need three months of repairs to be seaworthy again. But the *Victoria* fared far worse. The flagship toppled over and sank within minutes. Over 350 lives were lost, including Vice Admiral George Tryon. And all of it happened in front of a crowd gathered on the shore.

It was the last time anyone saw George Tryon alive.

Well, sort of.

Back home in Eaton Square, in London, on that very same afternoon, Tryon's wife was hosting a gathering at their home. Dozens of people were there, enjoying food and drink and conversation. They talked politics. They gossiped about local nobility. They discussed Tryon's career in the military, and his current whereabouts in the Mediterranean Sea.

And then, while everyone was watching, George Tryon walked into the room and into the gathering of friends. Everyone saw him, but it seemed as if Tryon himself didn't see them. His eyes were focused on something else, something off in the distance.

He stood there for a few moments, the center of everyone's attention and the source of many curious questions. And then . . . right before their eyes . . . he vanished.

A Study in Silk

MRS. BARGRAVE ANSWERED the knock at her front door, half expecting a delivery of some kind, but it wasn't. Instead, it was a face she hadn't seen in years.

Before she'd moved to Canterbury in 1703, she had called Dover her home. And during her time there she had become quite friendly with another woman in her neighborhood, a Mrs. Veal. They had been close friends, spending much of their time together, but had lost touch when Bargrave moved away.

That's not unusual for the time. In the pre-Internet era, it was a lot more difficult to maintain long-distance friendships. So the two women lost touch and fell apart, however innocent the breakup might have been. Yet here, arriving on her front steps just as her clock struck noon, stood Mrs. Veal herself. It was quite a surprise.

So the two settled into conversation in the sitting room. They talked about life, about changes, about new developments that the other woman would find interest in. The entire time, though, Bargrave kept leaning forward to feel the fabric of her friend's dress. It was brand-new, made of a lovely silk, and very pleasing to the touch. Veal told her—almost casually—that the secret was to heavily wash the silk, which gave it a scoured texture.

Mrs. Veal informed her friend that she had stopped by because she was about to embark on a long journey, and she wished to restore their friendship before doing so. And this was shocking news, because Veal rarely traveled. She was severely epileptic, and as a result, she spent most of her time in the care of her brother, who wouldn't permit her to travel alone.

Maybe Bargrave looked at her friend in a quizzical way. Maybe she actually asked her straight up. Either way, the conversation turned to Veal's health. The visitor wondered whether she looked more or less healthy than she had nearly three years before. According to Bargrave, her friend had visibly improved.

Next, they moved on to family. Bargrave had a daughter, and Veal asked to see her and say hello. So Bargrave left the room to fetch her. A few moments later, she returned empty-handed, and was apologizing for that as she stepped through the doorway. She stopped, though, when she saw her friend walking toward the front door.

It was 1:45 in the afternoon. Their visit had taken less than two hours, but now Mrs. Veal suddenly had to leave. So they said their goodbyes as they walked outside, and then Bargrave watched the other woman as she made her way down the length of the street. Then she was gone.

On September 10, 1705, just two days after that unexpected visit, Bargrave went to visit another couple in the area. The Watsons were also old friends, but they were also relatives of Mrs. Veal. They welcomed her inside, made small talk, and then Bargrave asked about Veal.

The couple glanced nervously at each other, and there was more than a bit of sadness in their expressions. And then Mrs. Watson spoke up.

"Your timing is unfortunate," she said. "Your Mrs. Veal recently passed away. Just three days ago, at noon on Friday, in fact. I'm so sorry to have to tell you."

Bargrave was taken aback. "That can't be," she told them. And then she described the visit Veal had paid her just two days earlier—the day *after* she was supposed to have passed away. To help give her experience something concrete to hang on, she mentioned the new dress that Veal had been wearing.

"Oh, yes," Mrs. Watson said at the mention of it. "I knew that dress well. In fact, I helped her make it."

And then, leaning forward slightly, Mrs. Watson added one new detail.

"No one knows this," she said, "but that silk was special. She and I washed it very heavily many times, giving it a wonderful scoured texture."

Quarantine

ABOUT TWENTY MILES to the west of the South African city of Umzinto, there used to be an old Catholic outpost called St. Michael's Mission. Along with serving as home to the missionaries working there, it was also the location of a small, peaceful orphanage.

In 1906, though, that peace was broken by an extraordinary event. One of the older children, a sixteen-year-old girl named Clara Germana Cele, began to act strangely. Although she'd never studied them, she suddenly became fluent in German, French, and Polish. Witnesses also reported that she somehow knew the darkest secrets of complete strangers, as if she could read their minds.

They said she could levitate off the floor, sometimes as high as five feet, but holy water would bring her back down. On more than one occasion, Clara even tossed a nun across the room as if she were a rag doll. And the noises she made sounded as if "a herd of wild beasts, orchestrated by Satan, had formed a hellish choir." When they realized that Clara couldn't be near objects that had been blessed by a priest, they finally had their answer: she was possessed, they said, by a demon.

Hers is one of countless possession stories told throughout history. They span centuries and cultures and religions. And all the while, people have been fascinated by them. Maybe it's the darkness. Maybe it's the loss of control. Perhaps it's just our love of a good, old-fashioned scary tale. People are obsessed with stories about possession.

Look no further than Hollywood for proof. Films like *The Exorcist* and *Rosemary's Baby*—along with every single episode of *Supernatural*—all hinge on the idea of dark forces taking control of innocent victims. It makes for great entertainment. Darkness sells, apparently.

These stories, it turns out, are almost always about individuals. One person, possessed by evil, and the results of the condition. But what happens when there are more than one? What if an entire community falls victim to demonic possession? It sounds unlikely—*impossible,* even.

But four hundred years ago, it actually happened.

UNDER QUARANTINE

Deep in the French countryside, about twenty miles south of the town of Chinon, is an ancient little village that's home to just a few thousand people. The streets are picturesque, and the surrounding landscape is gorgeous, but there are darker things in Loudun than you might expect.

In the early 1600s, Loudun sat on the border between two territories: that of the Protestants—also known in France as Huguenots—and that of the Catholics. Like elsewhere in Europe and England at the time, there was a lot of hostility between these two groups of Christians, but it was different in Loudun. There, things seemed to be peaceful. Side by side, Catholic and Protestant lived and worked together.

But being on the border between two regions meant that there was a lot of troop movement, and in the early 1600s French troops were plagued by typhus. It's an illness sometimes referred to as "camp fever" because it flourished in the overcrowded, unsanitary conditions of military campaigns. And although the inflow of soldiers most likely brought a boost to the local economy, it also brought disease.

The year 1632 was a hard one. The community had been battling the pandemic for over five months, and it was taking its toll on them. Some estimates report that about 26 percent of the population there died as a result of the illness. Because of that, two things were happening.

First, all of the people of wealth and importance were leaving town. Doctors, priests, anyone who could afford to, really—all of them were fleeing to the countryside. Second, those who remained behind set up quarantine measures to stop the spread of the disease. And one of the groups that closed themselves off from the rest of the world was a convent of Ursuline nuns.

It wasn't an old convent—maybe six years old at the time—and so it was full of relatively young members. Most of the women who lived there had come from wealthy, noble families. Which made sense. St. Ursula was said to have been the daughter of a powerful ruler who was killed while on a religious pilgrimage. Noble-born women of the time were drawn to her story, and as a result, the order flourished.

In September 1632, after months of quarantine and the death that surrounded it, the nuns began to report odd experiences. On the twenty-first of that month, one of the women woke up to find a man standing at the foot of her bed. He was weeping, and begged her to pray for him. And he had a book, which he kept offering to her.

Alarmed, the nun called for her roommate to wake up as well, but when she did, the man vanished. The two women had trouble sleeping, though, and stayed awake the rest of the night. And all the while, both of them claimed they could still hear the man, weeping and muttering quietly, as if he was still there, praying by himself in the shadows.

A few days later, another nun claimed to see a black sphere that floated up and down the corridors of the convent. It even ran into one of the women, knocking her to the floor and leaving marks on her leg. A week after that, someone saw a skeleton, walking around as if it were still alive.

But these events seemed to be the precursor to something

darker. It was that hot, sticky wind that blows in just before a tropical storm slams the coast. Except this storm would turn out to be far more frightening. And it began with seizures.

Many of the nuns began to have violent convulsions. When they could speak, they cried out that hands—*invisible* hands—were slapping and hitting them. They heard voices and witnessed ghostly figures in their rooms. Remember, this wasn't an isolated thing; the experiences were spread across a whole group of the women. And that caught the attention of Church leadership.

When the Catholic confessor Jean Mignon arrived on October 5, there were eight nuns exhibiting these unusual symptoms, including the convent's prioress, Jeanne des Anges. Actually, she seemed to be the worst of the lot, convulsing through the night, and screaming what seemed like nonsense the entire time.

Suspecting a demon, Jean Mignon demanded that it speak and identify itself, but he wanted to be careful. If, for some extraordinary reason, the prioress was faking it, he didn't want to make it easy to answer. So he spoke to the demon in Latin, a language he knew she did not understand. Amazingly, though, it replied, also in Latin. But the answer was frightening beyond anything he might have expected.

"Who are you?" he shouted.

The prioress looked at him, smiled, and then whispered three chilling words: "Enemies of God."

THE PACT

One of the common beliefs of the sixteenth and seventeenth centuries was that a person had to strike a deal with the Devil in order to obtain supernatural powers. People all across Europe were accused of witchcraft for hundreds of years, but the core accusation was always that these individuals had somehow struck a bargain with evil spirits.

So it wasn't odd for Jean Mignon to ask his next question: "How were you invited into this convent?" The demon, through the

mouth of Jeanne des Anges, replied, "A pact, authored by Urbain Grandier."

It was an answer that Mignon had no problem accepting as true. Why? Well, to understand that, we need to take a moment and get to know Urbain Grandier. Because not only was he real, he was right there in the convent.

Grandier was a priest. This guy was handsome, suave, even seductive. Think Jude Law in *The Young Pope*. He'd been in Loudun for at least fifteen years, and in that time he'd built himself quite a reputation as a ladies' man. Rumor had it that Grandier had fathered a child with the daughter of a local lawyer. She was married off to someone from out of town, they say. But that didn't stop his seemingly endless string of mistresses.

Just two years before the possessions began, Grandier had been brought before the court. Other priests claimed to have seen him with women, married and unmarried alike. Some of these women had even gone to Grandier's own room to visit him alone. But thanks to some powerful connections in town, he was released without conviction.

Which didn't sit well with the judge, a man who also happened to be the local representative for the Pope, the bishop of Poitiers. And the bishop, it turns out, was a close friend of Jean Mignon. Which begs a lot of questions, right?

Was there really an epidemic of demonic possession taking place? Or was it a plot between Jean Mignon and Jeanne des Anges to finally get rid of Grandier? I know, that's a lot of names, a lot of French, and a lot of intrigue. But real life is always more complicated than fiction.

Real or not, the evidence of demonic possession went on for months, and with it all came more exorcisms. Every time a priest asked who the author of the pact was, Grandier's name would come up. Over and over, the testimony against him, however unbelievable it might have been, was stacking up. But at the same time, these unusual experiences pointed toward something . . . well, *supernatural*.

Witnesses reported that some of the afflicted nuns would shout expletives, something unbecoming of noble women, let alone ladies of the Church. Some of them barked like animals, while others uttered long diatribes in broken Latin. Many of the nuns would expose themselves during their demonic fits, or contort into positions that the priests considered obscene.

Naturally, word of these events eventually spread outside the convent walls. With the town-wide quarantine finally removed, dozens of people visited the convent with hopes of seeing for themselves what was really taking place. News always has a way of spreading, just like a disease. In Loudun it passed from mouth to ear, person to person, and finally made its way out into the countryside.

That's about the time when Grandier stepped in and tried to establish his own quarantine. He didn't want news of the possessions and exorcisms to spread, and tried to shut off the convent from the rest of the world. But Jean Mignon and the prioress wouldn't allow it.

Let me say this: I know Grandier's story isn't the most frightening and dark. I get it. It's political and religious and nothing different from anything we can find in the news today. That doesn't make for the most interesting story, admittedly. But if these demonic possessions were the elephant in the room, so to speak, then Grandier was the noose from which that elephant was hanged.

In November 1633, the Loudun events finally reached the ears of King Louis XIII, who told his advisor about it all. And that advisor was none other than Cardinal Richelieu, a man with both immense political power and a deep personal grudge against—you guessed it—Urbain Grandier.

By mid-December, the authorities had arrived at the convent to help. But they weren't there to end the exorcisms. No, they came solely for one purpose: to arrest Grandier. He was immediately taken into custody, and by the seventeenth he was on trial.

But the word "trial" might be misleading. What happened next was more of an exhibition of the worst of human nature. Looking back, it even put the demons to shame.

KINDLING

The trial began like you might expect. Evidence was brought against Grandier, accusing him of a pact with the Devil. But as difficult to prove as that might sound today, the Loudun trial seems to have allowed almost anything to stand as evidence.

The nuns were all brought into the courtroom and given a chance to testify. Jeanne des Anges did more than speak, though. The prioress was said to have levitated two feet off the floor. Later, she somehow stretched her body to a height of seven feet before shrinking back to normal.

One of the nuns reported horrible dreams in which Grandier appeared to them and forced them to do unspeakable things. Once, when all of the nuns involved were in the courtroom together, they passed out in unison, collapsing to the floor in a bizarrely synchronized wave.

Not wanting to leave anything to chance or fraud, the court also separated the nuns and questioned them individually. But when they spoke, it was the demon inside them that communicated. And these demons knew things that the nuns wouldn't have. They knew, right down to the day, when some of the visiting priests had last confessed. They even knew what was being said between two exorcists in another room across the building. If the women were faking their symptoms, they were doing an amazing job at it. Uncanny, really.

But the court didn't just test the nuns. No, Grandier himself had to endure some very unusual treatment as well, all in an effort to prove whether or not he was in league with the Devil. And the primary way they did this was through a search for what they called the "Devil's mark," sometimes referred to as a "witch's mark."

These were thought to be markings made by the Devil himself on the people who struck bargains with him. These spots were numb and never felt pain. Conveniently, they were also said to resemble normal scars, dark moles, unusual birthmarks, or even freckles. Obviously, this made it impossible for the accused to prove their innocence, and the court knew this.

On December 7, 1633, they imprisoned Grandier, and then shaved his body and pricked him with needles all over, looking for the places where he felt no pain or didn't bleed. But they cheated. According to a historian writing about sixty years later, it was well known that the surgeon in charge simply turned his needle around in certain places to avoid causing pain.

The crown jewel of their evidence, though, was the pact: the actual paper Grandier was supposed to have signed in the presence of the Devil. The paper was covered in the text of the agreement, as well as the personal seals of seven demons, and signed, they said, by Grandier . . . using his own blood as ink.

All of this was enough to convict Grandier, and he was sentenced to death. We can thank Cardinal Richelieu for that. Because of his involvement, the case was never tried in a secular court. Instead, it was a committee of his own creation that handled the whole proceedings. Which meant Grandier's death sentence was incontestable. He had no chance of freedom. No hope. No chance to prove his innocence.

They tortured him before his execution. They used a device called the "boot" to crush both of his legs. They took all of his money and possessions and delivered them to the king. They beat him. They pressed pins into his skin so deeply that they struck bone.

And not once did he give in and confess. Where most people accused of witchcraft would give in and name other witches in an attempt to save themselves from pain, Grandier refused. Seventy-two people gave false evidence against him in court, and yet he never once returned the favor.

The day of his execution, they carried him out of the prison toward the place where he would die, sort of a gallows built over a large pile of brush and kindling. It was a simple yet cruel system. First he would be handed a lit candle. Then the trapdoor would drop open, hanging him. Once he was dead, the candle would fall from his hand and onto the kindling, where it would ignite and burn his corpse. It was, in essence, a deadly Rube Goldberg machine.

But once he was brought to the platform, the crowd became

hysterical. They wanted violent justice. They threw holy water at him when he tried to address the crowd. They mocked him. And so, in an effort to please the angry mob, the executioner simply lit the funeral pyre and walked away.

Fueled by the dry brush and a whole lot of hatred, that fire consumed Grandier alive.

AUTHENTICITY

This fascination with demonic possessions almost seems like it's been woven into the fabric of society. We can go back into the depths of history and find countless examples of it, in all shades and interpretations. Judaism, Christianity, Islam, even Buddhism. All of them have been a lens, providing a subtle twist on an old story. Even the Spiritualist movement of the nineteenth century added its own flavor.

Because of this long and winding thread woven into the tapestry of human history, many people can't help but see possession as a real thing. Its history *is* the evidence. The sheer volume, at least to them, has to account for something. People like the former official exorcist of the Diocese of Rome, Father Gabriele Amorth. Before he passed away in 2016, he claimed to have performed over 160,000 of them.

Others look to modern psychology, to diagnoses like schizophrenia or dissociative identity disorder. The human mind is complex and fragile. You don't need to be a psychologist to understand that, either. Looking around at our friends and family, many of us know firsthand how destructive mental illness can be.

Whatever the cause, it hasn't stopped people from reacting like monsters. The execution of Urbain Grandier was far from the first of its kind, and sadly, it wasn't the last. When faced with events that are unexplainable, frightening, or contrary to our belief system, people have a tendency to overreact. We quarantine. We ostracize. We lash out. Sometimes violently.

In 2005, a young woman visited a monastery in Romania. She was there to spend time with her brother, but during the Mass, she giggled uncontrollably. The local psychiatrist wanted to treat her for schizophrenia, but the monastery's priest had other plans. The woman was chained to a large cross and gagged before being left alone in a cold room for three days. She died as a result.

The execution of Grandier was supposed to stop the possessions, but it didn't. The prioress continued to convulse and shout in Latin. Others seemed to suffer the same symptoms around her. Then, in October 1637, she seemed to get better. It was a miracle, they said.

Healed of her condition, she went on a pilgrimage to Rome, then back to France, where she stopped in for a visit with, of all people, Cardinal Richelieu. After that, she traveled through France, telling her story and earning a living. When Jeanne des Anges retired back at the convent years later, she became the local mystic and claimed to be able to communicate with angels, all of which brought her quite a lot of fame.

How nice for her.

Modern historians have since revisited that paper document, the one that was presented at Grandier's trial as his actual signed pact with the Devil. They brought in handwriting experts and dug into contemporary documents in the Loudun archives in an effort to determine if he really did write it. Surprisingly, they found a match, but it wasn't Grandier.

It was none other than the prioress herself, Jeanne des Anges.

Desperate Measures

THE HUMAN BODY is a mystery to us. Well, for most of recorded history, at least. Yes, we've done our best to explore and decipher the secrets inside ourselves, but so much of it has been pure guesswork. Thankfully, the past century of medical research has multiplied that understanding exponentially, but for a very long time, we've been a slave to assumption.

No matter where you look, early folklore always had a focus on our well-being. Folklore dictated our agricultural techniques, our personal safety, and—of course—our health. And thanks to folk wisdom, our ancestors did incredibly unusual things to fight illness and pain.

They cut themselves to let the sickness out. They gave themselves mercury enemas for their constipation. They drank their own urine, drilled holes in their skulls to stop seizures, and chewed tree bark to relieve pain. If someone said it worked, there were always people willing to try it for themselves.

Of course, we've learned a lot since then. We now know that mercury is highly toxic, and that drinking your own urine has zero benefit for our bodies. Plus it's just gross. And while there's a lot of archaeological evidence that drilling holes in skulls rarely killed people, it also failed to *help* them.

Sometimes those old folk remedies actually worked, though. Ancient Egyptians discovered that the bark of the willow tree was the best way to relieve pain. It turns out that willow bark is rich in salicylic acid, an active ingredient still used today in aspirin. But accurate treatments like willow bark were more of a lucky guess than scientific know-how.

People are very good at grasping for straws. It's part of our hopeful nature. It's a reflection of our belief that human life can be hacked. We can find any cure, if we look hard enough.

Sometimes, though, people have looked a bit too hard, and it's led to tragic results.

Mixing a Cure

Beginning in the late 1600s and continuing well into the 1800s, America welcomed its first major wave of immigrants. Many of them came from southwestern Germany and settled in what is now Philadelphia. In fact, the area of the city known as German-town was once an independent community founded by the earliest of those German immigrants.

Over time, they became known as the Pennsylvania Dutch, which is a misleading term because they weren't Dutch at all. It was just a variation on the word *Deutsch,* which means "German." But along with their common language, these immigrants also brought a unique belief system with them, a mixture of Protestant Christianity and European folk magic. The result was a folk religion known as *spielwerk* or *brauche.* It was focused primarily on healing and curative practices, but don't think pharmaceuticals. This was a bit more, well, *unique* than traditional medicine. It was a mixture of passages from the Christian Bible, prayers, and recipes that would look a lot like spells to modern readers.

This practice leaned heavily on two primary sources for guidance. The first was the Bible, which no practitioner of *brauche* would ever be caught without. And for Protestant German immigrants, that makes a lot of sense. Bible passages were so powerful to German American Christians that many who fought in World War I actually carried small pages of scripture with them as an amulet of protection.

The second primary source was a book called *The Long Lost Friend,* published in 1820 by a German immigrant named John George Hohman. In essence, it was a collection of recipes, instructions, and spells that were all aimed at curing physical and spiritual ailments. But it was based on an even older book from 1788 called the *Romanus,* or *Little Book of the Roma,* full of unusual spells.

What sort of spells? Well, one was called "To Prevent Witches from Bewitching Cattle, to Be Written and Placed in the Stable." Another was "Against Bad Men and Evil Spirits, Which Nightly Torment Old and Young People, to Be Written and Placed on the Bedstead." And those are just the *titles.*

An alternative name for *The Long Lost Friend* was *Pow-wows,* a word borrowed from Native Americans, one that has a lot of magical connotation to it. As a result, all of this—the spells, the faith healing, the incantations to ward off evil—all of it became known by *that* name: they called it "pow-wowing."

And it turns out that pow-wowing was treated almost like a family legacy. It was common to find whole lineages of *brauchers,* families that had practiced this combination of folk magic and faith healing for generations.

Families like the Blymires. They'd been well-known pow-wow practitioners for at least three generations, so when John Blymire was born in 1896, he represented the fourth. And all of those years within the field had earned their family a reputation. They weren't superstars by any stretch of the imagination, but generations of dedication had at least earned them the respect and patronage of their neighbors.

John, though, had health troubles early in his life. At the age of five, just when a little boy should be growing like a weed, John began to lose weight. Not a little, either. John's condition was noticeable, which alarmed his parents. And of course, his father tried all of the natural remedies at his own disposal. But no matter what he did, John's rapid weight loss continued unchecked.

Which led John's father to a darker conclusion: his son, for whatever reason, had been hexed. And if he was going to save the boy's life, he needed to find a way to remove that evil curse. But this wasn't small magic. A hex was something powerful, something dangerous. So John's father decided that he needed the help of someone wiser, with a level of experience that surpassed his own.

There were a lot of choices out there, too. Pow-wowing seemed to have been accepted everywhere in Pennsylvania Dutch country. John's father could have taken his son to any of the popular, well-known healers in the region: Katherine George, Andrew Lenhart, John Rhoads, even Nellie Noll or the deeply revered Mountain Mary.

But there was only one person in the area who came to mind. While the others were respected, this man stood head and shoulders above everyone else. He was a legend, a leader, and quite possibly the most talented "hexenmeister" in the country.

If you needed a cure, everyone knew that Nelson Rehmeyer was the man to see.

FOR BETTER OR WORSE

Nelson Rehmeyer lived in an area of southern Pennsylvania known—appropriately—as Hex Hollow. He was born there in 1868, and by most accounts, he was a shy, introverted boy. As he grew up, he took on the family business of farming potatoes, and of course learning the ins and outs of pow-wowing.

When John Blymire and his father arrived at Rehmeyer's doorstep in 1901, Rehmeyer was thirty-three and had grown into a mountain. Descriptions say he was a tall, two-hundred-pound tower of intimidation, but that wasn't his fault. Inside, he was still the shy, private man he'd always been. It was his desire to help others that made having a public life a necessity for him.

Rehmeyer listened to John's father. He checked the boy over. And then he gave them a prescription. Mr. Blymire was to collect his son's urine in a jar, and then boil an egg in it. Once the egg was hard-boiled, he was told to poke three holes in the shell, and then find an anthill to place the egg on top of. Nelson assured him that after the ants had fully consumed the contents of the shell, the hex would be gone.

Yeah, I know. Most of us would probably have just laughed and found someone else to help us, but not John's father. He went home and did exactly what Nelson Rehmeyer told him to do. Because that's what you did. This was tradition. It was core to who they were as a culture. And, as crazy as it might seem, it worked.

John's weight loss stopped. And then life moved on, as it always does. John, perhaps emboldened by his encounter with Rehmeyer, started diving into pow-wowing on his own within a couple of years. Local legend says that he performed his first cure at the age of seven. He was a child prodigy, some say.

But there was a lot to learn. At the age of ten, John took a job on Rehmeyer's potato farm, and I can't help but assume he also sat at the older man's feet and learned all he could about pow-wowing. But while things were looking up for John, life was taking a darker turn for Rehmeyer.

His wife, Alice, wasn't a fan of his career choice as a faith healer. After doing her best to deal with his growing fame and all of the people who kept knocking on their door, she took their two daughters and moved into a nearby house. Alice and Nelson remained married for the rest of his life, but they never lived together in the same house after that.

In 1909, when John was just thirteen, he moved to the city of York, maybe twelve miles to the north. He took a job at a cigar factory, but the work was dark, filthy, and unhealthy. John made up for it by earning himself a reputation as a talented faith healer.

It's said that he helped cure one man's eye infection, and when a rabid dog threatened a few coworkers outside, he calmed the dog in a way that seemed almost supernatural to those with him. But all of that success was overshadowed by something more troubling: his weight loss had returned.

"A stronger power than I had got hold of me," John later said. "It tormented me almost every day of my life from then on. I couldn't eat, I couldn't sleep, my skin was getting loose on me." John even claimed that his own power to heal others had left his body.

So at the age of eighteen, John quit his factory job and poured all of his time and focus into finding a cure. Well, not all of his time. He somehow managed to fall in love with and marry a woman named Lily. But John's first love was pow-wowing, and finding a cure for his illness fell under that umbrella. Lily would always take second place to that.

Years went by. John consulted a number of other local healers, including Andrew Lenhart, who was known for telling more than a few married people that they'd been hexed by their spouse. There were even some murders as a result, although there's no evidence that Lenhart was ever charged with any crimes.

But it was enough to make John suspect that Lily might be the cause. She responded by having him examined by a psychiatrist, which resulted in a short stay in a mental health facility. That wasn't the help John thought he needed, so he escaped and came home.

The rest is a blur. Lily divorced him, and, needing a way to support himself, he returned to the cigar factory. And that's where he was when he finally decided to reach out to Nellie Noll, an ancient, well-respected pow-wow witch, to see what she might be able to do for him. In August 1928 John went to visit old Nellie.

She was probably ninety years old at the time. She'd seen almost everything over the course of her life, and after she examined John, she told him she could help. She handed him a dollar bill and asked him to stare at George Washington's face for a long while. When she took the dollar away, the face of the man who had hexed him was imprinted on his palm.

A face that John recognized. How could he not, after all? The silver hair. The dark suit. That tall, mountainous frame. It was none other than his old mentor, Nelson Rehmeyer.

John was shocked. His hero, the man who had healed him so many years ago . . . how could *that* man be the source of his hex? But there it was, as plain as day, right on his hand. John might have had respect for Rehmeyer, even a bit of hero worship, but his respect for the faith was deeper. If Nellie Noll said it was true, then it was true.

And now that he knew the source, it was time to do something about it.

For what he had planned, John was going to need help. It wouldn't be easy, after all. Old Nellie told him that the hex could only be removed one of two ways. Either he had to somehow get hold of a lock of Rehmeyer's hair and bury it, or—even more challenging—he had to steal the old man's copy of *The Long Lost Friend* and then burn it.

So John reached out to two friends from the area. The first was John Curry, who had been fourteen when he had worked at the factory with him. During their brief friendship, Curry came to appreciate and respect Blymire's skills as a healer, even working as his assistant for a time. And one of the cases the two men worked on was for the Hess family.

They lived near the Rehmeyers and had been experiencing unexplainable misfortunes for a long while. The common assumption was that a witch was involved, but no one could figure out just who that witch was—until Blymire suggested it was Rehmeyer. Wilbur Hess, a hulking eighteen-year-old, immediately offered his help.

On the afternoon of November 26, 1928, Blymire and Curry made their way to Rehmeyer's house, but the old man wasn't home. They walked to Alice's house, a short distance away, and she told them that Nelson had gone to visit a neighbor. So they waited for him to return.

When he did, he invited the two visitors inside. According to Blymire and Curry, they spent the evening talking about powwowing. It was so late when they finished that the two young men ended up spending the night there at Nelson's house. In the morning, satisfied they had learned enough to do what they needed to do, they left.

Back at the Hess farm, they enlisted Wilbur, and the three men prepared to return for a second visit that night. Close to midnight, Blymire knocked on Rehmeyer's door. He told the older man that he'd left something at the house by mistake, and asked if he could come in to retrieve it. Rehmeyer complied and let them in.

Once inside, the men surrounded Rehmeyer. They demanded that he hand over his copy of *The Long Lost Friend,* but the older man refused. And I think that shows us two things. First, Rehmeyer didn't think these men were a threat just yet. And second, his book was far too valuable to just give away. Many pow-wow practitioners considered their copy of the book to function almost like an amulet. It was powerful, and he wasn't giving it up.

So they attacked him. Blymire jumped on him and held him down while the others bound him with a length of rope they'd brought along. And then they dragged him to the kitchen, sat him on a chair, and continued to request the book.

The old man, however, was built of stronger stuff. He offered them his wallet, and even told them where they might find more money in the house, but no, he told them, you can't have the book.

All three men became furious. They beat him, using whatever they could find around them. One man hit him with a board. Someone else threw a chair. And at some point, driven by rage and frustration, Blymire took some of the rope and looped it around Nelson's neck.

Within a matter of minutes, Rehmeyer—the man who had once saved John Blymire's life, the man who had helped a community with his wisdom—was dead. And the three men were left standing over a blood-soaked body with a fog of regret and panic slowly descending on them.

Everything moved fast after that. Blymire cut a lock of the dead man's hair and tucked it into his shirt pocket. One of the others decided to make it look like a robbery, and retrieved the handful of change that Rehmeyer had told them was hidden in the house. And then they set the body on fire. If they could make it go away, perfect. If it took the whole house with it, even better.

Back outside, Blymire buried the lock of Rehmeyer's hair in the yard and then took a deep breath. He'd done it. He already felt better, more alive, and healthier than he had in years. For once, his future looked to be full of hope and possibilities, rather than pain and frustration. Everything was better.

Except it wasn't. While the men were returning to their homes that night, Rehmeyer's body failed to burn thoroughly. And rather than bringing the house down around it, only the kitchen showed signs of the damage. Which meant that when the mailman arrived the following morning, he didn't find the charred wreckage of a house.

He found a crime scene.

ON THE DECLINE

People do unusual things when they lack an understanding of how it all works. Folklore is the thing that fills the vacuum created by a lack of knowledge. It helps keep fear from rushing in, like a dam in a river. And for a very long time, across much of Pennsylvania, pow-wowing was the dam that held fear at bay.

Obviously, folklore surrounding witches is ancient and full of dozens of cultural nuances, but pow-wowing holds a special place in American history. It's given us that image of the local wise person who always seemed to know the right words for any problem. Or the proper medicine. Or the best way to ward off something evil.

But pow-wowing seems to have faded into the past for most Pennsylvania Dutch, thanks in no small part to the Blymire trial. After it was over, the authorities responded to the superstitious roots of the "York witch trial" by pushing for better education in science. The result was sort of like inoculating a country against measles. Soon enough, belief in pow-wowing existed only in the most stubborn, out-of-the-way places.

But there was one bit of magic left. You see, the moment she learned of her husband's death, everything clicked in Alice Rehmeyer's mind. The men who had visited that day looking for Nelson. The fire. The rope. All of it.

So she called the police and told them what she knew. Blymire and the others were arrested a short while later. By the beginning of 1929, all three men were on trial for murder, and they immediately confessed.

John made his case for the reason behind his actions, of course. He even declared it a success, right there in court in front of the judge. But none of that mattered in the trial. These men had killed someone in cold blood, and that came with consequences. Life was about to get a lot more difficult for John and his friends.

On January 19, 1929, all three were sentenced to terms in prison. Curry and Hess were paroled a few years later, but John stayed behind bars until 1953, when he was finally released and sent home.

He died at the age of seventy-six. No one attended his funeral.

I can't help but see the irony in the ways things ended for John Blymire. Powerful words spoken over him in a private ceremony. Words that would alter the shape and quality of his future. Words that brought hardship and pain. It wasn't a hex, I know, but I can't help thinking that his murder trial would've felt like one.

The Rehmeyer house is still there today, and you can drive past it if you know where to find it. Nelson's great-grandson lives there now, although locals think the house is inhabited by something else, too. Something darker. It's haunted, they claim, and always will be.

Killing someone in cold blood, after all, always has a way of leaving a mark.

Black and Wild

IN THE WORLD of fairy tales and adventure stories, we're often invited into a strange new land. A place of monsters and magic, of danger and destiny. That's what we love about these powerful stories. They transport us, they move us, they show us another world.

Fantasy is more mainstream today than it's ever been. From *The Lord of the Rings* to *Game of Thrones,* we love it all. But each new fictional world needs a guide, a voice to help the reader find their bearings and make sense of it all. And for a very long time, that voice has been the wizard.

Everyone has their favorite wizard. From the Arthurian Merlin and Shakespeare's Prospero to the more modern Gandalf and Dumbledore, the wizard is the voice of reason, our tour guide in a strange and dangerous place. They often speak for the author, and serve as a tutor for the uninitiated—readers and fictional characters alike.

We could spend a long time discussing why that is. Why it seems that, deep down, our brains cry out for a sage old voice, full of power and magic and depth, to walk us through a strange new world. But I'm not going to do that. Because some things are better left unspoken.

Wizards, you see, are the stuff of legend. We've invented them to help us cope, to help us understand, or to help us find our way.

They're a pillar of storytelling, and yet they're nothing more than make-believe. At least, that's what most of us *think*.

But history hides many secrets, and if you know where to look, you might be surprised by the sorts of individuals tucked away in those dusty pages. Real people. People who lived and breathed and walked among us, and who had a reputation for the otherworldly.

One such man existed in the middle of the sixteenth century. And if you consider the stories, you'll risk coming face-to-face with a startling conclusion: wizards just might be real.

A CALCULATED DESTINY

Roland and Jane Dee lived in the area of London known as Tower Ward during the first half of the 1500s. Roland was a business man who specialized in textiles, but thanks to his reputation and close proximity to the White Tower, he also had the opportunity to serve as the court tailor for King Henry VIII.

Their only child, John, was born in 1527. We don't know much about his childhood, but by the age of fifteen he was on his way to Cambridge, where he studied . . . well . . . *everything*. While there, he barely managed to get four hours of sleep each night due to the number of subjects he was studying. His mind was hungry. He wanted to know everything, to master it and connect it all.

So he poured himself into every topic available. Navigation, astronomy, engineering, theology, law, mathematics, medicine. Even astrology and cryptography. In the truest sense of the world, John was a polymath. But it still wasn't enough.

After Cambridge, he boarded a ship and sailed for the Netherlands, where he would study at the Old University of Leuven. And that's where he dug deeper into the one subject that intrigued him the most: the occult. When John finally returned to England in 1551, he brought a collection of European navigational equipment with him, as well as a solid reputation as a sorcerer.

That last bit was certainly his fault. Months before, he'd been hired to help with a particular problem in a stage production of *Pax,* the ancient comedy by the Greek philosopher Aristophanes.

It was a story that called for a large, flying scarab—a dung beetle, basically—but it was proving tricky to actually make one that was believable enough.

Not for John, though. He dug in, worked hard, and returned to them with a mechanical version. And it was a massive hit. Legend says that the audiences were so terrified by his animatronic beetle that they assumed he'd acquired his skills by selling his soul to the Devil himself. Rather than deny it, John stayed quiet, adding a whole new layer to his reputation. A perfect example of how silence can speak just as loudly as words.

But things had changed in England while he'd been away. Henry VIII had died in 1547, and although his nine-year-old son, Edward VI, took the throne, the boy king just couldn't compare. The economy began to fall apart. Riot and rebellion became commonplace. War broke out with Scotland. When John returned, the England he remembered was in turmoil.

Then, in 1553, young Edward died, and his half sister Mary succeeded him on the throne. Seeing his chance, John used his reputation to gain an audience, and then cast horoscopes for both Mary and her younger sister Elizabeth, offering them each a glimpse into their future. But it didn't seem to connect with the new ruler.

In fact, as Catholic Mary began to crack down on Protestant citizens, she didn't hesitate to arrest John's father. He was thrown in prison and stripped of his entire fortune, which was bad on many levels. John lost his father, and at the same time, he lost his inheritance, something he'd been counting on for a very long time.

You see, John had a dream: he wanted to spend the rest of his life furthering his studies, without having to worry about paying the bills. But thanks to Queen Mary, that dream had been torn out of his hands. And then things got worse.

Shortly after his father's arrest, John himself was brought to court for a crime of his own. And the charge? John Dee, they said, was guilty of "calculating." No, really. John was arrested for engaging in mathematics.

Remember, this was an era when the line between math and magic was a lot more blurry than it is today. And it could get you into a lot of trouble. Very few people were educated, and to most of them, math really was magic. It was divination and sorcery and conjuring all rolled into one. To use the darkest of magical descriptors, it was black and wild. So for the dark crime of "calculating," John found himself in prison.

When he was released three months later, he headed straight back to Queen Mary. He had a grand idea, but needed her approval. John wanted to build a national library, where old manuscripts and scientific records could be stored and used by scholars like himself. So he presented this plan to her.

Sadly, Mary passed on the idea, so John shifted to a backup plan. In 1556, he moved back to the London home of his mother and began setting up a personal library there. Over time, he would amass a collection of nearly four thousand books, many times larger than the libraries of Cambridge and Oxford combined.

See, who says you can't accomplish great things while living in your parents' basement?

All of that changed when Mary died and her sister Elizabeth took the throne, because Elizabeth, it seems, remembered John Dee. She remembered his horoscope, and his passion, and his wisdom. With her coronation approaching, Elizabeth asked John to pick the perfect date for the ceremony, and when it went off without a hitch, John's place at her side was secured.

Then, in November 1572, everything blew up. Well, in the sky, at least. That was the year something appeared overhead. It wasn't a comet, though—most people had seen those before and while they were exciting, they weren't new. No, this was much more significant, inspiring some and frightening others.

It was a brand-new star.

A Shining Light

We now know that this "new star" was actually a massive supernova in the constellation Cassiopeia. After it appeared, it remained there—visible to the naked eye—for well over a year. Astronomers from England to China all recorded it, and everyone seemed to have their own way of interpreting it.

To scholars like John, though, this new star's appearance had deep occult undertones. He made the detailed observations that you might expect from an astronomer, sure, but he also used the opportunity to make predictions, something much more in line with his wizardly reputation.

A new star, he said, meant the rise of a new empire, and at the center of it all was Queen Elizabeth. He viewed this new empire as a new Camelot, Elizabeth as the new King Arthur, and himself—of course—as the new Merlin. And he also had this bizarre belief that the New World, the one across the Atlantic Ocean that they were beginning to get a glimpse of, would be the jewel in the crown of this new, majestic "British Empire," as he called it.

For the next two decades, John and Elizabeth worked together to advance that vision of England. It was everything he'd hoped for. He was in his prime, publishing books and deepening his understanding of the world around him. And that success was spilling over into the political sphere, including heavy influence over England's colonization efforts in the New World.

John became advisor to many of the first explorers to sail from England to the New World. After all, he had the unique advantage of owning that collection of European navigational instruments, as well as a deep understanding of astronomy and geometry, all of which meant that there were few individuals in the world who knew as much about navigation as he did. If you wanted to get around in the mid-sixteenth century, John Dee was the closest to Google Maps you were going to get, and everyone knew that.

But as the world got bigger, John grew increasingly aware of just how little he truly understood. There were just so many questions he couldn't find answers to, so many challenges he couldn't overcome. And that frustration was pushing him deeper into occult territory.

So rather than seek out answers in this world, John tried to peer into the next. With tools like scrying mirrors and crystal balls, he pushed hard into the world beyond the veil, with the goal of making contact with the spirits there. If he couldn't find the answers to his questions in this world, maybe he could find them in the next.

And according to his own journal, those efforts were paying

off—if only slightly. One entry from May 25, 1581, describes an unusual encounter that involved seeing shapes and movement in his crystal ball. It was the first time it had happened, but it was also incredibly frustrating. He could only see the shapes. Communication, either receiving or sending, was completely nonexistent.

Remember who this man was: Cambridge-educated by the age of nineteen, advisor to the queen of England, and wizard in nearly every sense of the word. He was used to setting his mind to something and achieving it. Complex mathematics. Global navigation. Language and theology and law. And yet here he was, stumped by something. He'd failed.

To John, the reason was clear. It wasn't that he lacked the knowledge or focus; no, he simply lacked the natural ability to do it. This thing that he was attempting must require a special gift that some were born with, while others weren't. So John went looking for those gifted individuals.

Thankfully, there was no shortage of people in London who claimed to be able to do the thing that John was pursuing. One by one, these people were invited into his process and put to the test, only to fail just as consistently. They tried, of course, and they told a good story, but John never fell for it.

Then, in 1582, after months of frustration, he met someone special. Someone who claimed to be able to do all that John required, and more. His name was Edward Kelley, and although he was much younger than the experienced and educated scientist, he claimed to have the skills necessary for the task. So he got the job.

John went into this arrangement with a lot of hope. His dream of seeking out deeper knowledge in the world beyond our own had a deceptively simple requirement: to be able to hear the messages from the other side, and then send back replies. Kelley seemed to have potential, if his resumé was any indication.

The younger man claimed to be able to do a lot of things that most people couldn't. Adept in alchemy and necromancy, he told John that he could learn things from the dead, magically teasing out their past secrets while also predicting the future. Oh, and one more important skill.

Kelley, it seems, could talk to angels.

Kelley was a serial liar by trade, which made it a huge risk for him to set up shop right beside the smartest man in England. What little we know about him from history paints him as an overweight alcoholic con man with no ears.

That last part wasn't a deformity. You see, Kelley had been punished by the Crown. It was called "cropping," literally cutting off a person's ears as punishment for their crimes. Which meant there was no way for Edward Kelley to hide his past. John, for his part, didn't really seem to care. He just wanted the man to deliver on his promise.

They two men approached this task with reverence. They would fast and pray before each angelic session, and always went into it with an eye for knowledge and answers that could benefit humanity. For years, both men would reach out, Kelley would listen, and then write down what he heard.

The messages came from an assortment of angels, who identified themselves by names familiar to most of us. Michael. Gabriel. Raphael. And these messages filled volumes, too, sometimes consisting of English prose that was said to rival the very best of his day, while other times they were in the indecipherable language of the angels themselves.

In 1583, a Polish scholar and alchemist named Albert Laski reached out and told John about the riches that awaited him in Europe, and in Poland specifically: nobles and wealthy elite who were willing to fund the esoteric experiments of people like John Dee. So on September 21, 1583, he and Kelley packed up and headed to the Continent, leaving his home and enormous library in the hands of his brother-in-law, Nicholas Fromond.

The conversations with angels continued while they were on the road. For nearly six years, John Dee and Edward Kelley traveled through Europe, mostly in Poland and Bohemia, showing their work to people with the wealth to fund it. Think of it like a medieval version of *Shark Tank,* but with the constant risk of imprisonment or exile.

There were certainly high points in the journey. On April 17,

1585, he and Kelley were given an audience with King Stephen of Poland. In fact, the ruler became a repeat patron of theirs, sharing their deep interest in communicating with the angels. Later, the men were even given the chance to stay and work for the Holy Roman Emperor Rudolf II. That experience began on a positive note but ended with the two sorcerers being kicked out of the capital for "necromancy and other prohibited arts."

But something unusual happened while they traveled and worked there in Europe: John's reputation—decades in the making and practically legendary in certain circles—began to be eclipsed by that of Edward Kelley. It was Kelley who listened and spoke with the angels, after all. Kelley relayed their instructions, which covered a whole assortment of topics, from when and where to travel to how to bind new books of imparted wisdom.

Another unexpected moment occurred in 1587, when Kelley relayed a bizarre message. On Saturday, April 18, while in their temporary residence in the Bohemian city of Trebona, Kelley reported that Uriel had instructed him and John to exchange wives for a night. John, blinded by his relentless pursuit of favor with the angels, reluctantly complied.

Things fell apart quickly after that. John and his wife, Jane, found it more and more awkward to be around the Kelleys, which I'm sure comes as anything but a shock to us today. And that awkwardness wasn't the only thing growing between them: Jane Dee, it turns out, was pregnant.

When she gave birth in February 1588—nine months after that April night they referred to as their "cross-matching"—it was to a baby boy. John gave his new son the middle name Trebonianus, which means "a gift from God at Trebon." Some historians think the name hints at the boy's true father, while others are unsure. But the birth does seem to signal the end of their European adventures.

Within a year, Dee and his family were packing up to head back to England, and they arrived ten months later after a long, difficult journey. But his return home wasn't as rewarding as he'd hoped. He arrived at a house in disarray. His precious library, amassed over many decades and full of rare and annotated volumes, had been looted, as had his collection of scientific instruments.

Some things would later be recovered, but the losses kept stacking up. In 1594, his young son Michael died unexpectedly. A year later, Queen Elizabeth appointed him warden of Christ's College in Manchester, which turned out to be a frustrating and painful experience. Then, in 1604, his youngest son, Theodore, also passed away, followed by his wife, Jane, and three of their daughters— Madinia, Frances, and Margaret.

In the end, John Dee moved back to London in 1605 and lived his last remaining years in poverty, forced to sell off his library book by book so he could buy food. What came next didn't happen with the dramatic bang of one of his experiments, or even with the fanfare that he rightfully deserved. Instead, on March 26, 1609, the great light within John Dee just flickered and then went out.

And when it did, darkness flooded in.

OUT OF TIME

I can't help but wonder how John would fare in our modern times, where the battle between science and superstition is supposed to have ended decades ago. But has it really? Maybe he'd be right in his element, guiding us toward progress with steely determination. Maybe he would be overwhelmed. Or maybe he would just be sad that, even after all these long years, people really haven't changed that much.

There's so much to love about John Dee. He knew more about everything than most people alive at the time. His personal library was a legendary collection of everything he could get his hands on. The things he could do . . . well, people viewed it all as magic. And on some level, it really was.

He predicted the rise of the British Empire, he proposed a national library long before anyone else valued the idea, and he enabled much of the global navigation that consumed European culture for another century and a half. John Dee, at least as he was seen through the eyes of his contemporaries, was a wizard.

But if you asked him yourself, Dee would tell you he was a scientist. A scientist who just happened to live in a culture where advanced knowledge about the world around him was viewed as necromancy or witchcraft. If it was magic, it was black and wild.

It's interesting to note that John's surname, Dee, was of Welsh origin. It's a word that means, of all things, "black." And his mother's maiden name? Before she was Jane Dee, she was Jane *Wild*.

Black and Wild. John, it seems, was born for the life he lived.

John Dee, it turns out, also held one more role during his time in the service of Queen Elizabeth. There are some who think he served as a spy during England's war with the Spanish, which began in 1585. Espionage like that was common in his day, and during his adventures across Europe he encountered many others who were rumored to be spies for Elizabeth.

We know from historical documents that many Elizabethan spies would use a code name, rather than their real identity. The Earl of Leicester, for example, signed his letters to the Queen with two zeros. She, in turn, replied with communications signed with her own unique code name.

John Dee seems to have played along, and in doing so, he set in motion wheels that even his brilliant mind could never have predicted. He appreciated the symbolism of the two zeros, drawn on the page like a pair of eyes. Sometimes they would even have dots inside them to highlight that. But he added something else to perfect it, to fully represent himself as a man who sought perfection and piety.

Over three centuries later, one British author would discover these tantalizing bits while reading a biography of John Dee. When he set pen to paper soon after, he gave birth to a literary character that the entire world has grown to love. A spy, in fact, who used John Dee's own code name.

007.

Unholy Acts

WHEN FAITHFUL CATHOLIC Marthe Brossier began to have seizures and shout out vicious, hateful words, people around her took notice.

It wasn't because she was important; she wasn't. Marthe was the twenty-five-year-old daughter of a poor merchant in the French village of Romoantin. Not nobility, not a community leader.

Insignificant or not, it certainly looked as if Marthe's personality had suddenly changed. She cut her hair short and began to dress in the clothing of a man. And she'd become violent toward others, even those she loved. On at least one occasion, she physically assaulted her close friend Anne Chevreau, and accused Anne of bewitching her.

Oddly, it wasn't the village who demanded an exorcism for her, but Marthe herself. And if the records show us anything, it's that the exorcism went as you might expect. She convulsed and writhed on her bed, shouting hateful words. But the focus of her words, it seems, was the heresy of the Protestants.

You see, when her seizures began in 1598, the world around her was in a constant state of tension. The friction between the old world of the Catholic Church and the new uprising of Protestants known as Huguenots was causing trouble all across the country.

But rather than get better, Marthe's condition remained the same. And to make matters worse, she kept having her fits of demonic rage in public. In fact, most of the anti-Protestant rants that she shouted seemed to be happening in crowded spaces. And she didn't stay in one place, either. Marthe seemed to be enjoying the attention, and like all attractions, she began to take the show on the road.

She traveled all over France, with her father at her side. Angers, Saulmur, Clery, Orleans, and of course, Paris. In each new location, she would experience more of her demonic fits, and then her hateful proclamations would begin again. And always in a crowd. It was making people nervous.

Partly because the government was taking steps to get rid of that religious and political tension. Just days before Marthe and her father walked into Paris, Parliament had passed the Edict of Nantes, which called for equal civil rights for Protestants. It was fresh on everyone's mind, whether they were a fan of tolerance or not.

Some of the stories about Marthe's possession are difficult to explain away. The impossible twisting and contorting of her body. The writhing fits of violence. One account says that she was somehow able to speak even when her mouth was closed, and the words themselves seemed to come from someplace else.

In Orleans she managed to get a certificate of possession from a local priest. But other church officials weren't so keen on her. It took a while, but city after city began to post warnings, forbidding their priests to exorcise Marthe when she came to town. Whether or not her condition was real, they said, she was using it to raise money from the crowds who came to watch her. They didn't want to participate in that sort of entertainment.

In April 1599 the king had her arrested and imprisoned. It was an effort to stop the public disturbances once and for all. But after just forty days, she was released and sent back home under house arrest. The local priest was given the task of watching her, and he checked in on her at regular intervals.

For a while it worked. Her fits became less and less frequent. She stopped shouting about the heresy of the Huguenots while in large crowds. She was getting better. And then she was kidnapped by a true believer.

His name was Alexandre de la Rochefoucauld. He was the prior of an abbey to the south, and fully convinced that Marthe's condition was real and important. And so he came and spirited her away to Rome, in hopes of introducing her to the Pope. They managed to get there just days before the papal jubilee of 1600, where she received one of her famous public exorcisms.

The last time anyone saw Marthe was five years later, in Milan. She was, of course, still trying to be rid of her demonic illness. In front of crowds. For money.

My guess is that the people of Milan ate it up, and that she encountered the same enthusiasm in every other town she traveled to after that. But while many would have assumed she was not being entirely truthful, few would have guessed that there was actual proof that she was faking it all.

How do I know?

Because just after it had all begun, Marthe underwent a private exorcism in 1599 at the hands of Bishop Charles Miron, who splashed her with holy water while reading passages in Latin. Both techniques seemed to have had the desired effect: the young woman screamed with pain as the water touched her skin, and the Latin words landed on her like punches.

But Miron hadn't been entirely truthful with Marthe and her father. You see, the water he had used hadn't been blessed by a priest. It was just normal well water, nothing more. And the Latin that hurt Marthe so badly to hear?

It was Latin, but the text wasn't from the Bible, or even Miron's exorcism manual. It was a line of poetry written by the ancient Roman poet Virgil.

On the Run

I N 1887, AN organization was formed in London with the express purpose of studying the occult in all its forms and shapes. Today we might view the subject matter as paranormal or metaphysical, or maybe just a little bit *odd,* but in the late nineteenth century, it was at least slightly closer to acceptable to the general public.

This group, known as the Hermetic Order of the Golden Dawn, operated for almost two decades as a united society, but around 1901, things started to break down. The result was a split, a fracturing of the order into at least four smaller groups. And one of them was known as the Alpha and Omega.

By 1930 almost all of those groups were in steep decline, partly because of infighting, and partly because of the modern world's refusal to believe in the sorts of forces and hidden secrets that these societies built their communities around. But some still held on. In fact, the last of them finally shut its doors as recently as 1978.

In 1929, though, one of the members of Alpha and Omega went on a pilgrimage. Her name was Nora Marionetta Fornario, and she was driven by a deep interest in fairy lore. When she arrived on the island of Iona, off the western coast of Scotland, it appeared that she would be staying awhile, judging by all of the luggage she'd brought with her.

She took up residence with a local woman named Mrs. MacRae, and began going on daily walks all over the island. She was researching something, she told her hostess. Something powerful and dark. And while it was invisible to most people's eyes, this research was dangerous.

For weeks Fornario wandered across the island, all dressed up in black robes and brilliant silver jewelry. She would perform rituals designed to aid her research, and would come back hours later, oftentimes long after sunset. And as the seasons changed, drifting from summer into fall, so too did Fornario. She seemed to age slightly, as if she was carrying a heavy burden.

One morning many weeks after her arrival, Fornario arrived at breakfast in a state of distress. Mrs. MacRae remembers how the younger woman's jewelry was no longer bright and silvery, but black, as if it had been completely tarnished overnight. So she asked if anything was the matter.

Fornario told MacRae that she planned to leave that very day. But before she could run upstairs and began to pack for her departure, MacRae broke the bad news that the boat to the mainland didn't run on Sundays.

The young woman was overcome with rage. She claimed that she had been under constant attack by unseen forces since her arrival weeks before. If she didn't leave soon, she might never see London again. But with no boat to take her away from this place, she was trapped. Resigned to her fate, it seems, she went back out for another of her walks.

Fornario didn't return that morning. By the afternoon, a storm had rolled in and MacRae began to wonder if the woman was safe. But still she waited. Afternoon became evening, and soon enough evening became morning.

Only then did MacRae go for help. She told others about Fornario's disappearance, and a group was gathered to search for the young visitor. Despite the island's small size, it still took the search party two full days. Two long days of scouring every inch of the island. Two days of walking and shouting her name. Two days of hope. And then . . . they stumbled upon a mysterious scene.

There, in a shallow impression in a far-off field, a large cross-shaped symbol had been carved into the hard turf. The tool used was probably the unusual dagger that was found a few meters away. But despite the presence of a knife, there was no blood to be found.

In the center of the scene, sprawled out on top of the cross, was Fornario's naked body. Later, a medical examination would fail to shed new light on the true cause of death. The results were inconclusive, drifting somewhere between death by exposure and sudden heart failure. Not unheard of, but certainly unusual for a thirty-year-old woman.

Exposure would be a better explanation, especially given the weather. But neither of these theories explain what was found on Fornario's legs and feet: long red scratches and cuts. It looked to everyone there as if the young woman had been running before she finally fell to the ground and carved the cross beneath herself. But what she'd been running from was impossible to guess.

Whoever or *what*ever it was, Nora's killer will remain a mystery that only she could reveal to us now.

ACKNOWLEDGMENTS

Lore is the type of project that involves a lot of people working hard outside the spotlight, so allow me a moment to pull them back in and give them some attention.

First, many thanks to my research assistants, Marcet Crockett and Carl Nellis. Without the hours you've spent in libraries, these stories would have no heart. Thanks for trudging into the mines and bringing back ore for me to smelt and forge.

Second, to my Del Rey team. You inspire me, support me, and work tirelessly to grow Lore into something bigger than when you found it. For that, and everything else you do, I am beyond grateful.

Third, I can't ignore my own parents. You've spent a lifetime giving me permission to chase my dreams and create things that make the world a better place—like stories about serial killers and wizards. So, thanks for that.

Lastly, my wife. You are my partner and structural support beam, and you do so much outside of Lore to give me the space and time to write, speak, tour, and promote. Without you, none of this would have happened (it's all your fault, basically).

BIBLIOGRAPHY

The Castle

"H. H. Holmes," Biography, date unknown, https://www
.biography.com/people/hh-holmes-307622.
Harold Schechter, *Depraved* (Simon and Schuster, 2008).
Adam Selzer, *H. H. Holmes: The True History of the White City Devil*
(Skyhorse Publishing, 2017).
Erik Larson, *The Devil in the White City: Murder, Magic, and Madness
at the Fair That Changed America* (Crown Publishers, 2003).

Black Stockings

Josephine McDonagh, *Child Murder and British Culture, 1720–1900*
(Cambridge University Press, 2008), 189.
Carole G. Silver, *Strange and Secret Peoples* (Oxford University Press,
2000), 63.
William Robert Wilde, *Irish Popular Superstitions* (Ulan Press, 1852), 28.
Joan Hoff and Marian Yates, *The Cooper's Wife Is Missing* (Basic
Books, 2001).
Angela Bourke, *The Burning of Bridget Cleary* (Penguin Books, 1999).

Covered Mirrors

Steve Lehto, *American Murder Houses: A Coast-to-Coast Tour of the
Most Notorious Houses of Homicide* (Penguin, 2015).

Roy Marshall, *Villisca* (Graymalkin Media, 2014).

Bill James and Rachel McCarthy James, *The Man from the Train: The Solving of an Old Serial Killer Mystery* (Simon and Schuster, 2017).

ON THE FARM

Michael Newton, *The Encyclopedia of Unsolved Crimes* (Infobase Publishing, 2009), 164–65.

Andrea Maria Schenkel, *The Murder Farm* (Quercus, June 3, 2014).

"The Mysterious Unsolved Murders of Hinterkaifeck Farm," Mysterious Universe, September 17, 2014, http://mysterious universe.org/2014/09/the-mysterious-unsolved-murders-of -hinterkaifeck-farm.

"Unresolved: The Hinterkaifeck Murders," *The Ghost in My Machine,* November 10, 2014, https://theghostinmymachine.wordpress .com/2014/11/10/unresolved-the-hinterkaifeck-murders.

SUPPLY AND DEMAND

George MacGregor, *The History of Burke and Hare and of the Resurrectionist Times* (T. D. Morison, 1884).

"Burke and Hare," Encyclopedia.com, 2001, http://www .encyclopedia.com/topic/Burke_and_Hare.aspx.

Ruth Richardson, *Death, Dissection and the Destitute* (University of Chicago Press, 2000), 79–85.

Lisa Rosner, *The Anatomy Murders: Being the True and Spectacular History of Edinburgh's Notorious Burke and Hare and of the Man of Science Who Abetted Them in the Commission of Their Most Heinous Crimes* (University of Pennsylvania Press, 2009).

Hugh Douglas, *Burke and Hare* (Hale, 1973).

"Edinburgh's Mysterious Miniature Coffins," *Smithsonian,* April 2013, http://www.smithsonianmag.com/history/edinburghs -mysterious-miniature-coffins-22371426.

THAT AXMAN JAZZ

Todd C. Elliott, *Axes of Evil: The True Story of the Ax-Man Murders* (Trine Day, 2015).

Jay Robert Nash, *Open Files: A Narrative Encyclopedia of the World's Greatest Unsolved Crimes* (Rowman & Littlefield, 1983), 17–21.

Gary Krist, *Empire of Sin: A Story of Sex, Jazz, Murder, and the Battle for Modern New Orleans* (Crown Publishers, 2015), 285–98.

THE ALTERCATION

Johnathan Sutherland, *Unsolved Victorian Murders* (JMD Media Ltd., 2015), 95–99.

"The Strange Death of Thomas Farrant," Historic Mysteries, December 10, 2015, http://www.historicmysteries.com/thomas -farrant.

DRAINED

"Bela Kiss," Murderpedia, n.d., http://murderpedia.org/male.K/k /kiss-bela.htm.

Maria Bovsun, "Hungarian Man Murdered 24," New York *Daily News,* February 9, 2014, http://www.nydailynews.com/news /justice-story/killer-murdered-24-pickled-corpses-barrels -article-1.1607445.

Harvey Rosenfeld, *Depravity: A Narrative of Sixteen Serial Killers* (iUniverse, 2009), 117–132.

A MINER THING

William Fordyce, *The History and Antiquities of the County Palatine of Durham* (Fullarton and Co., 1857), 2:599–600.

HOMECOMING

Grady, David, "The Debonair Killer," *American Cowboy,* August 1996.

"Herman Webster Mudgett," Murderpedia, April 2017, http:// murderpedia.org/male.H/h/holmes.htm.

David Franke, *The Torture Doctor* (Hawthorn Books, 1975).

Erik Larson, *The Devil in the White City: Murder, Magic, and Madness at the Fair That Changed America* (Crown Publishers, 2003).

John Borowski, *The Strange Case of Dr. H. H. Holmes* (Waterfront Productions, 2005).

"Holmes Cool to the End," *New York Times,* May 8, 1896.

Harold Schechter, *Depraved: The Shocking True Story of America's First Serial Killer* (Pocket Books, 1994).

Frank P. Geyer, *The Holmes-Pitezel Case* (Publishers' Union, 1896).

ALL THE LOVELY LADIES

"Why Are Old Women Often the Face of Evil in Fairy Tales and Folklore?", NPR, January 2016, http://www.npr.org/2015/10/28/450657717/why-are-old-women-often-the-face-of-evil-in-fairy-tales-and-folklore.

"The Bloody Reign of Countess Elizabeth Bathory," The-Line-Up.com, n.d., http://www.the-line-up.com/blood-countess.

"Death of Countess Elizabeth Bathory," HistoryToday.com, August 2014, http://www.historytoday.com/richard-cavendish/death-countess-elizabeth-bathory.

"Elizabeth Báthory," *Britannica,* last updated January 5, 2018, http://www.britannica.com/biography/Elizabeth-Bathory.

"On the Trail of the 'Blood Countess' in Slovakia," CNN, updated October 30, 2014, http://www.cnn.com/2014/08/21/travel/blood-countess-slovakia/index.html.

LOST AND FOUND

"Mystery. Murder. And Half a Century of Suspense," *Independent,* August 1999, http://www.independent.co.uk/arts-entertainment/music/features/mystery-murder-and-half-a-century-of-suspense-745330.html.

"Three Students Discover Corpse," *New York Times,* January 30, 1984, http://www.nytimes.com/1984/01/30/nyregion/3-students-discover-corpse-in-a-carpet-found-on-street.html.

"The Bawdy Under the Bed," Snopes, updated July 2014, http://www.snopes.com/horrors/gruesome/bodybed.asp.

"Skeleton Found in Chimney 27 Years After Man Disappeared," ABC News, July 27, 2011, http://abcnews.go.com/US/skeleton-found-chimney-27-years-man-disappeared/story?id=14169501.

"Russian Grave Robber," *Daily Mail,* November 8, 2011, http://www.dailymail.co.uk/news/article-2058587/Anatoly-Moskvin-pictured-Russian-grave-robber-29-female-doll-corpses-flat.html.

"The Dripping Killer," *Crime Magazine,* October 2014, http://www
.crimemagazine.com/dripping-killer.

"Horrific Fate of Victorian Murder Victim," *Daily Mail,* July 2011,
http://www.dailymail.co.uk/news/article-2011513/Skull-David
-Attenboroughs-garden-murder-victim-Julia-Martha-Thomas
.html.

"The Dripping Killer," The Lineup, date unknown, http://www
.the-line-up.com/dripping-killer.

Negative Consequences

"'Queen of the Underworld' Sophie Lyons Burke Murdered," New
York *Daily News,* June 10, 2012, http://www.nydailynews.com
/news/justice-story/queen-underworld-sophie-lyons-burke
-murdered-article-1.1090881.

"Shot At," *Detroit Free Press,* March 19, 1881, 1.

"Con Woman," *Chicago Tribune,* July 13, 1947, 7.

Viviana A. Zelizer, "Human Values and the Market: The Case of
Life Insurance and Death in 19th-Century America," *American
Journal of Sociology* 84, no. 3 (November 1978): 591–610.

Thomas Samuel Duke, *Celebrated Criminal Cases of America* (James H.
Barry Company, 1910), 437–43.

Rosan A. Jordan and Susan J. Kalcik, *Women's Folklore, Women's
Culture* (University of Pennsylvania Press, 2015), 109–24.

"Scenes at the Indiana Murder Farm," *Times-Dispatch* (Richmond,
VA), June 1, 1908, 3.

"Ethics in Photo Editing," Ethics in Editing, April 1, 2009, https://
ethicsinediting.wordpress.com/2009/04/01/photo-manipulation
-through-history-a-timeline.

The Sweet Embrace

Harold Schechter, *Fatal: The Poisonous Life of a Female Serial Killer*
(Simon and Schuster, 2012).

"For 10 Years, 'Jolly Jane' Poured Her Poison," *Lowell Sun,*
November 2, 2011, http://www.lowellsun.com/ci_19247994.

Harold Schechter, *The Serial Killer Files: The Who, What, Where,
How, and Why of the World's Most Terrifying Murderers* (Random
House Publishing Group, 2003), 32–33.

Katherine M. Ramsland, *Inside the Minds of Healthcare Serial Killers: Why They Kill* (Greenwood Publishing Group, 2007), 23–26.

Robert Barr Smith, *Outlaw Women: The Wild West's Most Notorious Daughters, Wives, and Mothers* (Rowman & Littlefield, 2015), 155–60.

HALF-HANGED

John Putnam Demos, *Entertaining Satan* (Oxford University Press, 2004), 372.

Sylvester Judd, *History of Hadley* (H. R. Hunting, 1905), 228–31.

HOLE IN THE WALL

Julian Goodare, *The Scottish Witch-Hunt in Context* (Manchester University Press, 2002), 179–80.

Marion Gibson, *Witchcraft and Society in England and America, 1550–1750* (Continuum International Publishing Group, 2006), 1–9.

Rosemary Ellen Guiley, *The Encyclopedia of Witches, Witchcraft and Wicca* (Facts on File, 2008), 18–19.

Geoff Holder, *Poltergeist over Scotland* (History Press, 2013).

John Mitchell and John Dickie, *The Philosophy of Witchcraft* (Murray and Stewart, 1839), 96–97.

"The Curse of the Paisley Witches," The Spooky Isles, November 2013, http://www.spookyisles.com/2013/11/the-curse-of-the -paisley-witches.

FAMILIAR

Wallace Notestein, *A History of Witchcraft in England from 1558 to 1718* (American Historical Association, 1911), 175–79.

Jonathan Barry, Marianne Hester, and Gareth Roberts, *Witchcraft in Early Modern Europe: Studies in Culture and Belief* (Cambridge University Press, 1998), 237–56.

Craig Cabell, *Witchfinder General: The Biography of Matthew Hopkins* (Sutton, 2006).

AFTER SUNSET

Ray Bendici, *Speaking Ill of the Dead: Jerks in Connecticut History* (Rowman & Littlefield, 2012), 164–74.

Cheri Revai, *Haunted Connecticut: Ghosts and Strange Phenomena of the Constitution State* (Stackpole Books, 2006), 25–27.

PEG AND BUTTON

John James Babson, *History of the Town of Gloucester, Cape Ann* (Procter Brothers, 1860), 321.

Ednah Dow Littlehale Cheney, *Stories of the Olden Time* (Lee and Shepard, 1890), 13–18.

Peter Muise, *Legends and Lore of the North Shore* (History Press, 2014), 40.

"Essex County Chronicles," *Salem News,* October 19, 2009, http://www.salemnews.com/archives/essex-county-chronicles-early-inhabitants-lived-in-fear-of-mammy/article_0e577136-a749-51aa-b29b-0638e86618cf.html.

HIGH STAKES

"Uncovering Warwickshire's Sinister Secret," BBC.co.uk, September 2014, http://www.bbc.co.uk/coventry/features/weird-warwickshire/1945-witchcraft-murder.shtml.

RISE ABOVE

Amy Waters Yarsinske, *Virginia Beach: A History of Virginia's Golden Shore* (Charleston, SC: Arcadia Publishing, 2002), 61–62.

Belinda Nash and Danielle Sheets, *A Place in Time: The Age of the Witch of Pungo* (Virginia Beach, VA: W. S. Dawson Company, 2012), 108.

"What's in a Name: Virginia Beach's Witchduck Road," *Virginian-Pilot,* June 1, 2009, https://pilotonline.com/news/local/history/what-s-in-a-name-virginia-beach-s-witchduck-road/article_c2174c7a-aade-5834-aee5-2e9350550d98.html.

MAKING A MARK

"The Cora Tree," Brigands' Bay Homeowner's Association, accessed January 2016, http://brigandsbay.org/tree.asp.

"The Cora Tree," Did You See That?, March 27, 2015, http://didyouseethatinnc.blogspot.com/2015/03/the-cora-tree.html.

Charles Harry Whedbee, *Blackbeard's Cup and Stories of the Outer Banks* (John F. Blair, 1989), 80–87.

"More Coastal Legends," NCBeaches.com, 2007, https://www .ncbeaches.com/Features/History/TalesAndFolklore /MoreCoastalLegends.

Angus Konstam, *Blackbeard: America's Most Notorious Pirate* (Wiley, June 5, 2006).

"Blackbeard's Ghost," North Carolina Ghost Stories & Legends, http://www.northcarolinaghosts.com/coast/blackbeard-ghost .php.

"New Theory?," *Outer Banks Sentinel,* September 13, 2006, http:// www.obsentinel.com/opinion/new-theory/article_cb58064f -8106-5cfe-b435-6161f3aa7bdb.html.

A Stranger Among Us

Jacob Brown, *Brown's Miscellaneous Writings* (Cumberland, MD, 1896), 41.

First Impressions

"The Woman Who Married Her Dead Husband in Church," *Mental Floss,* August 2016, http://mentalfloss.com/article/83247/woman -who-married-her-dead-husband-church.

"Notes of the Month," *The Occult Review,* September 1919, 128.

T. E. C. Jr., "The Power of Maternal Impression Causes the Alleged Father's Name to Appear in Legible Letters in His Infant Son's Right Eye (1817)," *Pediatrics* 58, no. 6 (1976).

"Debunked," Skeptoid, September 23, 2011, https://skeptoid.com /blog/2011/09/23/debunked.

Dennis Todd, *Imagining Monsters: Miscreations of the Self in Eighteenth-Century England* (University of Chicago Press, 1995).

"The Rabbit Babies of Mary Toft," The Museum of Hoaxes, n.d., http://hoaxes.org/archive/permalink/mary_toft_and_the _rabbit_babies.

Clifford A. Pickover, *The Girl Who Gave Birth to Rabbits* (Prometheus Books, 2000), 41–46.

"The Amazing 'Mummy in the Cupboard' Case in North Wales," *Daily Post,* May 7, 2012, http://www.dailypost.co.uk/news/local-news/amazing-mummy-cupboard-case-north-2660600.

James Boswell and Paul Tankard, *Facts and Inventions: Selections from the Journalism of James Boswell* (Yale University Press, 2014), 314.

John S. Gibson, *Deacon Brodie: Father to Jekyll and Hyde* (Hyperion Books, 1993), 30.

William Roughead, *Deacon Brodie* (New York Review of Books, 2000).

"The Real Jekyll & Hyde?", BBC News, January 29, 2015, http://www.bbc.com/news/uk-scotland-31018496.

"The Real Dr. Jekyll, Deacon Brodie," Books Tell You Why, October 2013, http://blog.bookstellyouwhy.com/the-real-dr-jekyll-deacon-brodie.

Labor Pains

"New Discovery of World's Oldest Stone Tools," NPR, April 15, 2015, www.npr.org/sections/thetwo-way/2015/04/15/399937433/new-discovery-of-worlds-oldest-tools.

John Murray Spear and Simon C. Hewitt, *Messages from the Superior State* (Bela Marsh, 1853).

E. W. Wallis and M. H. Wallis, *A Guide to Mediumship and Psychic Unfoldment* (Health Research, 1901), 151.

Emma Hardinge Britten, *Modern American Spiritualism: A Twenty Years' Record of the Communion Between Earth and the World of Spirits* (Spiritualists' National Union, 1870), 217–29.

Bret E. Carroll, *Spiritualism in Antebellum America* (Indiana University Press, 1997), 106.

J. W. Daniels, *Spiritualism Versus Christianity; or, Spiritualism Thoroughly Exposed* (Miller, Orton, & Mulligan, 1856), 180.

Daniel Dunglas Home, *Lights and Shadows of Spiritualism* (Virtue & Company, 1877), 216–19.

Sideshow

"The Grave of Elmer McCurdy," Atlas Obscura, n.d., http://www.atlasobscura.com/places/grave-elmer-mccurdy-skb.

"How a Real Corpse Ended Up in a California Fun Park
Spookhouse," *Slate,* date unknown, http://www.slate.com/blogs
/atlas_obscura/2014/04/11/the_corpse_of_elmer_mccurdy
_and_how_it_ended_up_in_a_long_beach_fun_park.html.
"The Long, Strange, 60-Year Trip of Elmer McCurdy," NPR,
January 9, 2015, http://www.npr.org/2015/01/09/376097471
/the-long-strange-60-year-trip-of-elmer-mccurdy.

IN A PICKLE

Peter Muise, *Legends and Lore of the North Shore* (History Press,
2014), 50.
"Edward Harraden," Minor Descent, September 14, 2010, http://
minerdescent.com/2010/09/14/edward-harraden.

FROM WITHIN

"Why Sati Is Still a Burning Issue," *Times of India,* August 16, 2009,
http://timesofindia.indiatimes.com/home/sunday-times/Why
-sati-is-still-a-burning-issue/articleshow/4897797.cms.
"How Cremation Works," How Stuff Works, n.d., http://science
.howstuffworks.com/cremation1.htm.
John Knott, "Spontaneous Combustion," *American Medicine* 9
(1905): 653–60.
"A Fire Within," Doctors Review, December 2011, http://www
.doctorsreview.com/history/fire-within.
"Reeser Death Stumps Anthropologist," *St. Petersburg Times,*
July 28, 1951, 9.

TEACHER'S PET

Robert Rapley, *Witch Hunts: From Salem to Guantanamo Bay* (McGill-
Queen's Press, 2007).
Robert Dale Owens, *Footfalls on the Boundary of Another World*
(Trübner & Company, 1861), 348–55.
Noah Brooks, *Washington in Lincoln's Time* (Century Company,
1895), 220–22.

WHERE THERE'S SMOKE

"The Great Amherst Mystery: A Documented Haunting," Historic Mysteries, December 2015, https://www.historicmysteries.com/great-amherst-mystery.

Walter Hubbell, *The Great Amherst Mystery* (Brentano's, 1888).

Laurie Glenn Norris and Barbara Thompson, *Haunted Girl: Esther Cox and the Great Amherst Mystery* (Nimbus Publishing, 2012).

Walter F. Prince, "Critical Study of 'The Great Amherst Mystery,'" *Proceedings of the American Society for Psychical Research* 13 (1919): 89.

ICED

Konrad Spindler, *The Man in the Ice* (Orion, 2013).

THE HANDKERCHIEF

John H. Anthon, "A Course of Lectures on Medical Jurisprudence," *New York Medical Press* 2, no. 8 (1859): 555.

John Wilkes, *Encyclopaedia Londinensis,* vol. 19, *Pathology* (Milland House, 1823), 293.

CHRISTMAS MOURN

Vincent H. Gaddis, *Mysterious Fires and Lights* (David McKay Company, 1967), 217–18.

Michael Harrison, *Fire from Heaven: A Study of Spontaneous Combustion in Human Beings* (Skoob Books, 1990), 79–80.

THE U-TURN

Harry Eiss, *Divine Madness* (Cambridge Scholars Publishing, 2011), 51.

Christina Hole, *Haunted England: A Survey of English Ghost-Lore* (B. T. Batsford, 1950), 21–22.

A STUDY IN SILK

George A. Aitkin, "Defoe's 'Apparition of Mrs. Veal,'" *The Nineteenth Century* 37 (1895): 95–100.

"With Foreign and Inland Intelligence," *The Loyal Post*, December 24, 1705.

QUARANTINE

Moshe Sluhovsky, "The Devil in the Convent," *American Historical Review* 107, no. 5 (2002): 1379–411.

Edmund Goldsmid, *The History of the Devils of Loudun* (1887).

Michel de Certeau, *The Possession at Loudun*, trans. Michael B. Smith (University of Chicago Press, 2000).

Robert Rapley, *A Case of Witchcraft: The Trial of Urbain Grandier* (McGill-Queen's Press, 1998).

Jonathan L. Pearl, *The Crime of Crimes: Demonology and Politics in France, 1560–1620* (Wilfrid Laurier University Press, 2012).

"Witchcraft and the Occult, Possession at Loudun," University of Massachusetts (Gary Zabel), www.faculty.umb.edu/gary_zabel /Courses/Phil%20281b/Philosophy%20of%20Magic/Arcana/ Witchcraft%20and%20Grimoires/Loudun.html.

Mary Kate Hunter, "The Loudun Possessions: Witchcraft Trials at The Jacob Burns Law Library," *LH&RB* 16, no. 3 (2010): 1–7.

"Looking Back: The Possessions at Loudun," The British Psychological Society, February 2014, https://thepsychologist.bps. org.uk/volume-27/edition-2/looking-back-possessions-loudun.

DESPERATE MEASURES

"Superstition," Southern Illinois University professor emeritus Ronald Ray Schmeck, n.d., mypage.siu.edu/rae50/Superstition .html.

"Romanus-Büchlein," Twilit Grotto: Archives of Western Esoterica, n.d., www.esotericarchives.com/moses/romanus.htm.

David W. Kreibel, "Pow-wowing: A Persistent American Esoteric Tradition," *Esoterica* IV (n.d.): 16–28.

David W. Kriebel, *Pow-wowing Among the Pennsylvania Dutch: A Traditional Medical Practice in the Modern World* (Penn State Press, 2007), 115–21.

Gail de Vos, *What Happens Next? Contemporary Urban Legends and Popular Culture* (ABC-CLIO, 2012), 50–52.

Daniel Harms, *The Long-Lost Friend: A 19th Century American Grimoire* (Llewellyn Worldwide, 2012), 24–33.

BLACK AND WILD

Glyn Parry, *The Arch Conjuror of England: John Dee* (Yale University Press, 2012).

Benjamin Woolley, *The Queen's Conjurer: The Science and Magic of Dr. John Dee, Advisor to Queen Elizabeth I* (Macmillan, 2002).

Peter J. French, *John Dee: The World of an Elizabethan Magus* (Psychology Press, 1987).

John Dee, *John Dee* (North Atlantic Books, 2003).

"John Dee: The Man Who Spoke to Angels," *Telegraph,* January 10, 2016, http://www.telegraph.co.uk/books/authors/the-man -who-spoke-to-angels.

A. K. Sharma, *Prophecies & Predictions* (Pustak Mahal, 1993), 57–61.

Philip Gardiner, *The Bond Code: The Dark World of Ian Fleming and James Bond* (New Page Books, 2008), 91–101.

Daniel Ferreras Savoye, *The Signs of James Bond: Semiotic Explorations in the World of 007* (McFarland, 2013), 36–37.

UNHOLY ACTS

Sarah Ferber, *Demonic Possession and Exorcism in Early Modern France* (Routledge, 2004), 40–58.

D. P. Walker, *Unclean Spirits: Possession and Exorcism in France and England in the Late Sixteenth and Early Seventeenth Centuries* (University of Pennsylvania Press, 1981), 33–37.

Rosemary Ellen Guiley, *Encyclopedia of Demons and Demonology* (Infobase Publishing, 2009), 33–34.

Brian Levack, *The Devil Within: Possession and Exorcism in the Christian West* (Yale University Press, 2013), 146–47.

ON THE RUN

Steve Blamires, *The Little Book of the Great Enchantment* (Skylight Press, 2013), 278–80.

ABOUT THE AUTHOR

One of the most successful podcast producers in the world, AARON MAHNKE began his career in 2015. His first podcast *Lore* has been downloaded half a billion times, adapted for television by Amazon, and published as a major book series from Penguin Random House. Aaron has also produced a number of other wildly popular podcasts, including his chart-topping *Cabinet of Curiosities* and his award-winning supernatural audio drama, *Bridgewater*.

lorepodcast.com
facebook.com/lorepodcast
Instagram: @amahnke & @lorepodcast
Threads: @amahnke & @lorepodcast

ABOUT THE ILLUSTRATOR

M. S. CORLEY is a professional illustrator and book cover designer fascinated by folklore, the supernatural, and all things strange. Besides *The World of Lore: Monstrous Creatures* and *The World of Lore: Wicked Mortals,* he has also created illustrations for *Darkness There: Selected Tales* by Edgar Allan Poe, *Never Bet the Devil & Other Warnings* by Orrin Grey, and others. He haunts Central Oregon with his wife, daughter, son, and cat named Dinah.

mscorley.com
X: @corleyms